John Wesley

ON THE SERMON ON THE MOUNT

This engraving was drawn by T. A. Dean after an original
portrait of John Wesley by Lewis Vaslet (1742-1808).

*T*his engraving by T. A. Dean is based on an original portrait by Lewis Vaslet (1742–1808). Vaslet exhibited miniatures at the Royal Academy in the 1770s as "Lewis Vaslet of York." As an artist, he itinerated mostly in York, Bath, and Oxford where he gained commissions for portraits. He advertised himself as "artist in crayons (miniatures and likenesses)" and as a painter of "wild animal, gentlemans' seats, still-life & c." His oil paintings use pleasantly subdued colors, and his best crayon works are highly accomplished works of art. Vaslet's pastel drawing of Thomas Webb (c. 1795), American Methodism's first bishop, is a splendid illustration of his skill as an artist.

T. A. Dean, who drew this engraving, was a respected artist who also engraved numerous well-known people, including a popular portrait of King Henry VIII. Dean's engraving of Wesley was done with impressive skill and attention to detail. This engraving is at the John Rylands Library, Manchester, England.

—Kenneth Kinghorn

John Wesley
ON THE SERMON ON THE MOUNT

THE
STANDARD
SERMONS
IN
MODERN
ENGLISH

VOLUME II, 21-33

KENNETH CAIN KINGHORN

ABINGDON PRESS / Nashville

JOHN WESLEY ON THE SERMON ON THE MOUNT
THE STANDARD SERMONS IN MODERN ENGLISH, VOL. 2

Copyright © 2002 by Abingdon Press

This book is printed on recycled, acid-frree, elemental-chlorine–free paper.

Library of Congress Cataloging in Publication Data

Wesley, John, 1703-1791.
~~[Sermons on several occasions]~~
The standard sermons in modern English / [edited by] Kenneth Cain Kinghorn.
    p. cm.
Includes bibliographical references and index.
Contents: v. 1. John Wesley on the Sermon on the Mount, 21-33
ISBN 0-687-02810-8 (alk. paper)
1. Methodist Church—Sermons. 2. Sermons, English. I. Kinghorn, Kenneth C.
II.. Title.

BX8217.W54 K56 2002
252'.07—dc21

2001055256

02 03 04 05 06 07 08 09 10 11—10 9 8 7 6 5 4 3 2 1

MANUFACTURED IN THE UNITED STATES OF AMERICA

Contents

JOHN WESLEY'S
CHRISTIAN ETHICS

John Wesley was the principal leader of the eighteenth-century evangelical revival in England, a spiritual awakening that changed the face of Western Christianity. The Methodists in England and America successfully took the good news of the gospel to vast segments of the populace which the established churches had failed to reach. Through the Wesleyan sermons and hymns, the New Testament doctrine of salvation by grace came to life again, with an added emphasis on Christian ethics. This pivotal work of spiritual and social revitalization imprinted itself upon Protestantism and created the framework for modern evangelicalism.[1]

The sixteenth-century Protestant Reformation had established the doctrines of justification and the Christian's changed standing before God. Building on the foundations laid by the Reformers, Wesley's central theological contribution was his emphasis on the Christian's changed state. His insights into ethics flowed out of his belief that theological doctrine and religious experience must lead to radical changes in one's inward dispositions and outward actions. For Wesley, Christianity can be properly understood and communicated only in the light of its transforming power in individual lives and social contexts. Furthermore, Wesley combined the primacy of grace and the necessity of human responsibility. One of his favorite descriptions of Christianity was "faith working through love" (Gal. 5:6).

Wesley was, of course, not the first to teach the inseparability of theology and ethics. Yet, he developed and demonstrated this union so compellingly that he produced a lasting legacy. This volume contains John Wesley's famed discourses on Christ's Sermon on the Mount, found in Matthew's Gospel, chapters 5, 6, and 7. Although practical Christian behavior permeates all of Wesley's sermons, the discourses in the following pages especially clarify his teaching on personal and social ethics.[2] This book is the second volume of a three-volume edition of John Wesley's fifty-three Standard Sermons in modern English. Volume 1 of this collection (sermons 1-20) contains Wesley's sermons on Christian foundations; this present volume (sermons 21-33) includes his sermons on the Sermon on the Mount, and volume 3 (sermons 34-53) contains Wesley's sermons on Christian maturity.

Each of the sermons in this volume is an independent discourse, complete in itself. Together, these discourses contain John Wesley's most thorough exposition of Christian ethics. Simply stated, they describe the fruit of justifying faith. Wesley wrote, "Instead of teaching men that they may be saved by a faith which is without good works, without 'gospel-obedience and holiness of life,' we teach exactly the reverse, continually insisting on all outward as well as all inward holiness. For the notorious truth of this we appeal to the whole tenor of our sermons . . . in particular to those upon 'Our Lord's Sermon on the Mount,' wherein every branch of gospel obedience is both asserted and proved to be indispensably necessary to eternal salvation."[3]

Many have ranked John Wesley's series of sermons on Christ's Sermon on the Mount among the best ever written on these scriptures. In the view of Wesley scholar Edward H. Sugden,

> As a practical manual of Christian conduct, it would be hard to find anything so good as this noble series of thirteen sermons. Nothing could prove more conclusively that Wesley's enthusiastic preaching of justification by faith gave no excuse to his followers

for "making void the law through faith." Their ethical teaching glows throughout with spiritual fervour; and their appeal to the conscience is irresistible. They are the candle of the Lord, searching the innermost parts of the soul.[4]

It is impossible to read these sermons without attaining a better understanding of the basic teachings of Jesus Christ and developing an increased appreciation for the essential spirit of John Wesley. These classic messages constitute a collection of theological and ethical jewels of timeless worth.

The study of ethics is the consideration of ultimate issues pertaining to human conduct, with regard to our moral responsibilities to God, self, and others.[5] Ethics also deals with the means by which we can fulfill these obligations. The study of ethics falls into three branches—*philosophical* ethics, *theological* ethics, and *Christian* ethics.

Philosophical ethics approaches human responsibility from the standpoint of natural reason and experience. The varieties of philosophical ethics contain many points of view, a number of them contradictory.[6] From a Christian perspective, some philosophical assumptions and conclusions are entirely unacceptable. For instance, Niccolò Machiavelli (1469–1527) championed the idea that "might makes right" and he subordinated moral absolutes to political expediency. Dictators, of course, take this view. This ethical outlook, however, is not limited to such people as Napoleon, Hitler, Stalin, and Mao Tse-tung. Machiavelli's point of view is the fundamental position of politicians and legal scholars who deny that human rights are based on the God-given dignity of humankind, and see them as concessions to be granted (or taken away) by the state.[7]

Other systems of philosophical ethics, though, contain worthwhile insights. John Wesley showed appreciation for the ethics of some of the ancient "heathen." He lamented that the ethics of many Christians in his day did not come up to the standards of moral obligation set by these pre-Christian philosophers. At the same time, Wesley insisted that all ethics derived solely from human reason fall short of the revelation of God found in Jesus Christ and in scripture. Wesley's first sermon on Christ's Sermon on the Mount declares, "One cannot but observe...that Christianity begins just where heathen morality ends."[8]

Theological ethics is based on the conclusions of a religious outlook. While *philosophical* ethics pertains to the present life, the study of *theological* ethics deals with concerns about both the present life and life after death. For example, the theology of Hinduism sees reincarnation as a basis for ethical living, because good works in the present life supposedly improve one's status in future earthly re-embodiments. The ethics of Buddhism (a non-theistic "religion") extols self-discipline as the way to achieve tranquility and ultimate nirvana—which is the eventual annihilation of personal identity.[9] Moslem ethics is based on good works and the sacrifice of one's self for Islam in order to earn an entrance into Paradise. The ethics of the cult of Jehovah's Witnesses calls for sacrificial good works as a means of deserving a place in heaven. While Christian ethics is theological, theological ethics is not necessarily Christian.

Christian ethics is based on a distinctly *biblical* worldview. Wesley insisted that we could know religious truth only as God has revealed it through the (closed) biblical canon and the incarnate word in Jesus Christ:

> We can neither depend upon reason nor experiment [experience]. Whatsoever men know or can know...must be drawn from the oracles of God. Here, therefore, we are to look for no new improvements; but to stand in the good old paths; to content ourselves with what God has been pleased to reveal; with "the faith once delivered to the saints."[10]

In harmony with classical Christianity, Wesley refused to ground ethics in human will, natural conscience, sociological trends, inward impressions, or an individual's need and ability to earn the favor of God. Rather, he based ethics on God's prevenient, saving, and sanctifying grace as revealed in Jesus Christ. He also rooted ethics in God's moral law disclosed in sacred scripture. We can summarize Wesley's ethics under the general headings of (1) creation, (2) grace and free will, (3) law and gospel, (4) disciplined living, (5) personal and social transformation, and (6) the primacy of love.

I. Creation

Wesley rested his theology and ethics on the first four words of the Bible—*In the beginning God.* He believed that Christian theology does not start with the created, but with the Creator. As the Apostle John declared, "All things came into being through him, and without him not one thing came into being" (John 1:3). We did not spring from the natural order as a result of blind chance, indiscriminate accident, or random evolution. Rather, it was for a grand purpose that the Creator created creation. Wesley assumes that God the Creator has never removed himself from his creation. Rather, he maintains an integral relationship with the world, and he is moving it toward his ultimate purpose in history. Because God is sovereign, history is *his*-story.

The apex of God's creation is humankind, whom he created in his own image and likeness. God endowed humankind with unique moral attributes. Wesley echoed the theological consensus of classical Christianity when he stated:

> Man was created in the image of God: because he is not mere matter, a clod of earth, a lump of clay, without sense or understanding, but a spirit like his Creator, a being endued not only with sense and understanding but also with a will exerting itself in various affections. To crown all the rest, he was endued with liberty, a power of directing his own affections and actions, a capacity of determining himself, or of choosing good or evil.[11]

We measure human significance not on the basis of an earthly life span, but on the basis of *eternity;* not on the basis of *physical form* but on the basis of *spiritual capacity.* According to John Wesley, we understand our value and find meaning only in reference to God. The ethical implications of this assumption are profound and far-reaching.

Those cultures that lack a biblical understanding of human origins have no adequate basis for valuing human life, and they lack any satisfactory starting point for personal or social ethics. Despite our being physically small beings in the vastness of God's created order, we are at the center of God's providence and purpose in history.[12] John Wesley championed the unique dignity and infinite value of every individual because God created us in his own image and because he has a special purpose for humankind. Wesley teaches that God does not change his mind with succeeding generations. Therefore, today we understand theological truth and moral principles only in reference to God, whose being remains constant.

Wesley's belief in the incomparable worth of every person led him to become an advocate for human freedom. In 1774, he wrote *Thoughts upon Slavery,* one of the most influential tracts ever written against human bondage. Wesley's final letter was to William Wilberforce, a member of the House of Commons, encouraging him to work to abolish slavery in England: "Unless God has raised you up for this very thing, you will be worn out by the opposition of men and devils. But, 'if God be for you, who can be against you?' Are all of them together stronger than God? O 'be not weary in well doing!'"[13] By 1811 slavery had ended in Great Britain.

Wesley's view of human worth also led him into ministries to prisoners. For example, he wrote in his journal: "I visited one in the Marshalsea Prison; a nursery of all manner of wickedness. O shame to man, that there should be such a place, such a picture of hell upon earth! And shame to those who bear the name of Christ, that there should need any prison at all in Christendom!"[14] Wesley's prison work took three forms—bringing the knowledge of Jesus Christ to every inmate, providing financial relief to free some from prison debt, and working with others to bring about prison reform.

John Wesley also undertook measures to halt the national scourge of alcoholism which shattered the well-being of so many people. Wesley believed that the consumption of distilled liquors destroyed body and soul, and contributed to economic poverty as well. In a treatise titled "Thoughts on the Present Scarcity of Provisions" he contended that distillers diverted the farm produce needed to feed the hungry into alcoholic "poison." The resulting scarcity of grain drove up prices that the poor were unable to pay.[15] In 1743 Methodism's General Rules forbade "buying or selling spirituous liquors." Wesley helped pioneer the study of physiological consequences of alcohol on the body.[16] Historian J. Wesley Bready claimed, "Not till 1751, when the vehement temperance teaching of [Wesley's] Evangelical Revival had already been heard throughout the land, and when groups of converts in very considerable community were committed to total abstinence, was Law of any avail."[17]

In sum, Wesley grounded ethics in his belief that God created humankind in his image and likeness and that he conferred a unique worth upon everyone. Wesley called for Christians to work for the redemption and well-being of the bodies, minds, and souls of all people. He insisted that it is a false humility to claim that we are too sinful ever to be able to do good works that please God. Wesley rendered Philippians 4:13, "I can do all things through Christ strengthening me." Commenting on this verse, he wrote, "I can do all things—even fulfill all the will of God."[18]

II. Grace and free will

Wesley assumes that God does not work entirely apart from our responses to him. The theological term for human cooperation with God is "synergism," from the Greek word *synergos,* which means "working together." In short, Wesley's synergism balances God's sovereignty and human moral responsibility. He preached, "God worketh in you; therefore, you must work. You must be 'workers together with him'...otherwise he will cease working."[19] Wesley quoted St. Augustine, "He that made us without ourselves, will not save us without ourselves."[20]

Wesley was one with the Protestant Reformers in saying that because we are born with sinful natures, we have forfeited our moral likeness to God.

Knowest thou not, that thou canst do nothing but sin, till thou art reconciled to God? Wherefore, then, dost thou say, "I must do this and this first, and then I shall believe?" Nay, but first believe! Believe in the Lord Jesus Christ, the Propitiation for thy sins. Let this good foundation first be laid, and then thou shalt do all things well.[21]

15

From start to finish, our salvation is by grace alone. Yet, Wesley rejected the teaching that God predestines some to salvation and others to damnation. Many of the Reformers taught that only the sovereign God is active in our salvation, and helpless humankind is completely passive. Wesley affirmed the Nicene and Post-Nicene Church Fathers who insisted on human responsibility before God.

Wesley also rejected the theological position known as Pelagianism, a viewpoint that minimizes original sin and contends for our natural ability to turn to God. Wesley discarded this notion because it does not sufficiently take into account sinful human tendencies and our need for God's grace at every point in our lives. Yet, because Wesley stressed the importance of human response to God, critics have accused him of teaching Pelagianism. It becomes important, therefore, to emphasize that Wesley credited God alone for enabling us to repent, turn from sin, trust in the merits of Christ, and live holy lives. In Wesley's view, humankind has no inherent or natural ability to respond positively to God. We respond to God's redemptive agenda only because his grace enables us to do so.

Synergism appears often in the Old Testament, and King David stated it concisely: "Trust in the LORD, and do good" (Ps. 37:3). God calls us to *trust* and to *do*. St. Paul frequently underscored the synergism of God's initiative and human response. He wrote, "Work out your own salvation with fear and trembling; for it is God who is at work in you, enabling you both to will and to work for his good pleasure" (Phil. 2:12). Because of God's prior work in Timothy's life, St. Paul urged him, "Discharge your duties" (2 Tim. 4:5). For Christians, sin is not an unavoidable necessity. The victory of Jesus Christ enables us to overcome deliberate disobedience. When we surrender our wills to God this synergistic relationship enables God to "grant us that we, being rescued from the hands of our enemies, might serve him without fear, in holiness and righteousness before him all our days" (Luke 1:73-75).

On the one hand, Wesley based his ethics on God's gracious initiative and love. On the other hand, Wesley taught that God requires our response and obedience. Professor Kenneth Collins comments on this point: "Precisely because God has already acted, human *response,* not initiative, is possible."[22] The more grace God gives us, the greater is our responsibility. "From everyone to whom much has been given, much will be required; and from the one to whom much has been entrusted, even more will be demanded" (Luke 12:48). From conversion to glorification, Wesley acknowledges the prior work of God's grace at every point in the Christian life. Obedience to God leads to his blessing; disobedience restricts his work in and for us. This synergistic approach to personal and social ethics provides a solid theological reason for us to strive to become "faithful stewards of the manifold grace of God" (1 Pet. 4:10).

III. Law and gospel

Since the time of the apostolic church, two opposite and equally incorrect concepts of the place of the moral law have asserted themselves in every generation. Both of these mistaken concepts were especially evident in Wesley's day. In the name of faith, some set aside the requirements of the moral law. This opinion is called "Antinomianism," which comes from two Greek words—*anti* (against) and *nomos* (law). We may define Antinomianism as the belief that Christians are not obliged to teach or obey the moral law because Christ, on our behalf, has already fulfilled it completely. Antinomians believe that Christians are "robed in the righteousness of Christ" and that it is neither possible nor necessary to be subject to the moral law. Allegedly, God overlooks the sins of Christians because he regards only the righteousness of Christ. For Antinomians, Christ *imputes* righteousness to Christians, but he does not *impart* righteousness to them. Supposedly, he *counts* them righteous, but he does not *make* them righteous. This approach to religion asserts that all efforts to keep the moral law undermine the doctrine of salvation by grace alone. The Apostle Paul decisively dealt with this error: "Do we then overthrow the law by faith? By no means! On the contrary, we uphold the law" (Rom. 3:31). Rhetorically, St. Paul asked, "Should we continue in sin in order that grace may abound? By no means! How can we who died to sin go on living in it?"

The other flawed understanding of the moral law emphasizes that good works are a necessary means of gaining merit and earning God's favor. Those who depend on their good works to appease God and gain his approval are called "legalists" or "Pharisees." One recalls that the first-century Pharisees and scribes sought to "establish their own righteousness" (Rom. 10:3). Often, legalists require the scrupulous observance of trifling minutiae, which they append to the moral law. Frequently, legalists take pride in their religious achievements and judge others harshly for their "failures."

John Wesley believed that law and gospel are *both* important for the integrity of Christianity. And because his theology and ethics maintained a place for the moral law, some of his critics accused him of "legalism," "popery," and betraying "the grand Protestant doctrine of justification by faith alone."[23] Claiming that in Christ they were free from the moral law, some of them rejected any need for the means of grace and disciplined holy habits. Many of them fell into Antinomianism. Wesley recorded the following account in his journal:

> At eight I went to Edward Smith's, where were many not only of Epworth, but of Burnham, Haxey, Ouston, Belton, and other villages round about, who greatly desired that I would come over to them and help them. I was now in a strait between two; desiring to hasten forward in my journey, and yet not knowing how to leave those poor bruised reeds in the confusion wherein I found them. John Harrison, it seems, and Richard Ridley, had told them in express terms, "All the ordinances are man's inventions; and if you go to church or sacrament, you will be damned." Many hereupon wholly forsook the church, and others knew not what to do. At last I determined to spend some days here, that I might have time both to preach in each town, and to speak severally with those, in every place, who had found or waited for salvation.[24]

With patience and clarity, Wesley repeatedly made his case for using the God-ordained means of grace and keeping the moral law. He appealed to scripture, Christian antiquity, reason, and the experiences of countless numbers of Christians past and present.

Wesley taught that the moral law is the gospel presented in the form of a requirement, and the gospel is the law presented in the form of a promise.

> Yea, the very same words, considered in different respects, are parts both of the law and of the gospel: If they are considered as commandments, they are parts of the law; if as promises, of the gospel. Thus, "Thou shalt love the Lord thy God with all thy heart," when considered as a commandment, is a branch of the law; when regarded as a promise, is an essential part of the gospel—the gospel being no other than the commands of the law, proposed by way of promise. Accordingly, poverty of spirit, purity of heart, and whatever else is enjoined in the holy law of God, are no other, when viewed in a gospel light, than so many great and precious promises.[25]

The law points us to God's will and to our need for grace. In turn, the gospel points us to God's promise and power, which enable us to move toward the fulfillment of the law. The moral law tells us what we should do, and the gospel gives us the assurance that God makes it possible for us to do it. God's commands are an implied promise, and every promise is an implicit command. What God expects us to do, he enables us to do; and what God enables us to do, he obligates us to do. In these sermons Wesley writes, "On the one hand, the law continually makes way for, and points us to, the gospel; on the other hand, the gospel continually leads us to a more exact fulfilling of the law."[26] If the fulfilling of the moral law is both necessary and possible, God expects us to discipline ourselves to obey its commands and benefit from its promises.

IV. Disciplined living

John Wesley taught that *all* our decisions and actions are significant, whether great or small. And in every circumstance we can do God's will only by self-discipline. Christians do not coast into maturity and usefulness. Jesus said, "*Strive* first for the kingdom of God" (Matt. 6:33). He also said, "For the gate is narrow and the road is *hard* that leads to life, and there are few who find it" (Matt. 7:14). Wesley wrote, "I cannot think I ought to look for perfection in the future, and so sit still and be idle at present. I received the grace of God, which I now must occupy, or suffer loss."[27] Disciplined living is necessarily a part of Christian discipleship. Accordingly, Wesley calls us to stewardship, self-denial, and a diligent use of the means of grace.

Throughout his writings, Wesley emphasizes that we are not owners, but stewards. Our material possessions, time, and talent do not properly belong to us, but to God. We are not free to use God's blessings as we please. Rather, he will require of us a final accounting of how we used them. Stewardship involves every aspect of our lives, including our physical bodies, which Wesley refers to as "exquisitely wrought machines."[28] Accordingly, Christians should eat simple food and avoid gluttony, distilled alcohol, and any practice that damages the body or dulls the senses. Self-centered and lazy living is antithetical to Christian stewardship. The stewardship of our lives includes the faithful development and proper use of our mental, moral, and spiritual abilities. God has given us understanding, memory, imagination, affections, and will. He expects us to improve and employ these attributes in a life of devotion and service.

Wesley also emphasizes the importance of the stewardship of material things. He warns against squandering money on costly apparel, which can easily nourish pride, obscure eternal things, and diminish our ability to help those in need. Wesley warns that *having* money is not necessarily a justification for *spending* money: "No Christian can afford to waste any part of the substance which God has entrusted him with."[29] To be sure, money in itself is not evil. It is the *love* of money that is the root of all manner of evil. The love of money easily causes people to grasp for it, despite its deceptive allurement and tendency to cause harm to body and soul. The love of money all too often causes people to feel self-sufficient and to substitute the love of pleasure for the love of God. Stewardship also includes the wise use of talent, beauty, voice, personality, intelligence, education, time, position, and opportunity. Good stewards invest their God-given time and resources, working for the dignity and well-being of others.

In all his writings, John Wesley urges us to place service ahead of creature comforts and to prioritize duty over personal convenience. This way of living is possible only by self-denial, which Wesley called a "grand doctrine of Christianity."[30] He based that claim on a declaration of Jesus: "If any want to become my followers, let them deny themselves and take up their cross and follow me. For those who want to save their life will lose it, and those who lose their life for my sake will find it" (Matt. 5:14-16). Indeed, one can overcome sin only by denying the demands of the self. Wesley defined self-denial as "denying or refusing to follow our own will, from a conviction that the will of God is the only rule of action to us. And we see the reason thereof, because we are creatures; because 'it is He that hath made us, and not we ourselves.'"[31]

Wesley's discourses on the Sermon on the Mount emphasize that self-denial involves a willingness to take one's place among the minority of humankind and willingly endure misunderstanding and persecution. In the words of Jesus, "The gate is wide and the road is easy that leads to destruction, and there are many who take it. The gate is narrow and the road is hard that leads to life, and there are few who find it" (Matt. 7:13, 14). A sure characteristic of the way that leads to destruction is that it is easy and well traveled.

Wesley also insisted on the importance of the "single eye," a critical aspect of ethical living (Matt. 6:22). These sermons teach that wholehearted commitment is required for success in any venture. If we are not dedicated to an undertaking, we will fail in its achievement. With respect to our relationship to God, we can know no peace until we are singly devoted to loving and serving him. In Wesley's ninth discourse on the Sermon on the Mount he states, "This is a plain, sure rule; uneasy care is unlawful care. With a single eye to God, do all that in you lies to provide things honest in the sight of all men: And then give up all into better hands; leave the whole event to God."[32] Wesley insists that unless our eye is single toward God we will be damned.

It is not surprising that in Wesley's day many people rejected self-denial, because over the centuries certain fanatics have carried asceticism to irrational extremes. Wesley makes it clear that self-denial does not mean excessive mortification or taking perverse delight in artificially contrived suffering. Wearing haircloths, sleeping uncovered in the cold, deliberately allowing insect stings, and sprinkling ashes on one's food are not the kinds of self-denial that John Wesley advocated. Those who neglect their physical needs to the point of compromising their health are not practicing Christian self-denial. Wesley does not advocate self-inflicted suffering as a means of becoming more holy. The only true self-denial is that which pertains to placing God's will ahead of our own comfort, desires, or preferences.

Wesley linked self-denial with the discipline of taking up one's cross. Self-denial means renouncing the priority of personal pleasure; bearing one's cross means willingly to accept discomfort or pain for the advancement of God's kingdom and the well-being of others. Wesley defined taking up one's cross:

> We are . . . properly said to "bear our cross," when we endure what is laid upon us without our choice, with meekness and resignation. Whereas, we do not properly "take up our cross," but when we voluntarily suffer what it is in our power to avoid; when we willingly embrace the will of God, though contrary to our own; when we choose what is painful, because it is the will of our wise and gracious Creator.[33]

Self-denial and cross bearing are necessary if one wants to be a disciple of Christ: "It is always owing to the want either of self-denial, or taking up his cross, that any man does not thoroughly follow Him, is not fully a disciple of Christ."[34] Thus, disciplined living is a necessary component of Wesleyan ethics.

John Wesley insisted that a disciplined life include the faithful use of the means of grace. The means of grace are the practices which God typically uses to nourish our spiritual lives.[35] Wesley said that those means are "outward signs, words, or actions, ordained of God, and appointed for this end, to be the ordinary channels whereby he might convey to men, preventing, justifying, or sanctifying grace."[36] Some rejected the use of the means of grace, arguing that we would come to depend on them rather than Christ. These people believed that using the means of grace would give the impression that they were trying to earn salvation by something they did or said. Wesley disagreed with such reasoning. He strongly advocated using these ordinances for the reason that God ordained them and because the Bible stipulates their use. Regarding those who despised the means of grace, Wesley charged that they were "glad of any pretence to cast aside that wherein their soul has no pleasure, to give over the painful strife, and sink down into an indolent inactivity."[37]

Wesley placed the means of grace into two categories—the "instituted" and the "prudential" means of grace. The instituted means of grace are those practices that Christ specifically commanded. They include the Christian sacraments, prayer, searching the scriptures, fasting, and Christian conversation. The prudential means of grace are those practices that scripture and experience show to be wise and prudent for Christian disciples. There are three headings for these practices—doing no harm, doing good, and using all the ordinances of God. The specific items under the headings of doing no harm and doing good are by no means an eighteenth-century form of legalism. The particular points have their foundations in explicit scriptural admonitions, not in legalistic inventions. These specific ethical guidelines constitute a concise yet comprehensive system of social ethics.

At this point, we should note that one of the prudential means of grace in Wesley's ethics is *Christian conference,* a term for frequent communication with others of "like precious faith" (2 Pet. 1:1 KJV). Wesley understood that a sustaining community is necessary if Christians are to overcome discouragement, ridicule, and opposition.[38] Mutual encouragement and support provide immeasurable help to those who seek to live for Christ in a non-Christian world.[39] To this end, Wesley developed class meetings, band meetings, love feasts, watch night services, and a liturgy for the renewal of one's covenant with God.

Of course, the means of grace do not work automatically, nor do they earn us merit. Furthermore, Wesley allowed that God can (and sometimes does) work outside the means of grace. Yet, he stressed that God's *ordinary* way of imparting grace into our lives is through the means that he himself has ordained. The "indolent inactivity" mentioned above can be overcome only by disciplined stewardship, self-denial, and the use of the means of grace.

V. Personal and social transformation

Wesley's ethical teachings are predicated on regeneration and sanctification as God's work within us to make us holy in heart and life. Wesley believed that we must be spiritually transformed if we are to do genuine good works.

> All works done before justification are not good, in the Christian sense, forasmuch as they spring not of faith in Jesus Christ . . . they are not done as God hath willed and commanded them to be done, we doubt not . . . but they have the nature of sin.[40]

Good works flow from the conviction that through the power of the new birth God both *counts* us righteous and *makes* us righteous. Wesley refers to the effects of the new birth as "the fruit of the Spirit." The principal fruit of the Spirit is a cluster of renewed dispositions described by Paul as "love, joy, peace, patience, kindness, generosity, faithfulness, gentleness, and self-control" (Gal. 5:22, 23). Wesley listed these qualities often, especially calling attention to the primacy of love.

In these thirteen sermons on Christ's Sermon on the Mount John Wesley grounds Christian ethics in the renewal of the soul "after the image of God" and the "mind that is in Christ Jesus" (Phil. 2:5). As early as October, 1738, Wesley had clarified the meaning of being "in Christ." For such a one, "it is the design of his life . . . to regain the image of God; to have the life of God again planted in his soul; and to be 'renewed after his likeness, in righteousness and true holiness.'"[41] Wesley's ethical concerns flow out of this conviction. For Wesley, Christian experience results in a transformation of the heart that expresses itself in holiness and good works.

24

This view contrasts with some segments of the Protestant tradition. It must be remembered, of course, that the sixteenth-century Protestant Reformers lived in a time when most people were seeking to earn God's favor by good works. As a result, these reformers believed that God had called them to champion the biblical doctrine of salvation by faith, apart from human merit or the works of the law. Martin Luther believed that the only righteousness Christians have is an "alien righteousness," which is the righteousness of Christ *imputed* to them by faith. He also believed that conversion was a lifetime process, not completed until after death. Therefore, he and certain other sixteenth-century Reformers taught that Christians dare not claim any *imparted* righteousness.[42] The Reformers believed that, for Christians, righteousness is a future hope to be realized in the next life.

In the eighteenth century, however, John Wesley encountered many who emphasized faith to the point of denying the need for good works. He taught that if faith is the root of salvation, good works are its fruit. God frees us from both the guilt of sin (in justification) and the power of sin (in sanctification). Wesley often quoted the apostle Peter: "As he who called you is holy, be holy yourselves in all your conduct; for it is written, 'You shall be holy, for I am holy'" (1 Pet. 1:15-16). Wesley frequently pointed out that God does not declare us to be righteous unless (at least to some degree) we *are* righteous. With St. Paul, Wesley taught that "if anyone is in Christ, there is a new creation: everything old has passed away...everything has become new" (2 Cor. 5:17). In a collage of scripture quotations, Wesley declares

> Reckon ye yourselves to be dead unto sin, but alive unto God, through Jesus Christ our Lord. Let not sin therefore reign, even in your mortal body, but yield yourselves unto God, as those that are alive from the dead. For sin shall not have dominion over you— God be thanked, that ye were the servants of sin—but being made free—the plain meaning is, God be thanked, that though ye were, in time past, the servants of sin, yet now—being free from sin, ye are become the servants of righteousness.[43]

For Wesley, moral transformation is not the cause of the new birth, but it is the result of the new birth.

Wesley disallowed a separation of inner holiness and outward service. He would not divide what he believed that God himself had joined.[44] In his fourth discourse on the Sermon on the Mount Wesley wrote:

> The root of religion lies in the heart, in the inmost soul; that this is the union of the soul with God, the life of God in the soul of man. But if this root be really in the heart, it cannot but put forth branches. And these are the several instances of outward obedience, which partake of the same nature with the root; and, consequently, are not only marks or signs, but substantial parts, of religion.[45]

In short, right belief must lead to right actions.

Wesleyan ethics takes into account the reality that Christians are obliged to live among non-Christian people in a secular environment. God calls Christians to transform the world through their love, service, and witness. The Wesleyan way does not call for a retreat from the world. Rather, it reiterates Christ's teaching that Christians are the salt of the earth and the light of the world (Matt. 5:13, 14). Christian ethics requires believers to develop a sensitive awareness of the needs of others and to find practical ways of serving them—whether or not they treat us well or respond to the call of God upon their lives. Wesley wrote, "'Do good to them that hate you.' Let your actions show that you are as genuine in love as they are in hatred. Return good for evil. 'Do not be overcome by evil, but overcome evil with good.' If you can do nothing more, at least 'pray for those that persecute you.' You can never be incapacitated from acting this way, nor can all the hostility and violence of others keep you from praying for them."[46]

Wesley's Methodism demonstrably elevated the economic and social levels of the poor. If one measures the economic equality and cultural developments in England before and after the Wesleyan revival, it is difficult to overstate the vast good accomplished through the application of Wesley's ethics to a depraved environment.[47] An often-quoted statement of Wesley sums up his attitude toward personal and social ethics:

> "Holy solitaries" is a phrase no more consistent with the gospel than holy adulterers. The gospel of Christ knows of no religion, but social; no holiness but social holiness. "Faith working by love" is the length and breadth and depth and height of Christian perfection. "This commandment have we from Christ, that he who loves God, love his brother also;" and that we manifest our love by doing good unto all. . . . And in truth, whosoever loveth his brethren, not in word only, but as Christ loved him, cannot but be "zealous of good works." He feels in his soul a burning, restless desire of spending and being spent for them. "My Father," will he say, "worketh hitherto, and I work." And at all possible opportunities he is, like his Master, "going about doing good."[48]

God intends that his mysterious and unfathomable grace before conversion will eventually be manifested in works of piety and works of charity after conversion. God wills that the inner dynamic of faith should be revealed in the outward expression of good works. True virtue, therefore, resides both in one's *will* (inward devotion) and in one's *work* (outward service).

VI. The primacy of love

Finally, the keystone of Wesley's personal and social ethics is love. For Wesley, the epitome of religion and the sum of Christian perfection appear in the words of Jesus: "'You shall love the Lord your God with all your heart, and with all your soul, and with all your mind.' This is the greatest and first commandment. And a second is like it: 'You shall love your neighbor as yourself.' On these two commandments hang all the law and the prophets" (Matt. 22:37-40). Perhaps no theologian in the history of Christianity has made love more central. Professor Leon Hynson writes, "How did it happen that of all the thinkers in nearly two millennia of Christian history who pondered the meaning of love, Wesley should achieve such a maximum view of the concept? Who else has surpassed Wesley in his appreciation of holiness as love, socially active, catholic in temper, personally integrative, unitive, liberating?"[49] Clearly, love is the keystone and continuing inspiration for John Wesley's ethics.

Although the mystics extolled the importance of love, they tended to disparage the material creation. Wesley's love for God was as exalted as that of the mystics. However, this love was combined with love for the creation—especially humankind, which God made in his own image and likeness. And, as stated, Christian love for others necessarily expresses itself in social relationships. Wesley allowed that times for private prayer and meditation are appropriate, but he rejected the notion that love will lead one to live as a hermit. We can practice Christian virtues such as peacemaking, patience, gentleness, and kindness only as we interact with "ungodly and unholy" people, not when we live isolated lives. Wesley declared, "The words of our Lord; who is so far from directing us to break off all commerce with the world, that without it, according to his account of Christianity, we cannot be Christians at all."[50]

Only through love can Christian believers function effectively in the environment of this world, which is marred by sin, selfishness, and disorder. Based upon his understanding of the nature of love, Wesley insisted that it is not possible to conceal it. He wrote, "Your holiness makes you as conspicuous as the sun in the midst of heaven." Wesley appealed to the words of Jesus: "You are the light of the world. A city built on a hill cannot be hid. No one after lighting a lamp puts it under the bushel basket, but on the lampstand, and it gives light to all in the house. In the same way, let your light shine before others, so that they may see your good works and give glory to your Father in heaven" (Matt. 5:14-16).

Wesley insisted that a Christian's love express itself both to fellow believers and to those who lack Christian faith or devotion. With regard to relationships between fellow Christians, Wesley urged tolerance and forbearance. He recognized that among Christians there will be differences of ministries and opinions. Christians do not all think and act alike. Wesley called upon believers to refrain from condemning fellow Christians, if their hearts are devoted to Jesus Christ. To be sure, this "catholic spirit" does not imply doctrinal indifference or "speculative latitudinarianism."[51] Wesley insisted that the notion that one doctrine is as good as another is the "spawn of hell." Wesley calls for Christians to love each other and, when possible, to worship and work together for God's glory and for social betterment. To John Wesley, waging a religious war was neither Christian nor sane.[52] As much as he might disagree with those who betrayed the essentials of Christianity, the idea of harming them physically was unthinkable.

Love for and service to others begins with God's love for us in Christ. Wesley often quoted the Apostle John: "We love because he first loved us" (1 John 4:19). Christians return God's love to him and extend this love outward to others. Wesley personally demonstrated practical expressions of Christian love. He established a free dispensary for meeting the medical needs of the poor. To counter high interest rates, he set up a lending society for the poor. He worked in cooperation with the Society for the Reformation of manners to curtail public vices such as the desecration of Sunday, drunkenness, prostitution, and gambling. He established an orphanage and a boarding school for the children of the poor. He personally exemplified the truth that love necessarily leads to service, especially caring for those who are the most needy.

In summary, Wesley's ethical teaching begins and ends with God the creator, whose essence is love. God's gracious provision for abundant life calls for continuing human response to his grace and accountability to his commands. When believers respond positively to prevenient grace, they become new creations in Christ. Christians receive freedom from both the guilt and power of sin. Building on this theological foundation, these thirteen sermons expound upon Christ's Sermon on the Mount with unassuming authority, seasoned insight, and distinctive simplicity.

Wesley's ethics assumes that Christians have the responsibility to serve God by serving others. Furthermore, God's will is not elusive or vague. The Sermon on the Mount clarifies the ethical principles contained in Christ's teachings to his followers. Unmistakably, there are some things that Christians *should* do and other things that they *should not* do. In the introduction to his first discourse on Christ's Sermon on the Mount, Wesley said, "The Son of God, who came from heaven, is here showing us the way to heaven....He is teaching us the true way to life everlasting; the royal way which leads to the kingdom; and the only true way—for there is none besides; all other paths lead to destruction."[53]

Christ promised "blessedness" (or happiness) to those who obey his commands and overcome their circumstances—always through his grace. On the one hand, John Wesley's ethical principles give full expression to the concept that Christians are to count every small deed important because Christ fills it with significance. On the other hand, Christians are to count every important thing as small and easy because of God's anointing and power.[54] In a word, Wesley's ethical principles are the same as those of Paul: "The only thing that counts is faith working through love" (Gal. 5:6). Those things that God *requires* us to do, he *enables* us to do. And those who live by the ethics described in the Sermon on the Mount know both holiness and happiness, for theirs is the kingdom of God.

Notes

1. Mark A. Noll, *Turning Points: Decisive Moments in the History of Christianity*, 2nd ed. (Grand Rapids: Baker Academic Books, 2000), p. 221-28.

2. John Wesley's *Notes upon the Old Testament* also contains extensive expositions of the Ten Commandments, which are the essence of the moral law.

3. Thomas Jackson, *The Works of John Wesley*, 14 vols. (London: The Wesleyan Conference Office, 1872), 9:102.

4. Edward H. Sugden, *Wesley's Standard Sermons*, 2 vols. (London: The Epworth Press, 1961), 1:313.

5. "Ethics" comes from the Greek words *athos*, "character" or *ethos*, "custom."

6. As examples, the Epicureans posited feeling as the basis of ethics; Plato highlighted human intelligence; Aristotle based ethics on human will; Kant rooted ethics in natural conscience.

7. E. Clinton Gardner, *Biblical Faith and Social Ethics* (New York and Evanston: Harper Bros., 1960), p. 323.

8. Albert Outler, ed., *The Works of John Wesley*, 4 vols. (Nashville: Abingdon Press, 1984, 1985, 1886, 1987), Bicentennial ed., "Sermon on the Mount," Discourse 1 (I, 9), 1:480.

9. Saphir P. Athyal, "Buddhist Ethics," *Baker's Dictionary of Christian Ethics*, ed. Carl F. H. Henry (Grand Rapids: Baker Book House, 1973), pp. 75-76.

10. Jackson, *Wesley's Works*, "Of the Gradual Improvement of Natural Philosophy," 11:487.

11. Outler, *Wesley's Sermons,* "On the Fall of Man," (§1), 2:400-01.

12. William R. Cannon, *The Theology of John Wesley* (New York; Nashville: Abingdon Press, 1946), p. 179.

13. John Telford, *The Letters of the Rev. John Wesley, A.M.,* 8 vols. (London: Epworth Press, 1931), 8:265.

14. W. Reginald Ward and Richard P. Heitzenrater, eds., *Wesley's Journal and Diaries* (Nashville: Abingdon Press, 1988, 1995), Bicentennial ed. (February 3, 1753), 20:444-45.

15. Jackson, *Wesley's Works,* 11:53-59.

16. Richard M. Cameron, *Methodism and Society in Historical Perspective* (New York; Nashville: Abingdon Press, 1961), p. 51.

17. J. Wesley Bready, *England: Before and After Wesley* (London: Hodder and Stoughton, 1938), p. 150.

18. *Explanatory Notes upon the New Testament,* Phil. 4:13.

19. Outler, *Wesley's Sermons,* "On Working out our own Salvation" (III, 7), 3:208.

20. Saint Augustine, Sermon 169, on Phil. 3:3-16, xi. Outler, *Wesley's Sermons,* "The General Spread of the Gospel" (§12), 2:490.

21. Outler, *Wesley's Sermons,* "The Righteousness of Faith" (III, 1), 1:214.

22. Kenneth Collins, *A Faithful Witness: John Wesley's Homiletical Theology* (Wilmore, Ky.: Wesley Heritage Press, 1993), p. 165.

23. Thomas Jackson, *The Works of John Wesley,* 14 vols. (London: The Wesleyan Conference Office, 1872), 10:449.

24. Ward and Heitzenrater, *Wesley's Journal and Diaries* (June 6, 1742), 19:274.

25. Outler, *Wesley's Sermons,* "Sermon on the Mount," Discourse 5 (II, 2), 1:554.

26. Ibid. (II, 3), 1:554.

27. Jackson, *Wesley's Works,* 1:514.

28. Outler, *Wesley's Sermons,* "The Good Steward," (I, 4), 2:285.

29. Outler, *Wesley's Sermons,* "Sermon on Dress" (I, 17), 3:256.

30. Outler, *Wesley's Sermons,* "Self-Denial" (I,1), 2:240.

31. Ibid. (I, 2), 2:242.

32. Outler, *Wesley's Sermons,* Sermon on the Mount, Discourse 9 (§17), 1:641.

33. Ibid. (I, 11), 2:244.

34. Ibid. (II, 1), 2:245.

35. See Randy L. Maddox, *Responsible Grace: John Wesley's Practical Theology* (Nashville: Kingswood Books, Abingdon Press, 1994), pp. 192-213.

36. Ibid., "The Means of Grace" (II, 1), 1:381.

37. Ibid. (I, 6), 1:380.

38. James D. Nelson, "Christian Conference," *Wesleyan Spirituality in Contemporary Theological Education* (Nashville: General Board of Higher Education and Ministry, the United Methodist Church, 1987), pp. 47-53.

39. Rupert E. Davies, *The Methodist Societies I: Nature and Design,* Bicentennial edition of the *Works of John Wesley* (Nashville: Abingdon Press, 1989), A Short History of the People Called Methodists (§9), 9:430.

40. Outler, *Wesley's Sermons,* "Justification by Faith" (III.5), 1:192-93.

41. Ward and Heitzenrater, *Wesley's Journal and Diaries* (October 6-14, 1738), 19:17.

42. Paul Althaus, *The Theology of Martin Luther,* trans. from the German by Robert C. Schultz (Philadelphia: Fortress Press, 1966), pp. 227-28.

43. Outler, *Wesley's Sermons,* "The Marks of the New Birth" (I, 4), 1:419, 420.

44. See Umphrey Lee, *John Wesley and Modern Religion* (Nashville: Cokesbury Press, 1936), p. 196.

45. Outler, *Wesley's Sermons,* "Sermon on the Mount," Discourse 4 (III, 1). 1:541-42.

46. Outler, *Wesley's Sermons,* "Sermon on the Mount," Discourse 3 (III, 13). 1:529.

47. Waldo Beach and H. Richard Niebuhr, *Christian Ethics: Sources of the Living Tradition* (New York: Ronald Press, 1955), p. 364.

48. Jackson, *Works of John Wesley,* 14:321.

49. Leon O. Hynson, *To Reform the Nation: Theological Foundations of Wesley's Ethics* (Grand Rapids: Francis Asbury Press of Zondervan Publishing House, 1984), p. 93.

50. Outler, *Wesley's Sermons,* "The Sermon on the Mount, Discourse 4" (I, 6), 1:536.

51. Outler, *Wesley's Sermons,* "Catholic Spirit" (III, 1), 2:92.

52. Outler, *Wesley's Sermons,* "The Lord our Righteousness" (§1), 1:449.

53. Outler, *Wesley's Sermons,* "Sermon on the Mount," Discourse 1 (§3), 1:470.

54. Blaise Pascal (1623–62) wrote, "Do small things as if they were great, because of the majesty of Christ, who does them in us and lives our life, and great things as if they were small and easy, because of his almighty power." Quoted in Alban Kraitsheimer, *Pascal* (Oxford: Oxford University Press, 1980), p. 72.

UPON OUR LORD'S SERMON ON THE MOUNT

Discourse 1

As early as 1725, John Wesley preached sermons from the sixth chapter of Matthew. Thereafter, he spoke frequently on the Sermon on the Mount, one of his favorite sections of scripture. During his missionary journey to Georgia in 1735, he preached from this section of the Bible to the members of the crew of the ship *Simmonds*. When he began field preaching in 1739, he did so in part because Jesus spoke out of doors when he delivered the Sermon on the Mount. Fittingly, on Wesley's initial venture into field preaching, he spoke from this passage of Scripture.[1] In his mature years, Wesley referred to this sermon of Jesus as "the noblest compendium of religion which is to be found even in the oracles of God."[2]

With this discourse, Wesley begins a series of thirteen expositions on the Sermon on the Mount. The underlying assumption of these sermons is that justifying faith must lead to a transformation of one's being. This new life in Christ results in a life that consists of right relationships and actions. Wesley included these thirteen discourses in his Standard Sermons because of his concern for Christian ethics. In his preaching he emphasized that God both counts us righteous (in justification and adoption) and makes us righteous (in regeneration and sanctification). Wesley said, "The 'new man' must imply... 'a good heart, which after God is created in righteousness and true holiness'; a heart full of that faith which, working by love, produces all holiness of conversation."[3]

In Wesley's day, the specter of Antinomianism loomed large. Some teachers so emphasized justification by faith alone that they discounted the importance of good works. As noted in the introduction to this volume, the Antinomians went so far as to caution *against* doing good works, on the theory that such deeds compromised the gospel of salvation by grace alone. These teachers attacked Wesley as a "heretic" for teaching that good works must follow conversion to Christ. Wesley reported that such theological opponents as William Cudworth, James Relly, and their associates abhorred him "as much as they do the Pope; and ten times more than...the devil."[4] Claiming the freedom of grace, the Antinomians set aside the moral law, duty, and discipline. Wesley led the Methodist preachers in maintaining a balance between faith and works. The second Annual Conference of Wesley's preachers, held in Bristol in 1745, dealt forthrightly with the threat of Antinomianism:

Q. 26 Doth faith supersede (set aside the necessity of) holiness or good works?

A. In no wise. So far from it that it implies both, as a cause doth its effects.

Defending Methodism's emphasis on faith and works, Wesley wrote:

And to this day, instead of teaching men that they may be saved by a faith which is without good works, without "gospel-obedience and holiness of life," we teach exactly the reverse, continually insisting on all outward as well as all inward holiness. For the notorious truth of this we appeal to the whole tenor of our sermons, printed and unprinted; in particular to those upon "Our Lord's Sermon on the Mount," wherein every branch of gospel obedience is both asserted and proved to be indispensably necessary to eternal salvation.[5]

Thus, Wesley taught that true faith and genuine obedience will lead to good works, because the message of Christ leads to inward and outward righteousness. Early in his post-Aldersgate ministry, Wesley concluded, "God accepts us both here and hereafter only for the sake of what Christ has done and suffered for us. This alone is the cause of our justification. But the condition thereof is, not faith alone, but faith and works together."[6] Faith is the root of justification, and good works are its fruit.

These messages on Christ's Sermon on the Mount apply the teaching of Jesus to all who desire to live in the world as he directed. To this end, the focus of the thirteen discourses in this volume follow the pattern developed by Jesus in Matthew's Gospel. (1) The sum of true religion is a biblical balance between inner character and outer works. (2) The instructions of Jesus in his sermon pertaining to right behavior are concrete illustrations of inward dispositions. (3) The substance of genuine religion is both a negative avoidance of evil and a positive expression of righteous living. (4) The end result of evil is disharmony and unending misery, while the end result of righteousness is abundant life and eternal rewards.[7]

For Wesley, ethical living consists of more than theoretical principles or abstract theories such as one finds in the ancient Greek and Latin philosophical writings. Rather, one must demonstrate holy attitudes and deeds. For Wesley, holiness of heart and life arise out of a "divine temper" that God gives to those who truly love him and earnestly desire to do his will. In short, the Sermon on the Mount tells us how God wants us to live on the earth and brings to light the blessed benefits of obedience in this life and in the life to come.

Sermon 21

UPON OUR LORD'S SERMON ON THE MOUNT

Discourse 1

When Jesus saw the crowds, he went up the mountain; and after he sat down, his disciples came to him. Then he began to speak, and taught them, saying: "Blessed are the poor in spirit, for theirs is the kingdom of heaven. Blessed are those who mourn, for they will be comforted." (Matthew 5:1-4)

1 Beginning from the time when "John had been arrested," our Lord had now traveled throughout Galilee. He began "teaching in the synagogues and proclaiming the good news of the kingdom and curing every disease and every sickness among the people." As a natural consequence of this ministry, "great crowds followed him from Galilee, the Decapolis, Jerusalem, Judea, and from beyond the Jordan." "When Jesus saw the crowds," which no synagogue could contain, "he went up the mountain." On the mountain, there was room for all who came to him "from every quarter." According to Jewish custom, "after he sat down, his disciples came to him. Then he began a solemn discourse and taught

them. The phrase, "opened his mouth," was an expression signifying the start of a solemn discourse.

2. Let us recognize who is speaking here, so that we may consider how we should listen. The speaker is the Lord of heaven and earth, the Creator of everything. As such, he has the right to command the universe that he has made. The Lord is our Governor whose kingdom is from everlasting, and he rules over all things. He is the great lawgiver who can properly enforce all his laws. He "is able to save and to destroy"; yes, he is able "to punish with eternal destruction, separated from the presence of the Lord and from the glory of his might." In his eternal wisdom, God the Father "knows how we were made," and he understands our innermost being. God knows how we stand in our relationship with him, with one another, and with every person that he has made.

Consequently, he knows how to apply every law that he decrees to all the circumstances in which he has placed us. God "is good to all, and his compassion is over all that he has made." The God of love, who emptied himself of his eternal glory, came from his Father to declare his will to us, and then he returned to the Father. Jesus Christ has been sent from God "to open the eyes of the blind" and "to give light to those who sit in darkness." It was Christ himself, the great prophet of the Lord, about whom God solemnly spoke long ago: "Anyone who does not heed the words that the prophet shall speak in my name, I myself will hold accountable." Referring to Jesus Christ, the apostle Peter declared, "And it will be that everyone who does not listen to that prophet will be utterly rooted out of the people."

3. What, then, is the teaching of Jesus? Here in the Sermon on the Mount the Son of God who came *from* heaven is revealing to us the way *to* heaven. He is showing us the road to the place that he has prepared for us, as well as to the glory that he had before the world existed. In his own words Jesus is teaching us the true way to life everlasting, the royal road that leads to his kingdom and the only true way to live. There is no other way, because all other paths lead to destruction. Based on the character of Jesus, the one who speaks to us, we are fully confident that he has made known the full and perfect will of God.

Jesus has not spoken a single letter too much; he declared nothing more than he had received from the Father. Nor did he speak too little—he has not neglected to declare the whole purpose of God. And most certainly, he has not spoken any wrong thing— nothing contrary to the will of him that sent him. All his words are true and right concerning everything, and forever and ever his words will stand firm.

We can easily observe that in explaining and confirming his dependable and truthful words, Jesus takes care to refute the mistakes of the Scribes and Pharisees. The teachings of the Jewish teachers of that age were incorrect commentaries by which they had perverted the word of God. Jesus also refuted all the fundamental mistakes that would ever arise in the Christian Church that are incompatible with salvation. In advance, Jesus corrected all the comments through which Christian teachers (so called) of any age or nation would "pervert the word of God," by teaching careless souls to "invite death by the error of their lives."

4. Now, we are logically led to notice who it is that Jesus is teaching. He is not teaching just the apostles. If he had been, he would not have needed to "go up the mountain." A room in the house of Matthew or any of his disciples would have contained all the twelve disciples. And certainly it does not appear that the disciples who came to him on the mountain consisted only of the twelve. Without any force imposed on the expression, the term "his disciples" can be understood to mean *all* that wanted to learn from him.

But let us put this matter beyond any doubt and make it undeniably clear. Where it is said, "he began to speak, and taught them," the word *them* includes all the multitudes that went up the mountain with him. We need only to observe the concluding verses of the seventh chapter of Matthew. "Now when Jesus had finished saying these things, the crowds were astounded at his teaching, for he taught them (the multitudes) as one having authority, and not as their scribes."

Jesus taught the way of salvation not only to the crowd that was with him on the mountain. He also taught everyone who would ever be born—the entire human race. He taught the children yet unborn, all the generations to the end of the world who would ever hear the words about this life.

5. Everyone will acknowledge that in some of the parts of the Sermon on the Mount Christ was speaking to everyone. No one, for instance, denies that his statement about poverty of spirit relates to all humankind. However, many people have conjectured that other parts of this teaching of Christ concerned only the apostles, or the first Christians, or the ministers of Christ. These people allege that Christ's words were never intended for the general populace, and therefore ordinary people have nothing to do with these words of Jesus.

But may we not judiciously inquire as to who told them that some parts of this discourse concerned only the Apostles, or the Christians of the apostolic age, or the ministers of Christ? Mere assertions are not sufficient proof to establish a point of such great importance. So then, has our Lord himself taught us that some parts of his discourse do not concern all humankind? If such had been the case, he would have told us so. He would not have omitted such necessary information. Has he told us so? Where? In the discourse itself? No, the sermon does not contain the slightest suggestion of it. Has Jesus said so elsewhere? In any other of his discourses? We cannot find a single word that even suggests this possibility in anything he ever said to the multitudes or to his disciples. Has any one of the apostles or other inspired writers left such a teaching on record? Definitely not. There is no assertion of this kind to be found in the entire Bible. Who, then, are so much wiser than God, wiser "beyond what is written"?

6. Perhaps some will say that reason requires us to limit the range of people to whom this sermon is addressed. If reason does demand that we limit the sermon's application to only some Christians, but not to others, it must rest on one of two explanations: (1) without restricting the sermon's reach, it would be obviously absurd to apply it to everyone, or (2) other parts of scripture require us to restrict its application. However, neither theory is true.

When we examine the various considerations, it will become evident that it is not at all absurd to apply everything that our

Lord gave in this sermon to all humankind. Neither will a universal application of this sermon contradict anything else that Jesus has said or everything that we find in any other scripture. Furthermore, it will become evident that either the entire sermon is to be applied to *everyone,* or else to *no one.* All the members of the human race are connected to each other as stones in an arch. You cannot remove one stone without destroying the whole structure.

7. Finally, in the Sermon on the Mount we may observe the *manner* of our Lord's teaching. As in all circumstances, in this sermon "never has anyone spoken like he spoke." Jesus did not speak as the holy men and women of old, although "moved by the Holy Spirit" they "spoke from God." Jesus did not speak as the apostles Peter, James, John, or Paul spoke. They were indeed wise master-builders in his church. However, on the scale of heavenly wisdom, "the servants are not greater than their master." Indeed, Jesus spoke here in a manner unlike at any other time or on any other occasion.

It does not appear that it was ever his intent at any other time or in any other place to lay down at once the entire plan of his religion. In no single place or time did Jesus give us a full perspective of Christianity and describe expansively the nature of holiness without which no one will see the Lord. On a thousand different occasions Jesus described particular aspects of holiness. But nowhere else other than in this sermon did he intentionally give an extensive view of religion as a whole.

Indeed, we have nothing else of this kind in the entire Bible, unless one should consider that short sketch of holiness that God gave in the Ten Commandments to Moses on Mount Sinai. Yet there is a great difference between the Ten Commandments and the Sermon on the Mount! "For if there was glory in the ministry of condemnation, much more does the ministry of justification abound in glory!"

8. Above all, observe here the amazing love that the Son of God shows in revealing his Father's will to us! Jesus does not bring us again to the mount that burned with "a blazing fire, and darkness, and gloom, and a tempest." He does not speak as when he "thun-

dered in the heavens," when the Most High "broke through with clouds of hailstones and coals of fire."

Here, in this sermon Jesus now addresses us in "a sound of sheer silence." He said, "Blessed (or happy) are the poor in spirit." Blessed are those who mourn, the meek, those that hunger for righteousness, the merciful, and the pure in heart. They are blessed in the end, and along the way. They are happy in this life, and in the life everlasting! It is as if Jesus had said, "Who is the one who yearns to live and desires to see good days? Look! I am showing you the thing for which your soul hungers! Understand the way that you have so long sought without success. Here is the way of true pleasure, the path to serenity, and the road to joyful peace. It is the way to heaven below and heaven above!"

9. At the same time, notice with what authority he teaches! Understandably, the people said that he taught "not as the scribes." Observe the manner, the demeanor with which he speaks (it cannot be expressed in words)! Jesus did not speak as Moses, the servant of God; not as Abraham, God's friend; not as any of the prophets; nor as any other human being. Jesus' teaching is something more than human or anything connected with any created being. The teaching of Jesus is that of the Creator of everything! God has appeared upon the earth. The Being of beings, Yahweh, the self-existent, supreme God who is over all things and blessed forever!

10. This divine discourse was delivered in the most excellent order, and every succeeding part illustrates those parts that precede it. Ordinarily (and appropriately), Christ's sermon is divided into three principal sections. The first section comprises chapter 5 of Matthew's Gospel; the second section comprises chapter 6, and the third section comprises chapter 7. In the first division of the Sermon on the Mount, the entirety of all true religion is laid down in eight specific things. The rest of Matthew 5 explains these maxims and guards them against false human interpretations.

The second section of the sermon contains rules for the correct attitudes that we are to maintain in all our outward actions. These motives are to be untainted by worldly desires or anxious concerns, even for life's necessities. The third section cautions against the main hindrances to true religion, and then the sermon closes with an application.

I. The sum of true religion

1. First, in Matthew chapter 5 our Lord lays down the sum of all true religion in eight points. He explains these points and secures them against false interpretations.

Some people have theorized that Christ lays out these eight points as successive steps which Christians are to take in their journey to the promised land. Others assume that the eight points that Christ sets down apply to all Christians at all times. And why can we not acknowledge both interpretations? What incompatibility is there between the two approaches?

It is undoubtedly true that poverty of spirit and all the other attitudes mentioned here are at all times found (in a greater or lesser degree) in every genuine Christian. And it is equally true that genuine Christianity always begins with poverty of spirit and progresses in the order given here until the Christian is "made proficient" and "equipped for every good work." We begin with the foundation of these gifts of God, but we do not desert this gift when God calls us to "move up higher." "Only let us hold fast to what we have attained," while we "hold firm" and "press on" toward what still lies before us—the highest blessings of God in Christ Jesus.

2. Poverty of spirit is the foundation of everything, and it is here that our Lord begins. He opens his sermon by saying, "Blessed are the poor in spirit, for theirs is the kingdom of heaven."

It may not be illogical to assume that our Lord looked at those who were around him and observed that there were not many rich people there. Rather, his listeners consisted of the poor of this world. He took that opportunity to make a transition from temporal things to spiritual things. He said, "Blessed (or "happy" as the word should be translated here and in the succeeding verses) are the poor in spirit." Jesus does not say they are poor with regard to outward circumstances. It is not impossible that some of the poor may be as far from happiness as a monarch upon his throne. Jesus spoke about being poor in *spirit*. Whatever one's outward circumstances may be, those who are blessed have that disposition of heart. Poverty of spirit is the first step to all real, substantial happiness, either in this world or in the world to come.

3. Some have concluded that, here, the poor in spirit refers to those who love poverty and are free from covetousness and the love of money. That is, those who fear, rather than desire, riches. Perhaps those who hold to this view have entirely confined their thoughts to the literal term—"poor." Or, perhaps they have taken into account that significant observation of St. Paul that "the love of money is a root of all kinds of evil." Because of these considerations, many Christians have completely divested themselves of all riches and possessions. Thus, the vows of voluntary poverty have arisen in the Church of Rome, assuming that such a conspicuous degree of this fundamental grace must be a huge step toward the "kingdom of heaven."

However, these people do not seem to have observed the following. (1) The expression of St. Paul about money must be understood with some qualification, or else it is not true. The love of money is not the *exclusive* root of all evil. There are a thousand other roots of evil in the world, as distressing experience shows us daily. Paul's meaning can only be that money is the root of very many evils—perhaps of more than any other single vice. (2) The sense of the phrase "poor in spirit" will by no means express all of our Lord's present intention, which is to lay a general foundation for the entire structure of Christianity. The foundation on which to build the structure of Christianity does not consist only of guarding against one particular vice. Even if voluntary poverty were presumed to be one part of our Lord's intention, it could not possibly be the whole. (3) Voluntary poverty cannot be supposed to be any part of Jesus' meaning, unless we charge him with conspicuous repetition. If poverty of spirit were exclusively freedom from covetousness, the love of money, and the desire for riches, it would coincide with what he mentions again. It would be only a part of being pure in heart.

4. Who then are "the poor in spirit"? Without question, poverty of spirit belongs to the humble—those who truly understand themselves and are convinced of their sinfulness. The poor in spirit are those to whom God has given that initial repentance that precedes faith in Christ.

Those who are poor in spirit can no longer say, "I am rich, I have prospered, and I need nothing." They understand that they are "wretched, pitiable, poor, blind, and naked." The poor in spirit are convinced that they truly are spiritually poor and that they have no spiritual good residing in them. They say, "I know that nothing good dwells within me," only whatever is evil and abhorrent. The poor in spirit have a deep sense of the loathsome leprosy of sin, which they inherited at birth. This sin blankets the entire soul, and completely corrupts its every endowment and capacity.

The poor in spirit see more and more of the wrong dispositions that spring from that evil root. They see their pride and arrogance of spirit, their constant tendency to think of themselves more highly than they ought to think. They understand their egotism and thirst after the esteem and honor that come from others. Those that are poor in spirit see in themselves their hatred, envy, jealousy, revenge, anger, hostility, harshness, inbred hostility against God and others, all of which appear in ten thousand forms.

The poor in spirit understand their love of the world, their self-will, and the foolish and harmful desires that cling to their innermost souls. They are conscious of how deeply they have transgressed by their words. If their words are not profane, immodest, untrue, or unkind, yet their conversation is not "useful for building up" and does not "give grace to those who hear." God regards all these things as corrupt and grievous to his Holy Spirit. Being poor in spirit causes people to be ever aware of their deeds. If one were to confess them all, they are "more than can be counted." One might as well try to number the drops of rain, the sand of the sea, or the days of eternity.

5. One's guilt is now before one's face. The poor in spirit know that they deserve punishment. Guilt involves the carnal mind, which includes the entire, universal corruption of one's nature. How much more does guilt include all our evil desires and

thoughts and each of our sinful words and actions! Those that are pure in heart do not doubt for a moment that the least of their sins deserves the damnation of hell, where "the worm does not die and the fire is not quenched." Above all, the poor in spirit feel the heavy guilt of "not believing in the name of the only Son of God." They cry, "How can we escape if we neglect so great a salvation?" "Those who do not believe are condemned already" and "they must endure God's wrath."

6. "What will they give in return for their life," which is given up to the just vengeance of God? "With what will one come before the Lord?" How will one pay him whom he owes? Even if, from this moment, one were to perform the most perfect obedience to every command of God, this obedience would not atone for a single sin, for any previous act of disobedience. We owe God all the service we are able to perform, from this moment to all eternity. Even if we could obey in this way, it would not make amends for what we ought to have done previously. Therefore, the poor in spirit see themselves as utterly helpless to atone for past sins, unable to make any amends to God, or to pay any ransom for the soul.

Suppose God were to forgive everything that is past, on the single condition that we would not sin anymore and that in the future we would entirely and constantly obey all his commands. The poor in spirit would understand that it would gain them nothing, because it is a condition that they could never fulfill. They know and feel that they are not able to obey even the outward commands of God. We *cannot* obey them so long as our hearts remain in their natural sinfulness and corruption. "A bad tree cannot bear good fruit."

However, we cannot cleanse our own sinful hearts. "For mortals it is impossible." Therefore, we are completely at a loss even to begin walking in the path of God's commandments. Mortals do not know how to advance one step forward in God's way. Enveloped by sin, sorrow, and fear, without finding a way to escape, we can only cry out, "Lord, save us! We are perishing!"

7. Therefore, as poverty of spirit pertains to the first step we take in running the race that is set before us, it is a correct sense

of our inner and outer sins and our guilt and helplessness. Some have called this awareness "the virtue of humility," thereby teaching us to be proud of knowing that we deserve damnation! However, our Lord's term is quite different; it conveys no thought to the hearer other than that of sheer need, naked sin, helpless guilt, and utter misery.

8. In seeking to bring sinners to God, the great Apostle Paul spoke in a way that appropriately addressed this issue. He said, "The wrath of God is revealed from heaven against all ungodliness and wickedness of humankind." He immediately leveled this charge against the heathen world, and he demonstrated that all are under the wrath of God. Next, he explained that the Jews were no better than the heathen, putting them under the same condemnation. St. Paul delivered his message not so that sinners would attain "the noble virtue of humility." Rather, he spoke as he did in order that "every mouth may be silenced, and the whole world may be held accountable to God."

St. Paul proceeded to show that sinful humankind is as helpless as it is guilty. Such is the clear meaning of the following quotations:

- No human being will be justified in God's sight by deeds prescribed by the law. But now, apart from law, the righteousness of God has been disclosed (Rom. 3:20, 21).
- We hold that a person is justified by faith apart from works prescribed by the law (Rom. 3:28).

These statements all move toward the same aim, which is to keep us from pride. Paul humbles us to the dust, without teaching us to think about this kind of humility as a "virtue." Paul seeks to evoke a full, piercing conviction of our utter sinfulness, guilt, and helplessness. This awareness strips sinners of everything and tosses them, lost and undone, on the strong helper, Jesus Christ the righteous.

9. One is compelled to observe here that Christianity begins just where heathen morality ends. Poverty of spirit means conviction of sin, renouncing the self, abandoning one's own righteousness (the very first point in the religion of Jesus Christ), and leaving

behind all pagan religion. This understanding was permanently hidden from the wise of this world. The Latin language, even with all the improvements of the Augustan age, did not produce a single word for humility. (It is well known that the Latin word, from which we borrow "humility" has a different meaning.) No, not until the great Apostle Paul coined a word for "humility" can we find such a word even in the lavish Greek language.

10. O, that we will feel what they were not able to express! Sinner, awaken! Understand yourself! Understand and feel that you were "born a guilty sinner when your mother conceived you." Know that from the time you could discern good from evil that you yourself have been adding sin upon sin to your life! Bow down under the mighty hand of God, as one who is convicted of eternal death. Abandon, renounce, and abhor all fantasies of ever being able to help yourself! Let your entire hope center on being washed in Christ's blood and renewed by his almighty Spirit. "He himself bore our sins in his body on the cross!" Then you can testify, "Blessed are the poor in spirit, for theirs is the kingdom of heaven."

11. This poverty of spirit marks the kingdom of heaven (or kingdom of God) that is within us, which is "righteousness and peace and joy in the Holy Spirit." And what is "righteousness," other than the life of God in the soul, the same mind in you that was in Christ Jesus, and the image of God stamped upon the heart, now renewed after the likeness of him that created it? What is righteousness, but loving God because he first loved us, and, for Christ's sake, loving everyone else?

And what is "peace" (the peace of God) other than a calm tranquillity of soul and sweet rest in the blood of Jesus that leaves no doubt that he accepts us? This peace excludes all fear, other than the loving, childlike fear of offending our Father who is in heaven.

This inner presence of God's kingdom also entails "joy in the Holy Spirit." God's Spirit seals upon our hearts "the redemption that is in Jesus" and his righteousness that is imputed to us for "sins previously committed." Christ now gives us "the pledge of our inheritance"—the "crown which the Lord, the righteous judge, will give on that day." This blessing is appropriately called "the kingdom of heaven," because heaven is now opened in the soul. It marks the first springing up of those "rivers of delight" that flow at God's right hand forevermore.

12. For the poor in spirit, "theirs is the kingdom of heaven." I speak to all whom God has enabled to become "poor in spirit" and to feel themselves lost. Through the gracious promise of him "who never lies," we have a claim to heaven. The blood of the Lamb has purchased our title to heaven for us. Heaven is very near; you are on the brink of heaven!

After only one other step, you will enter into the kingdom of righteousness, and peace, and joy! Are you full of sin? "Here is the Lamb of God who takes away the sin of the world!" Are you completely without God? Look to your "advocate with the Father, Jesus Christ the righteous." Are you unable to atone for the least of your sins? Christ is "the atoning sacrifice for your sins." Here and now, believe on the Lord Jesus Christ, and all your sins will be blotted out! Are you completely unclean in soul and body? Here is the "fountain for sin and impurity!" Arise, and wash away your sins! Through your unbelief, hesitate no more at God's promise! Give glory to God! Dare to believe! At this moment, cry out from the depths of your heart,

> *Yes; I yield, I yield at last,*
> *Listen to Thy speaking blood,*
> *Me with all my sins I cast*
> *On my atoning God.*[8]

13. When you completely depend on Christ, you "learn from him" to be "humble in heart." This spiritual attitude is true, genuine, Christian humility. It flows from a sense of God's love brought to us in Christ Jesus. In this sense, poverty of spirit begins where a sense of guilt and of the wrath of God ends. Poverty of spirit is a continual awareness of our total dependence on God for every good thought, word, or deed. It is the conviction of our utter inability to produce any good thing, unless "every moment God waters it." Poverty of spirit is an aversion to human praise, knowing that all praise is due only to God.

Added to this humility is loving remorse and acute shame before God for the sins that we know he has forgiven and for the sin that still remains in our hearts (although we know our sin is not charged to our condemnation). Although we are not under God's condemnation, we daily feel a deeper and deeper conviction of inbred sin. The more we grow in grace, the more we understand the desperate wickedness of our hearts. More and more, we advance in the knowledge and love of God through our Lord Jesus Christ, as great a mystery as this may appear to those who do not know the power of God unto salvation. At the same time, increasingly we sense our alienation from God, the malice within our carnal minds, and the necessity of our being entirely renewed "in true righteousness and holiness."

II. Purity of intention

1. To be sure, the one who is just beginning to understand the inner kingdom of heaven has scarcely any concept of these things. New believers may say, "As for me, I said in my prosperity, 'I shall never be moved.' By your favor, O Lord, you have established me as a strong mountain." They feel that sin is so utterly crushed beneath their feet that they can scarcely believe that sin still remains within them. They think that even temptation is silenced, and calls no more to them. Temptation cannot approach; it stands far away. These new believers are borne aloft in the chariots of joy and love. They "mount up with wings like eagles." However, our Lord knows well that this triumphant state does not usually continue very long. Consequently, to the promise of the kingdom of heaven, Jesus adds, "Blessed are those who mourn, for they will be comforted."

2. We cannot conceive that this promise of comfort belongs to those that anguish over some worldly matter or who mourn and lament some mere earthly trouble or disappointment, such as the loss of reputation or friends, or the lessening of wealth. Equally so, those have no claim on the kingdom of heaven who trouble themselves with fears about some transitory harm or fret to the point of becoming heartsick over some deferred earthly thing. Let

us not think these people can "expect to receive anything from the Lord." God is not in all their thoughts. Therefore, they "go about like a shadow. Surely for nothing they are in turmoil." The Lord says to them, "This is what you shall have from my hand: you shall lie down in torment."

3. The mourners of whom our Lord speaks in his Sermon on the Mount are those that mourn for quite a different reason. Jesus speaks of those that mourn after God. When God enables them to "taste the goodness of the word of God and the powers of the age to come," they "rejoice with an indescribable and glorious joy." As for the overly confident new believers, God now "hides his face, and they are dismayed." They cannot see God through the dark cloud. Instead, they see temptation and sin rising again, which they foolishly assumed were gone, never to return. Now, temptation and sin pursue them at full speed, hemming them in on every side. It is not strange if their soul becomes distraught within them and trouble and depression seize them. Satan will not fail to take advantage of the occasion, saying something like the following:

Where now is your God? What has become now of the blessedness about which you spoke? You claim to have entered the kingdom of heaven? Has God really said, "Your sins are forgiven?" Surely, God has not said this to you. It was only a dream, a mere delusion, a figment of your own imagination. If your sins are forgiven, why are you so depressed? Can a pardoned sinner be unholy, as you are?

If, instead of immediately crying to God, these new believers try to dispute with Satan (who is wiser than they are), they will become depressed indeed. They will know sorrow of heart and anguish that cannot be expressed. Even when God shines again upon the soul and takes away all doubt about his past mercy, those who are weak in faith may still be tempted and distraught because of what is yet to come. They especially face a challenge when inward sin revives and powerfully pushes at them so that they will fall. Then again, they may cry out:

I have a sin of fear, that when I've spun
My last thread, I shall perish on the shore![9]

Oppressed Christians fear that they might "suffer shipwreck in the faith," and "their last state is worse than the first."

> *Lest all my bread of life should fail,*
> *And I sink down unchanged to hell!*

4. Certainly, this affliction "always seems painful rather than pleasant at the time, but later it yields the peaceful fruit of righteousness to those who have been trained by it." Therefore, "blessed are those who mourn" in this way. Let them "wait for the Lord" and not allow themselves to be "turned aside from the way" by the useless counselors of the world. The tempted ones will prevail if they resolutely reject all the comforts of sin, folly, and pride. They must turn aside from all the idle diversions and amusements of the world. These pleasures "perish with use" and only tend to benumb and stupefy the soul so that it will neither be aware of the self or of God. Blessed are those that "press on to know the Lord" and steadfastly refuse all other comforts.

They will be comforted by the encouragement of God's Spirit and by a fresh manifestation of his love. They have a strong inner witness that God accepts them in his Beloved Son, and this assurance will never again be taken from them. This witness is the "full assurance of faith," and it swallows up all doubt and agonizing fear. God gives them a confident hope of enduring substance, and "through grace he gives them eternal comfort."

We will not debate whether it is possible for any who were once enlightened and made partakers of the Holy Spirit to "fall away." It is enough, here, to say that by the power now resting upon them, "Who will separate us from the love of Christ? ... For I am convinced that neither death, nor life ... nor height, nor depth, nor anything else in all creation, will be able to separate us from the love of God in Christ Jesus our Lord."

5. The entire process of mourning for an absent God and recovering the joy of his approval seems to be foreshadowed in what our Lord said to his Apostles the night before his time of suffering:

"Are you discussing among yourselves what I meant when I said, 'A little while, and you will no longer see me, and again a little while, and you will see me'? Very truly, I tell you, you will weep and mourn, but the world will rejoice; you will have pain, but your pain will turn into joy. When a woman is in labor, she has pain, because her hour has come. But when her child is born, she no longer remembers the anguish because of the joy of having brought a human being into the world. So you have pain now; but I will see you again, and your hearts will rejoice, and no one will take your joy from you." (John 16:19-20)

6. By the return of the Holy Spirit, this mourning comes to an end and is lost in holy joy. Still, there is another most blessed kind of mourning that remains in the children of God. They still mourn for the sins and miseries of humankind; they "weep with those who weep." They weep for those that do not weep for themselves; they weep for those that sin against their own souls. Christians also mourn for the weakness and unfaithfulness of those who, at least in part, are saved from their sins. St. Paul said, "Do you think anyone is weak without my feeling his weakness? Does anyone have his faith overturned without my being concerned for him?"

Christians also grieve about the dishonor continually done to God, the sovereign power over heaven and earth. At all times they have an awful sense of this affront to God, and it brings a deep solemnity upon their spirit. It is a seriousness that is deepened because the eyes of their understanding are opened. They constantly see the vast ocean of eternity, without a bottom or a shore, which has already swallowed up millions and millions of people and is yawning to devour those that yet remain. While here on earth, Christians see the house of God eternal in the heavens. They also see hell and destruction without a covering. Therefore, they feel the importance of every moment, which appears briefly and then is gone forever!

7. To the world, however, all this wisdom of God is counted foolishness. People of the world regard the entire matter of mourning and poverty of spirit as stupidity and insensibility. In fact, it is good if they pass a favorable judgment on eternal concerns, and not decide that Christian mourning over sin is mere moping and gloom, if not complete insanity and confusion.

And it is no wonder that those who do not know God would pass judgment in this way. Suppose two persons were walking together, and one of them suddenly were to stop. And with the strongest signs of fear and astonishment, he cries out, "We stand on a frightening precipice! Look, we are on the verge of being shattered to pieces! If we take another step we will fall into that huge abyss! Stop! I will not continue further for all the world!" The other person, who thought of himself as able to see as clearly as his companion, looked ahead and saw no danger at all. What would he think of his companion, other than that he was confused or that he had gone out of his mind, and that too much religion (if he were not guilty of "much learning") had certainly made him insane!

8. Let not the children of God, "those who mourn in Zion," be deterred by any of these things. You whose eyes are opened, do not be troubled by those who continue onward while remaining in darkness. You do not "go about like a shadow." God and eternity are real things. Heaven and hell are very much indeed open before you, and you stand on the brink of the great gulf. It has already swallowed up more than words can express—nations, tribes, peoples, and languages. And it still yawns to devour the fickle, wretched people of the world.

"O shout out, do not hold back." Lift up your voice to him who holds both time and eternity. Pray that you and your sisters and brothers will be counted worthy to escape the calamity that will come like a whirlwind! Pray that you will be brought safely through all the waves and storms into your desired haven! Weep for yourselves until God wipes away the tears from your eyes. And even then, weep for the tribulations that will come upon the earth, until the Lord of all puts a stop to misery and sin. Then, he will wipe away the tears from all faces, and "the earth will be full of the knowledge of the Lord as the waters cover the sea."

Notes

1. W. Reginald Ward and Richard Heitzenrater, eds., *The Works of John Wesley,* Bicentennial Ed., Vols. 18-23, Journals and Diaries (Nashville: Abingdon Press, 1988–1995), April 1, 1739, 19:46.

2. Ward and Heitzenrater, *Wesley's Journal and Diaries*, October 17, 1771, 22:293.

3. Ward and Heitzenrater, *Wesley's Journal and Diaries*, July 31, 1739, 19:84.

4. John Telford, *The Letters of the Rev. John Wesley, A.M.*, 8 vols. (London: The Epworth Press, 1931), April 2, 1761, 4:144.

5. Thomas Jackson, *The Works of John Wesley*, 14 vols. (London: The Wesleyan Conference Office, 1862), 9:102.

6. Ward and Heitzenrater, *Wesley's Journal and Diaries*, December 13, 1739, 19:128.

7. See Sermon #30, §1.

8. Charles Wesley, "Waiting for Christ the Prophet," stanza 5, *Poet. Wks.*, 2:265.

9. John Donne, "A Hymn to God the Father," stanza 3, lines 1-2, in Edward Gosse, *The Life and Letters of Jon Donne, Dean of St. Paul's*, 2 vols. (Gloucester, Mass.: Peter Smith, 1959), 2:196.

10. Charles Wesley, "Groaning for Redemption," stanza 3, *Poet. Wks.*, 2:161).

UPON OUR LORD'S SERMON ON THE MOUNT

Discourse 2

This sermon is based on one of John Wesley's favorite scripture texts. Once, after he preached this message in Wales, he wrote in his journal, "At six almost the whole town (I was informed) came together, to whom I explained the six last Beatitudes; but my heart was so enlarged, I knew not how to give over, so that we continued three hours. O may the seed they have received, have its fruit unto holiness, and in the end everlasting life!"[1]

This discourse opens with the good news that "the winter is past" and the one who comforts those who mourn has come to disperse the clouds. In Wesley's words: "Joy comes when he that comforts the mourners has returned, 'that he may abide with them for ever.' At the brightness of his presence the dark clouds of doubt and uncertainty disperse, the storms of fear flee away, the waves of sorrow subside, and the spirit again rejoices in God our Savior. Then, these words will be completely fulfilled, and those whom God has comforted will bear witness."

Specifically, this sermon offers hope to three kinds of people— the meek, those who hunger and thirst for righteousness, and the merciful. Wesley begins his exposition with a discussion of the phrase "Blessed are the meek." In another sermon, Wesley states, "There is no disposition...which is more essential to Christianity than meekness."[2] Only the truly meek are able to discern what is good and evil. Because they trust God, they are willing to accept his providential working, even when treated unfairly or unjustly. The reward of the meek is great, for eventually they will inherit the earth. In his *Explanatory Notes upon the New Testament*, Wesley further elaborated on this beatitude: "They shall have all things really necessary for life and godliness. They shall enjoy whatever portion God hath given them here, and shall hereafter possess the new earth, wherein dwelleth righteousness." Wesley declares, "Meekness brings composure to the mind. It keeps steady with regard to anger, sorrow, and fear. It preserves balance in every circumstance of life and does not turn aside to the right hand or the left."

Wesley often speaks about "hungering and thirsting after righteousness." For instance, he wrote in his journal, "I endeavoured to stir them up once more to hunger and thirst after righteousness, after the whole image of God, without which they will still remain cold, languid, weary, heartless, dead."[3] Those who hunger and thirst for righteousness desire to know God even more strongly than hungry and thirsty people crave food and drink. Spiritually hungry and thirsty souls cannot be content with outward religion alone. They yearn for an inner religion that touches the soul. Wesley highlights the statement of Jesus that those who hunger and thirst for righteousness are blessed because God will fill their souls with righteousness. Wesley teaches that this righteousness is precisely the holiness that Jesus describes throughout the entirety of his Sermon on the Mount.[4]

Finally, Christ calls us to show mercy toward others, precisely because God is merciful to us. And being merciful brings the great reward of receiving both God's mercy and the mercy of others. This sermon shows that the foundation of showing mercy is love. Elsewhere, Wesley stated, "This common term, 'merciful,' is a distinguishing mark of brotherly love, and Jesus uses it here for the whole of religion. In the full sense of the term, 'the merciful' are those that love their neighbors as themselves." Concerning the merciful, Wesley wrote, "Whatever mercy therefore we desire from God, the same let us show to our brethren. He will repay us a thousand fold, the love we bear to any for his sake."[5] Wesley wrote in a letter, "O that God would stir up the hearts of all that believe themselves his children, to evidence it by showing mercy to the poor, as God has shown them mercy! Surely the real children of God will do it of themselves; for it is the natural fruit of a branch in Christ."[6]

The sermon closes with a benediction that reads as though it were written by an apostle: "The Lord God fill your heart with such love for every soul, that you will be ready to lay down your life for the sake of others! May your soul continually overflow with love, overpowering every unkind and unholy disposition, until God calls you up into the region of love, there to reign with him forever and ever!"

UPON OUR LORD'S SERMON ON THE MOUNT

Discourse 2

"Blessed are the meek, for they will inherit the earth. Blessed are those who hunger and thirst for righteousness, for they will be filled. Blessed are the merciful, for they will receive mercy." *(Matthew 5:5-7)*

I. Blessed are the meek

1 Blessedness comes when "the winter is past," and "the time of singing has come, and the voice of the turtledove is heard in our land." Joy comes when he who comforts the mourners has returned, "that he may abide with them for ever." At the brightness of his presence the dark clouds of doubt and uncertainty disperse, the storms of fear fly away, the waves of sorrow subside, and the spirit again rejoices in God our Savior. Then, these words will be completely fulfilled, and those whom God has comforted will bear witness to the words of Jesus, "Blessed are the meek, for they will inherit the earth."

58

2. Who are "the meek"? The meek are not those who never grieve for anything. Such people do not understand reality and they are not distraught over the evils that occur in the world. They do not discern evil from good. Furthermore, the meek are not those whose senseless apathy shelters them from the distresses of life. By nature or aptitude, such people have the qualities of livestock and stones. They are not annoyed at anything, because they feel nothing. These worldly philosophers are totally unconcerned about matters pertaining to God's kingdom. Consequently, apathy is as far from meekness as it is from humanity itself. One can hardly imagine how any of the Christians of the purer ages of the church, especially any of the Fathers of the Church, could confuse apathy with meekness. To do so would be to confuse one of the most profane errors of heathenism with one of the components of true Christianity.

3. Nor does Christian meekness denote a lack of enthusiasm for God. The lack of religious fervor has no more to do with meekness than do ignorance and apathy. Christian meekness keeps clear of every extreme, whether in excesses or shortcomings. Meekness does not nullify the affections—it balances them. The God of nature never intended that grace would abolish the affections. Instead, God intends that they be brought under proper discipline and retained there. Meekness brings composure to the mind. It keeps steady with regard to anger, sorrow, and fear. It preserves balance in every circumstance of life and does not turn aside to the right hand or the left.

4. Although meekness is the proper way to understand ourselves, it also pertains to our relationships with God and with our neighbors. When meekness refers to how we relate to God, it is usually termed "relinquishment," which denotes a peaceful submission to his complete will concerning us. Even though submission to God may not be pleasing to our natural instincts, meek Christians continually say, "It is the Lord; let him do what seems good to him." When we consider more carefully how meekness applies to ourselves, we call it "patience" or "contentment." When meekness applies to our relationships with others, it is kindness toward what is good and compassionate toward what is evil.

5. Those who are truly meek can clearly discern what is evil, and they can also endure it. They are aware of everything that is evil, and yet meekness maintains control in their lives. The meek are exceedingly "zealous for the Lord of Hosts." At the same time, in every thought, word, and deed their zeal is always guided by knowledge and tempered by love for God and others.

The meek do not want to extinguish any of the emotions that for wise ends God has implanted within their natures. However, they maintain mastery over all their emotions. They keep them in check and engage them only in the service of God's work. Even the discordant and more combative emotions can be applied to the noblest purposes. When employed against sin and regulated by faith and love, even hatred, anger, and fear can serve as "walls and bulwarks" for the soul so that the Evil One cannot assault it and bring it harm.

6. It is evident that meekness (a divine disposition) is to abide in us and grow in us daily. For as long as we remain upon earth, occasions for exercising and increasing meekness will never be lacking. "For you need endurance, so that when you have done the will of God, you may receive what was promised." We need the virtue of submission so that in all circumstances we may say to God, "Not what I want but what you want." Also, we need to behave "kindly to everyone," and especially toward evil and unthankful people. Without meek submission to God, evil will overwhelm us, instead of our overcoming evil with good.

7. Meekness does more than restrain our outward acts (as the ancient scribes and Pharisees taught). In every age, unworthy teachers who have not learned from God will unfailingly focus entirely on outward acts. Our Lord guards against this error. In the following words, Jesus reveals the true magnitude of this mistake:

> "You have heard that it was said to those of ancient times, 'You shall not murder'; and 'whoever murders shall be liable to judgment.' But I say to you that if you are angry with a brother or sister, you will be liable to judgment; and if you insult a brother or sister, you will be liable to the council; and if you say, 'You fool,' you will be liable to the hell of fire." (Matt. 5:21, 22)

8. In this scripture, under the heading of murder, our Lord places the anger that goes no farther than the heart. This anger does not show itself by any outward unkindness, no, not even so much as an ill-tempered word. Jesus said that God would judge those who are "angry with a brother or sister." Because we are all joined together as sisters and brothers, this warning applies to our attitudes toward any living person. Those who feel any unkindness in their hearts, any spirit contrary to love, those who are angry without a sufficient cause or any cause "will be liable to judgment." In that moment of anger, one will be exposed to "the righteous judgment of God."

But would one not be inclined to prefer the reading of those manuscripts that omit the words, "angry *without a cause*"? Is not the question entirely superfluous? If anger at persons is an attitude contrary to love, how can there be *any* cause for it that will justify it in the sight of God?

We concede that one should have anger toward sin. In this regard, we may be angry, yet we do not yield to sin. As to anger against sin, our Lord himself is once recorded to have been angry. "He looked around at them with anger; he was grieved at their hardness of heart." He grieved over the sinners, but was angry at their sin. In God's eyes, doubtless, this kind of anger is legitimate.

9. Jesus said, "If you say, 'You fool' you will be liable to hell-fire." This statement means that God will judge whoever gives way to the kind of anger that causes him or her to speak any word of contempt. Commentators have observed that the word *Raca* is a Syriac word, which correctly means "empty," "vain," or "fool-ish." This word is as harmless a declaration as we can use toward another person that displeases us. And yet our Lord assures us that whoever uses it "will be liable to the council," which means that we will be answerable for what we say. Offenders will be liable to an even more severe sentence from the Judge of all the earth.

Jesus declared, "If you say, 'You fool,' you will be liable to hell-fire." This kind of language concedes a foothold to the devil, and it is the same as breaking into vilification and purposely using censorious and contemptuous speech. The instant one uses this kind of language, he or she is liable to the highest condemnation. It should be observed that our Lord describes all these modes of speech as deserving of the severest punishment.

In the day of Jesus, the first offense made one "liable to judgment." It led to strangling, which was usually inflicted on those who were condemned in one of the lower courts. The second offense, making one "liable to the council," led to stoning, which was frequently inflicted on those condemned by the great Council at Jerusalem. The third offense led to "the hell of fire," which meant to be burned alive. This sentence was inflicted only on the highest offenders, and it was carried out in the "valley of the sons of Hinnom." (We translate "hinnon" as *hell*).

10. Our Lord next takes care to nullify a vain though common fantasy that people tend to imagine. Many presume that God will excuse their failing in some duties because they are scrupulous in others. Jesus explains that it is impossible for any sinner to bargain with God. He will not accept one duty in the place of another, nor will he accept partial for complete obedience. Jesus warns us that performing our duty to God will not excuse us from our obligation to our neighbor. He cautions us that if we are lacking in love, our works of piety, as they are called, will never accredit us with God. In fact, the lack of love will make all our good works an abomination to the Lord.

Suppose you bring your gift to the altar, and at the altar you remember that your brother or sister has something against you because of your unkind behavior in calling him or her *raca* (or fool). As long as your conscience is defiled with the guilt of unrepented sin, do not think that your gift will atone for your anger or that your gift will make you acceptable before God. "Leave your gift there before the altar and go; first be reconciled with your brother or sister" (at least do all you can to be reconciled), "and then come and offer your gift."

11. Let there be no delay in what so closely concerns your soul. "Come to terms quickly with your accuser," now, immediately, "while you are on the way to court with him." If it is possible, be reconciled before he or she leaves your sight. Otherwise, "your

accuser may hand you over to the judge." Your accuser may also appeal to God, the Judge of everyone.

The judge will summon the guard, "and you will be thrown into prison," that is, into hell, the judgment of the Great Day. "Truly I tell you, you will never get out until you have paid the last penny." However, "paying the last penny" is impossible for you ever to do. You have nothing with which to pay. Therefore, if you are once cast into that prison, "the smoke of your torment goes up forever and ever."

12. Meanwhile, "the meek shall inherit the earth." Observe the foolishness of worldly wisdom! Again and again, the wise of this world warn the meek that there will be no survival for them on earth if they do not take offense at mistreatment and if they meekly allow themselves to be ill-treated. Worldly advisers insist that the meek will never be able to obtain the common necessities of life or to keep even what they have. The meek are told that they can expect no serenity, peaceful ownership, or enjoyment of anything.

This teaching would be entirely true if there were no God in the world or if God did not concern himself with us. However, "God will rise up to establish judgment, to save all the oppressed of the earth." Then, God will laugh to scorn all this heathen wisdom. "Human wrath serves only to praise the Lord!" God takes particular care to provide the meek with "everything needed for life and godliness." Despite human power, deceit, or malevolence, God protects for the meek the provisions he has given them. And the things that he guards for them, he richly furnishes them for their enjoyment. Whether these provisions are little or much, they are pleasant to the meek. "By endurance they will gain their souls." Thus, they will truly possess whatever God has given them. They are always content, always happy with what they have. Because it pleases God, it pleases them. The hearts, desires, and joys of the meek are in heaven. Accordingly, it may truly be said that they "inherit the earth."

13. Moreover, there seems to be still a further meaning in the words, "the meek will inherit the earth." That is, the meek will have a more exalted part in the "new earth, where righteousness

is at home." In the twentieth chapter of the book of Revelation, St. John has given a general description of this inheritance (although we will know the full particulars in the hereafter). That apostle wrote:

> I saw an angel coming down from heaven.... He seized the dragon, that ancient serpent ... and bound him for a thousand years. ... I also saw the souls of those who had been beheaded for their testimony to Jesus and for the word of God. They had not worshiped the beast or its image and had not received its mark on their foreheads or their hands. They came to life and reigned with Christ a thousand years. (The rest of the dead did not come to life until the thousand years were ended.) This is the first resurrection. Blessed and holy are those who share in the first resurrection. Over these, the second death has no power, but they will be priests of God and of Christ, and they will reign with him a thousand years. (Rev. 20:1-6)

II. Hungering and thirsting for righteousness

1. This far in the Sermon on the Mount, our Lord is more directly engaged in removing the obstacles to true religion. One such obstacle is pride, the first and main hindrance of all religion. Poverty of spirit removes all pride. Other obstacles are frivolity and thoughtlessness. These things prevent any religion from taking root in the soul, until they are removed by holy mourning. Still other obstacles to true religion are anger, impatience, and discontent, which also are all healed by Christian meekness.

First, God must remove these hindrances. They are evil diseases of the soul that continually generate false cravings within us and fill us with unhealthy appetites. When God removes these hindrances, a genuine appetite for a heaven-born spirit returns. The soul hungers and thirsts for righteousness. As Jesus said, "Blessed are those who hunger and thirst for righteousness, for they will be filled."

2. We already observed that righteousness consists of the image of God within us—"the same mind in us that was in Christ Jesus." Righteousness is every holy and heavenly disposition combined. Righteousness springs from, and ends in, love for God as our

Father and Redeemer. It also includes love for all others for the sake of Christ.

3. Jesus said, "Blessed are those who hunger and thirst for righteousness." In order fully to understand this expression, first we should notice that hunger and thirst are the strongest of all our bodily appetites. In like manner, once they are spiritually awakened in the heart, the hunger and thirst of the soul for the image of God are the strongest of all our spiritual appetites. Indeed, they swallow up all other desires in that one great desire—to be renewed in knowledge according to the image of the creator.

Second, we should notice that from the moment we begin physically to hunger and thirst, those appetites never cease. They become increasingly intense and unrelenting, and unless we eat and drink, we will die. In the same way, from the moment we begin spiritually to hunger and thirst after the same mind that was in Christ, these spiritual appetites never cease. Rather, they cry for satisfaction with more and more intensity. For as long as there is any spiritual life remaining in us, these appetites cannot cease hungering and thirsting until they are satisfied.

Third, we may observe that only food and drink satisfy physical hunger and thirst. Hungry people give no regard to the entire world around them. They care nothing for all the elegance of clothing, all the trappings of government, all the treasure on earth, thousands of gold and silver pieces, or even the offer of any amount of fame. All these things are of no account to a hungry person. That one would still say, "These are not the things I want. Give me food, or else I die." It is the very same way with those souls that truly hunger and thirst after righteousness. They can find comfort in nothing but God. The human spirit cannot be satisfied with anything else. Whatever you offer the hungry soul besides God is valued lightly. Whether one has riches, or honor, or pleasure, one still says, "This is not the thing which I want! Give me love, or else I die!"

4. It is just as impossible to satisfy the hungry soul that thirsts for the living God with worldly religion as it is to satisfy the hungry soul with what the world counts as "happiness." The religion of the world includes only these three things:

(1) *Doing no harm.* That is, we must abstain from outward sin, at least from such scandalous transgressions as robbery, theft, common swearing, and drunkenness.
(2) *Doing good.* The religion of the world calls for us to relieve the poor and to be charitable (as it is called).
(3) *Using the means of grace.* This aspect of the religion of the world includes going to church and partaking of the Lord's Supper.

If people have these three marks, the world accounts them as "religious persons."

However, will mere "religion" satisfy the soul that hungers after God? Never. Outward religion does not provide food for the soul. We want a religion of an exalted kind, a religion higher and deeper than outward duties. We can no more find nourishment in a poor, shallow, formal religion, than we can satisfy our hunger "with the east wind." It is true that outward religion is careful to "abstain from every form of evil." Its adherents are zealous of good works and they attend all the ordinances of God. But the soul does not long for these things. Good works constitute only the outer shell of the inner religion for which one insatiably hungers.

The religion we hunger for is the knowledge of God in Christ Jesus. It is the "life that is hidden with Christ in God," being "united to the Lord and becoming one spirit with him," having "fellowship with the Father and with his Son," "walking in the light as God is in the light," and being "purified just as he is pure." This is the religion and the righteousness after which the soul thirsts. We cannot rest until we rest in God.

5. Jesus said that those who hunger and thirst for righteousness "will be filled." They will be filled with the things for which they yearn, including righteousness and true holiness. God will satisfy them with the blessings of his goodness and with the happiness of his chosen people. He will feed them with the bread of heaven and with the manna of his love. God will give them "drink from the river of his delights." Those who drink of this water will never thirst, except for more and more of the water of life. This thirst for more of God will continue forever.

The painful thirst, the fond desire,
Thy joyous presence shall remove,
While my full soul doth still require
Thy whole eternity of love.[7]

6. Whoever you are, to whom God has granted to "hunger and thirst for righteousness," call out to him so that you will never lose that immeasurable gift. Pray that this divine appetite will never cease. If many people reprove you and direct you to stop pleading with God, do not follow their advice. Indeed, pray so much the more, "Jesus, Master, have mercy on me! Let me not live, except to be holy as you are holy!"

Isaiah asked, "Why do you spend your money for that which is not bread, and your labor for that which does not satisfy?" Can you hope to dig happiness out of the earth or to find it in the things of the world? O, trample under foot all the world's pleasures, spurn its honors, count its riches as dung and dross—everything that is beneath the sun. Seek after "the surpassing value of knowing Christ Jesus" and for the complete renewal of your soul in the image of God in which it was originally created.

Beware of permitting what the world calls religion to quench that blessed hunger and thirst. The religion of the world consists of form and outward show, things that leave the heart as worldly and sensual as ever. Let nothing satisfy you except the power of godliness, a religion that is spirit and life, and living in God and God living in you. True religion consists of being an "inhabitant of eternity," entering "within the veil" by the "sprinkled blood," and sitting "with him in the heavenly places in Christ Jesus."

III. Blessed are the merciful

1. The more we are filled with the life of God, the more tenderly we will be concerned for those who remain without God in the world, still dead through trespasses and sins. This concern for others will not lose its reward. "Blessed are the merciful for they will receive mercy." The word *merciful* used here by our Lord more directly implies a compassionate and kindhearted person—one

who does not despise those who do not hunger after God, but earnestly grieves for them. This common term, *merciful,* is a distinguishing mark of brotherly love, and Jesus uses it here for the whole of religion. In the full sense of the term, the merciful are those who love their neighbors as themselves.

2. Without this kind of love, we gain nothing, even though we "speak in the tongues of mortals and of angels, have prophetic powers, understand all mysteries and all knowledge, have all faith, so as to remove mountains, give away all our possessions, and hand over our bodies to be burned." Because of the immeasurable importance of this love, God in his wisdom, through the Apostle Paul, has given us a full and particular account of it. By considering Paul's description of love, we will most clearly understand who are the merciful that will obtain mercy.

3. *Charity* is best translated as *love,* because it is a far clearer and less ambiguous word. It means loving our neighbors as Christ has loved us. Love is patient toward all people. Love endures all the weaknesses, ignorance, errors, infirmities, stubbornness, and weak faith of the children of God. As well, love endures all the malice and wickedness of the children of the world. Love suffers all these things, not only for a time or a short season, but also to the end. Love continues feeding the enemy when he hungers. If he thirsts, love still gives him drink, in this way continually heaping coals of melting love, on his head.

4. And in every step toward the desirable aim of "overcoming evil with good," "love is *kind,*" a word that is not easily translated. Love is gentle, amiable, and harmless. It stands at the greatest distance from peevishness, harshness, or bitterness of spirit. Love immediately inspires the sufferer with the most good-natured kindness and the most fervent and tender affection.

5. Consequently, "love is not envious." It is impossible for love to covet; love is the complete opposite of that depraved attitude. Envy cannot be present in the one whose love engenders a tender affection for everyone. The one who loves earnestly desires for every soul that God has made all temporal and spiritual blessings and good things in this world and the world to come. Love cannot be upset over God's bestowing any good gift upon any

human being. If people who love have received God's blessings, they do not bemoan others receiving the same benefits. Indeed, they rejoice when others are also blessed. If people who are loving do not have all these benefits, they bless God that at least others have them. They are more willing for others to receive blessings than for themselves to have them. The greater one's love, the more one rejoices in the blessings of all humankind. The greater one's love, the farther one is from every kind and degree of envy.

6. Love is not boastful. This statement coincides with the very next word—*arrogant*. Love is not rash or hasty in judging; it wil not hastily condemn anyone. It does not pass a severe sentence based on a limited or hasty understanding. It first weighs all the evidence, particularly that which is brought in favor of the accused. Those who truly love their neighbors are not like the majority of people who even in cases of the most trivial nature, "see a little, presume a great deal, and so jump to the conclusion."[8]

Those who love their neighbors do not act in this way. They proceed with alertness and prudence, paying attention to every step. They readily subscribe to that rule of the ancient heathen: "I am so far from lightly believing what one man says against another, that I will not easily believe what a man says against himself. I will always allow him second thoughts, and many times counsel too."[9] O, how do modern Christians compare to the ancient heathen!

7. It follows that love is not arrogant. Love does not influence or permit anyone "to think of himself more highly than he ought to think, but to think with sober judgment." Yes, love humbles one's soul unto the dust. Love dissolves all self-adulation, a cause of pride. Love prompts us to rejoice and to become as nothing, to be unimportant and paltry, the lowest of all, the servant of all. Those who "love one another with mutual affection" cannot help but "outdo one another in showing honor." Those who have the same love that was in Christ, are "in full accord," and "in humility regard others as better than themselves."

8. Love is not rude. It is not discourteous or willingly insulting to anyone. Love "pays to all what is due them, respect to whom

respect is due, honor to whom honor is due." Love extends courtesy, politeness, compassion to the entire world, and it "honors all" in their various stations. A late writer, Joseph Addison, defines good breeding, the highest degree of which is politeness, as "a continual desire to please in all areas of one's conduct." If this definition of love is true, there are none so well bred as Christians, who love all humankind. The Christian cannot keep from wanting to "please everyone" "for the good purpose of building them up." And this desire cannot be hidden; it will necessarily appear in all the Christian's interchanges with others. Christian love is "genuine." It will appear in all the Christian's actions and conversation. Yes, love will constrain the Christian, though without duplicity, to "become all things to all people, that by all means he can save some."

9. In becoming all things to others, "love does not insist on its own way." In striving to please all people, the lover of humankind has no view to his or her own temporal advantage. Those who love others covet no one's silver, or gold, or clothing. They desire nothing other than the salvation of their souls. Yes, in some sense, they may be said not even to seek their own spiritual or temporal advantage. Although they are earnestly seeking to save their souls from death, as it were, they forget themselves. As long as the zeal for the glory of God dominates their concerns, they do not think of themselves. No, through an overflowing of love, they may at times almost seem to forget themselves in both soul and body. With Moses, they cry out to God, "Alas, this people has sinned a great sin.... But now, if you will only forgive their sin—but if not, blot me out of the book that you have written." Or, with St. Paul, they say "I could wish that I myself were accursed and cut off from Christ for the sake of my own people, my kindred according to the flesh."

10. It is no marvel, then, that such love is not irritable. Let it be observed that the word "easily provoked," strangely inserted in the translation, is not in the original text. Paul's words are absolute—*love is not irritable*. It is not goaded into unkindness toward anyone. Indeed, there will be frequent instances of outward provocations of various kinds. But love does not surrender

to provocation; it triumphs over every circumstance. In all trials, love continues to look to Jesus and is more than a conqueror in his love.

It is not improbable that our translators inserted the word *easily* provoked as it were, to excuse the apostle Paul, who they supposed might, in contrast, appear to be lacking in the very love that he so beautifully describes. From a phrase in the Acts of the Apostles, which is very inaccurately translated, the translators seem to have assumed that this flaw was in St. Paul. When Paul and Barnabas disagreed concerning John Mark, our translation reads, "The disagreement became so sharp that they parted company."

This reading naturally prompts us to suppose that both parties were equally intense in their disagreement. Some assume that St. Paul, who was undoubtedly correct with regard to the point in question, was as much exasperated as Barnabas was. (Clearly, it was quite unsuitable to take John Mark with them again, because he had previously deserted them.) Some assume that Paul demonstrated anger by leaving the work for which he had been set apart by the Holy Spirit. But the original text implies no such thing, nor does it assert that St. Paul was irritated at all.

The text simply says, "the disagreement became so sharp." As a consequence of the eruption of strong emotions, Barnabas left St. Paul, joined with John Mark, and went his own way. "But Paul chose Silas and set out, the believers commending him to the grace of the Lord" (which is not said of Barnabas). Paul went through Syria and Cilicia, "strengthening the churches," as he had planned. But let us return to our subject.

11. Because "love is not resentful," it averts a thousand aggravations that otherwise would occur. Indeed, merciful Christians cannot avoid knowing about many things that are evil; they cannot help seeing them with their own eyes, and hearing them with their own ears. Love does not blind one's eyes, making it impossible for one to see that evil things do occur. Neither does love take away one's understanding any more than one's reasoning, so that one is unable to recognize evil.

For instance, when Christians see someone strike a neighbor or hear someone blaspheme God, they cannot disbelieve what was done or spoken; they cannot doubt that such offenders are evil. Nonetheless, they "think no evil." The word *think* does not refer either to our seeing and hearing or to the first and involuntary acts of our understanding. Rather, the term refers to our willingly thinking what we do not need to surmise. "Thinking no evil" means refusing to infer evil where it does not appear. It has to do with our deducing things that we do not observe, our assuming what we have neither seen nor heard.

Genuine love absolutely exterminates "thinking evil" of others. Root and branch, it tears up all inventing what we have not known. Love casts out all jealousies, evil speculations, and willingness to believe evil. Love is honest, open, and lacking suspicion. And as love cannot contrive evil, neither does love fear evil.

12. Love "does not rejoice in wrongdoing"—as common as it is, even among those who bear the name of Christ and who do not hesitate to rejoice when their enemies fall into affliction, error, or sin. Indeed, those who are zealously attached to any faction find it difficult to avoid this attitude! How difficult it is for them not to delight in any fault that they discover in members of the opposite party, whether it is a real or supposed blemish in their principles or their practice!

What fanatical defender of a cause is clear of these attitudes? Yes, who is so serene as to be altogether free from rejoicing in the downfall of others? Who does not rejoice when adversaries make false steps that they think will advance their own causes? Only persons of love refuse to rejoice in the mistakes of others. Only persons of love weep over the sin or folly of their enemies and take no pleasure in hearing or repeating it. Instead, they desire that it will be forgotten forever.

13. Love "rejoices in the truth," wherever it is found. Love delights in "the truth that is in accordance with godliness," bringing forth its proper fruit, which is holiness of heart and conduct. Persons of love rejoice to find that even those who oppose them, whether in points of opinion or practice, are nevertheless lovers of God and are in other respects irreproachable. Those who love are

glad to hear good things about others; they speak all the good they can, consistently with truth and justice.

Indeed, on the whole, those who love find glory and joy wherever good is diffused throughout the world. As citizens of the world, Christians claim a share in the happiness of all its inhabitants. Because Christians are fellow human beings with all people, they are concerned about the welfare of everyone. Those who love enjoy whatever brings glory to God and promotes peace and goodwill among all others.

14. "Love bears all things." (Without doubt, this verse should be translated *covers* all things. Otherwise the text would read the same as "endures" all things, which appears later in this verse.) Because people of mercy do not rejoice in iniquity, they do not willingly divulge it. Whenever Christians see, hear, or know about evil, they nevertheless conceal it as much as possible, without becoming "a partaker in the sins of others."

Wherever or in whomever Christians see anything that they do not approve, love does not allow it to escape from their lips, except to mention it to the persons concerned, so as to win them if possible. Those who love others are so far from making their faults or failings the subject of conversation that they never speak at all about an absent person, except to speak favorably. A busybody, slanderer, gossip, or evil-speaker is the same as a murderer. One would just as well cut a neighbor's throat as to destroy his or her reputation. One would just as well think of entertaining oneself by setting fire to a neighbor's house by "shooting deadly firebrands and arrows" and saying "I am only joking."

Love makes only one exception to repeating evil about a neighbor. Sometimes we are convinced that for the glory of God or the good of the neighbor (which amounts to the same thing) an evil should not be covered. In this case, for the benefit of the innocent, we are constrained to declare the guilty deed.

However, even in this case, (1) those who love others will not speak at all, until superior love constrains them. (2) They cannot repeat an evil based on a general, confused view of doing good or promoting the glory of God. They must speak only from a clear view of a particular end or certain good that they are seeking.

(3) Still, they cannot speak unless fully convinced that it is necessary to do so, and that a good purpose cannot be satisfied, at least not as effectively, by any other means. (4) In these cases, those who love others speak with the utmost sorrow and reluctance. They do so as the extreme and most severe medicine, a desperate remedy in a desperate case. We can liken it to using a kind of poison only to expel another poison. Consequently, (5) love speaks of evil as sparingly as possible. And we should speak only with "fear and trembling," for dread of transgressing the law of love by speaking too much and doing more harm than by not speaking at all.

15. Love "believes all things." Love is always willing to think the best about others and to put the most favorable construction on everything. Those who love are always ready to believe whatever may tend toward the benefit of another person's character. Love is easily convinced of (what it earnestly desires) the innocence and integrity of everyone, at least of the sincerity of other people's repentance when they miss the way. Love is glad to excuse whatever is imperfect, to condemn the offender as little as possible, and, without betraying the truth of God, to make every possible allowance for human weakness.

16. When love can no longer believe the best about others, it "hopes all things." Is an evil reported about someone? Love hopes that the account is not true and that the thing reported was never done. Is it certain that it *was* done? Perhaps it was not done under the circumstances that were reported. Allowing that possibility, there is room to hope it was not as bad as it is represented. Was the action unquestionably evil? Love hopes the motivation was not evil. Is it clear that the motivation was also evil? It might not spring from the settled nature of the heart, but rather from a burst of emotion or from some fiery temptation that pushed the person beyond his or her control.

Suppose that the report cannot be doubted, and all the actions, intents, and dispositions are equally evil. Love still hopes that God will at last bare his arm and gain the victory. Love hopes that "there will be more joy in heaven over" this "one sinner who repents than over ninety-nine righteous persons who need no repentance."

17. Finally, love "endures all things." The quality of fortitude completes the character of the one who is truly merciful. Christians endure not just some things, many things, or most things. Love utterly endures *all* things. Whatever the injustice, hostility, and cruelty that others inflict, love is able to endure. Christians call nothing unbearable. They never say of anything, "This cannot be borne."[10] No, Christians can do and endure all things through Christ who strengthens them. Nothing that the Christian suffers can destroy love or diminish it in the least. It is impervious to everything.

Love is a flame that burns even in the midst of a great ocean. "Many waters cannot quench love, neither can floods drown it." It triumphs over all things. "Love never ends," either in time or in eternity.

> *In obedience to what heaven decrees,*
> *Knowledge shall fail, and prophecy shall cease.*
> *But lasting charity's more ample sway,*
> *Nor bound by time, nor subject to decay,*
> *In happy triumph shall for ever live,*
> *And endless good diffuse, and endless praise receive.*[11]

So shall "the merciful receive mercy." The merciful receive mercy by the blessing of God on all their ways, and God multiplies a thousandfold within them the love they give to their sisters and brothers. Also, they receive "an eternal weight of glory beyond all measure" in "the kingdom prepared for them from the foundation of the world."

18. For a short time you may say, "Woe is me, that I am an alien in Meshech, that I must live among the tents of Kedar."[12] You may pour out your soul and lament the loss of true, genuine love on the earth. Love in the world is indeed lost! You may well say, "See how these Christians love one another" (although not to the degree found in the ancient church)!

Some Christian kingdoms tear out each other's insides, devastating one another with fire and sword! There are Christian armies that are sending each other by the thousands and ten thousands alive into the grave! There are Christian nations that are ablaze with internal conflict, party against party, faction against faction! There are Christian cities where deceit, fraud, oppression, wickedness, even robbery and murder never leave the streets! There are Christian families that are torn apart with envy, jealousy, anger, domestic quarrels without number and without end! Indeed, what is most dreadful and most to be lamented of all, these Christian churches that bear the name of Christ, the Prince of Peace, wage continual war with each other!

"Tell it not in Gath." It is a pity! How can we hide it from the Jews, Moslems, or pagans? They convert sinners by burning them alive, and they are "drunk with the blood of the saints." Does this charge belong only to "Babylon the great, mother of whores and of earth's abominations?" Truly not. Reformed Churches (so called) have to an extent learned to tread in Babylon's steps. When they have power in their hands, Protestant churches also know to persecute, even to the shedding of blood. In the meantime, how they also condemn each other, and assign each other to the lowest hell! What wrath, conflict, hostility, and bitterness are found everywhere among them, even when they agree on essentials and only differ in opinions or in the details of religion!

Who are they that "pursue what makes for peace and for mutual upbuilding?" O God! How long? Shall your promise fail? Do not fear that it will. "Do not be afraid, little flock." Hoping against hope, believe in hope! "It is your Father's good pleasure" yet to "renew the face of the ground."

Surely, "the evil of the wicked will come to an end" and "the inhabitants of the world will learn righteousness." "Nation shall not lift up sword against nation, neither shall they learn war any more." "The mountain of the Lord's house shall be established as the highest of the mountains," and "the kingdom of the world will become the kingdom of our Lord." "They will not hurt or destroy on all God's holy mountain," and they "shall call your walls Salvation, and your gates Praise." They shall all be without defect or blemish, loving one another, just as Christ has loved us.

Even if the harvest has not yet arrived, become a part of the firstfruits. Do you love your neighbor as yourself? The Lord God fill your heart with such love for every soul, that you will be ready to lay down your life for the sake of others! May your soul continually overflow with love, overpowering every unkind and unholy disposition, until God calls you up into the region of love, there to reign with him forever and ever!

Notes

1. Ward and Hietzenrater, *Wesley's Journal and Diaries*, October 19, 1739, 19:108.

2. Outler, *Wesley's Sermons*, "Sermon on the Mount," Discourse 4 (I, 3), 1:534.

3. Jackson, *Wesley's Works*, May 17, 1787, 4:375.

4. *Explanatory Notes upon the New Testament*, Matt. 5:6.

5. *Explanatory Notes upon the New Testament*, Matt. 5:5, 7.

6. Jackson, *Wesley's Works*, 3:307.

7. Charles Wesley, "Pleading the Promise of Sanctification," stanza 22, *Poet. Wks.*, 2:322.

8. Attributed to John Locke (1632–1704).

9. Attributed to Seneca (c. 54 B.C.–65 A.D.).

10. Prayer of Manasseh, v. 5, Old Testament Apocrypha.

11. Matthew Prior, "Charity," lines 31-36 in *The Poetical Works of Matthew Prior*, 2 vols., John Mitford, ed. (London: Bell and Daldy, 1835).

12. Ps. 120:5.

UPON OUR LORD'S SERMON ON THE MOUNT

Discourse 3

On Sunday, August 26, 1739 at 6:45 A.M. John Wesley preached this sermon on the Bowling Green in Bristol. The congregation numbered about 4,000. The Bowling Green was near the center of the city, and Wesley preached there often. At 5:00 P.M. on the same day he preached about two miles from Bristol at Rose Green, on a flat area at the summit of a rise. The congregation consisted mostly of coal miners. On that occasion, Wesley's pulpit was a heap of refuse that workers had removed from the mines. He estimated the evening crowd to be about five-thousand. In such settings as these, Wesley often preached from Christ's Sermon on the Mount.

Most eighteenth-century English clergymen regarded preaching outside the church as scandalous; some even pronounced the practice "harmful." Wesley, however, defended field preaching, and he refused to permit critics to deter him from this practice. The common people flocked to hear him speak in the fields and marketplaces. Wesley wrote in his journal, "I wonder at those who still talk so loud of the indecency of field-preaching. The highest indecency is in St. Paul's church, when a considerable part of the congregation are asleep, or talking, or looking about, not minding a word the Preacher says. On the other hand, there is the highest decency in a churchyard or field, when the whole congregation behave and look as if they saw the Judge of all, and heard him speaking from heaven."[1]

In a letter to the Earl of Dartmouth, Wesley wrote, "(i.) If there is a law, that a Minister of Christ who is not suffered to preach the Gospel in the church should not preach it elsewhere, I do judge that law to be absolutely sinful. (ii.) If that law forbids Christian people to hear the Gospel of Christ out of their parish church, when they cannot hear it therein, I judge it would be sinful for them to obey it. (iii.) This preaching is not subversive of any good order whatever. It is only subversive of that vile abuse of the good order of our Church, whereby men who neither preach nor live the Gospel are suffered publicly to overturn it from the foundation; and, in the room [place] of it, to palm upon their congregations a wretched mixture of dead form and maimed morality."[2] Wesley considered the teachings of Christ's Sermon on the Mount to be the antidote to "dead form and maimed morality."

This sermon begins with the affirmation that the distinguishing mark of heart purity is love. Elsewhere, Wesley comments that the pure in heart will see God "in all things here [and] hereafter in glory."[3] Here, he contends, "Although false teachers say little about love, this virtue remains essential for holiness. Love does not allow uncleanness into one's life. Love would cut off one's own hand rather than engage in unholy activities." Wesley encourages his readers to seek the purity of holy love, because, in the words of Jesus, those who have pure hearts will see God.

In the second division of the sermon, Wesley discusses the blessedness of peacemakers. The fullest expression of making peace is doing good to all people to the utmost of one's ability. Peacemakers take delight in any opportunity to minister to the souls and bodies of others. Furthermore, the ability to live as a peacemaker comes from God, who gives this grace to Christians so that they will become his instruments of reconciliation in the world.

Just before the American War of Independence, Wesley wrote a letter to Thomas Rankin, his "assistant" in America. In that correspondence, Wesley added a note to the American preachers: "You were never in your lives in so critical a situation as you are at this time. It is your part to be peace-makers; to be loving and tender to all; but to addict yourselves to no party. In spite of all solicitations, of rough or smooth words, say not one word against one or the other side. Keep yourselves pure: Do all you can to help and soften all: But beware how you adopt another's jar [body of beliefs]."[4]

This sermon also explains that the spirit of the world is not compatible with the spirit of Christ. Consequently, the fallen world system will invariably persecute the pure in heart who work to bring peace among all people. Wesley warns, "Peace-makers...take all opportunities of doing good to all men. This is the grand reason why they have been persecuted in all ages, and will be till the restitution of all things.... The men of the world sincerely think... the more the peace-makers are enabled to propagate lowliness, meekness, and all other divine tempers, the more mischief is done.... Consequently, the more are they enraged against the authors of this, and the more vehemently will they persecute them."[5] Although they are persecuted, the peacemakers are blessed because theirs is the kingdom of God. Elsewhere, Wesley wrote, "One would imagine a [peacemaker] of this amiable temper and behaviour would be the darling of mankind. But our Lord well knew it would not be so, as long as Satan was the prince of this world. He therefore warns them before of the treatment all were to expect, who were determined thus to tread in his steps, by immediately subjoining, Happy are they who are persecuted for righteousness' sake."[6]

Wesley concludes the sermon with a discussion of how God's children should respond to the persecution that is bound to come to them in the present world. (1) Love your enemies. (2) Bless them that curse you. (3) Do good to those who hate you. (4) Pray for those who spitefully use you and persecute you. The sermon ends with words of encouragement: "These principles comprise the fundamentals of Christianity.... Let us not rest until every line of this religion is transcribed into our hearts. Let us watch, and pray, believe and love, and 'exercise self-control in all things' until every part of it appears in our souls, graven there by the finger of God. Let us persevere until we are 'holy as he who calls us is holy and we are perfect as our heavenly Father is perfect.'"

Sermon 23

UPON OUR LORD'S SERMON ON THE MOUNT

Discourse 3

"Blessed are the pure in heart, for they will see God. Blessed are the peacemakers, for they will be called children of God. Blessed are those who are persecuted for righteousness' sake, for theirs is the kingdom of heaven. Blessed are you when people revile you and persecute you and utter all kinds of evil against you falsely on my account. Rejoice and be glad, for your reward is great in heaven, for in the same way they persecuted the prophets who were before you."

(Matthew 5:8-12)

I. Purity of heart

1 The Sermon on the Mount highly commends loving one's neighbor! Elsewhere, scripture states that love is "the fulfilling of the law" and "the aim of instruction." Without love, everything we have, do, and suffer is without value in the sight of God. Furthermore, the love of neighbor accounts for nothing

unless it springs from our love for God. This fact requires us, therefore, carefully to examine the foundation on which our love for our neighbor rests. We must determine if our love for others is really built upon our love for God and if "we love because he first loved us." God's love alone is the basis of our becoming "pure in heart." This love is the foundation that will never be displaced: "Blessed are the pure in heart, for they will see God."

2. "The pure in heart" are those whose hearts God has purified "just as he is pure." Through faith in the blood of Jesus, they are purified from every unholy affection and cleansed "from every defilement of body and of spirit, making holiness perfect in the fear of God." Through the power of God's grace and the deepest poverty of spirit, God purifies them from every unkind and violent passion. Through their meekness and gentleness, God removes every desire except to please and enjoy him. Increasingly, the pure in heart want to know and love God, and a hunger and thirst for righteousness fully occupies their entire souls. Now they "love the Lord their God with all their heart, and with all their soul, and with all their mind, and with all their strength."

3. However, the false teachers of all ages have given only slight regard to purity of heart. They have taught people barely to abstain from those outward defilements that God has specifically forbidden. All the while, these teachers did not deal with the heart. Failing to give heed to inner purity, in effect these false teachers sanctioned hidden impurities.

Our Lord has given us a noteworthy teaching about neglecting the heart: "You have heard that it was said, 'You shall not commit adultery.'" In explaining this commandment, the blind leaders of the blind in the time of Jesus insisted only that one abstain from the outward act. However, Jesus said, "I say to you that everyone who looks at a woman with lust has already committed adultery with her in his heart." God "desires truth in the inward being." He searches hearts, and there he tests our obedience. "If you cherish iniquity in your hearts, the Lord will not listen to you."

4. God permits no excuse for clinging to anything that is an inducement to impurity. Therefore, "if your right eye causes you to sin, tear it out and throw it away; it is better for you to lose one

of your members than for your whole body to be thrown into hell." If persons that you cherish as much as your right eye become an occasion of your offending God or a means of arousing an unholy desire in your soul, do not delay forcibly to separate from them. "And if your right hand causes you to sin, cut it off and throw it away; it is better for you to lose one of your members than for your whole body to go into hell." If any other people that seem as necessary to you as your right hand become a cause of sin or an impure desire, force yourself to a complete and decisive separation from them. Even if the sin (or desire) does not go beyond the heart and never results in word or action, leave the company of these people. Cut them off instantly, and give them up to God. Any loss of pleasure, material things, or friends is preferable to the loss of your soul.

There are only two appropriate steps to take before you make such an absolute and final separation. First, attempt to drive out the unclean spirit by fasting and prayer. Also vigilantly abstain from every action, word, and momentary look that you have found to be a cause of evil. Second, if you are not delivered by this means, seek counsel from the one who watches over your soul. At the least, ask advice from those who have experience in the ways of God about the time and manner of your separation. Do not confer with just anyone, for fear that you will receive "a powerful delusion, leading you to believe what is false."

5. Marriage itself, as holy and honorable as it is, may not be used as an excuse for giving in to all your desires. Indeed, "It was also said, 'Whoever divorces his wife, let him give her a certificate of divorce.'" The man did not need to state a cause, other than that he did not like her or that he liked another woman better. After one gave his wife a certificate of divorce, the matter was settled. However, Jesus declared, "I say to you that anyone who divorces his wife, except on the ground of unchastity (meaning unfaithfulness), causes her to commit adultery; and whoever marries a divorced woman commits adultery." The word for adultery signifies unchastity in general, either in the married or unmarried state.

These words clearly forbid all polygamy. Our Lord explicitly declares that it is adultery for any woman with a living husband

83

to marry again. By consistency of reason, it is adultery for any man to marry again, so long as his wife is living. The command applies to divorced couples, unless the divorce was due to adultery. Only in that case are there no scriptures forbidding remarriage.

6. Purity of heart is what God requires and what he produces in those who trust in his beloved son. In this regard, "blessed are the pure in heart, for they will see God." God "will reveal himself to them" in ways that he does not reveal himself "to the world." Also, he will disclose himself to them in ways that he does not always reveal even to his own children. He will bless the pure in heart with the clearest communications of his Spirit, in the most intimate "fellowship with the Father and with his Son Jesus Christ." God will cause his presence to go continually before them, and the light of his face to shine upon them.

The pure in heart ceaselessly pray, "Show me your glory," and God grants their petition. Because the veil of flesh is being made as it were transparent, by faith they now see God. They see him in everything that surrounds them, in all things that he has created and brought to pass. They see God in the height above and in the depths below—they see "the fullness of him who fills all in all."

The pure in heart see all things as being full of God. They see him in the expanse of the heavens, in "the moon moving in splendor," in the sun "like a strong man running his course with joy." They see God "making the clouds his chariot, and riding on the wings of the wind." They see God "preparing rain for the earth" and "crowning the year with his bounty," giving "the grass to grow for the cattle, and plants for people to use." They see the creator of everything wisely commanding it all, and "sustaining all things by his powerful word." "O Lord, our Sovereign, how majestic is your name in all the earth."

7. Especially, the pure in heart see God in all his providences relating to their souls and bodies. They see God's hand always over them and working good. He weighs and measures all things, numbering the hairs of their heads, putting a fence around about them and all that they possess. According to the depth of his wisdom and mercy, God arranges all the circumstances of their lives.[7]

8. In a special way, the pure in heart see God in the means of grace that he provides. They find God through these means, whether they go into the great congregation to "ascribe to the Lord the glory due his name" and worship him in "holy splendor" or go into their rooms and "shut the door and pray to their Father who is in secret."

They see God whether they search the scriptures, or hear the ambassadors of Christ proclaiming glad tidings of salvation, or eat of the bread and drink of the cup that "proclaim the Lord's death until he comes." In all these ways that God has appointed, they find a close access to him that cannot be expressed. As it were, they see God face-to-face and talk with him "face to face, as one speaks to a friend." This fellowship is a fit preparation for those mansions above where the pure in heart will see him as he is.

9. How very far from seeing God were "those of ancient times" who heard "You shall not swear falsely, but carry out the vows you have made to the Lord." They interpreted this command to mean, "You must not swear falsely when you swear by the Lord God. You must perform the vows you make to *him,* but he does not regard any other vows you make to others." The Pharisees made this interpretation. In ordinary conversation, they allowed all kinds of vows, but they considered them only a small thing, because they had not made the vow in the special name of God.

However, our Lord absolutely forbids all common oaths and, of course, deceptive promises. He explains the abuse of both kinds of promise-making. He appeals to the awesome consideration that every person belongs to God, who in prevenient grace is present everywhere, in everyone, and over everyone. Thus, Jesus declared, "But I say to you, do not swear at all, either by heaven, for it is the throne of God, or by the earth, for it is his footstool." To swear by anything is the same as swearing by God who "sits above the circle of the earth."

Furthermore, God is as intimately present in earth as in heaven. Jesus forbade swearing "by Jerusalem, for it is the city of the great King." (The name of God was well known throughout that city.) Jesus also said, "Do not swear by your head, for you cannot make one hair white or black." Even the hairs of your head do not belong to you. God is the exclusive agent of everything in heaven and earth. In all your discourse with each other "Let your 'Yes' be 'Yes' and your 'No' be 'No.'" (In a straightforward way, simply affirm or deny something.) "Anything more than this comes from the evil one." Everything more than a simple yes or no comes from the devil, and swearing oaths is a mark of Satan's children.

10. Here, it is apparent that our Lord does not forbid the swearing in judgment and truth when we are required to do so by a magistrate in court. (1) From the context of his teaching, Jesus was condemning the abuse of affirming things to be true. Namely, he is talking about deceptive swearing, and ordinary swearing. Affirming the truth before a magistrate is not at all under consideration (2) Jesus was talking about ordinary conversation, when he set forth the principle, "Let your word be 'Yes,' or 'No.'" (3) By his own example, Jesus used an oath, when required by a magistrate. When the High Priest said unto him, "I put you under oath before the living God, tell us if you are the Messiah, the Son of God." Jesus immediately answered in the affirmative: "You have said so." (This expression means, "What you say is true.") Jesus continued, "But I tell you, from now on you will see the Son of Man seated at the right hand of Power and coming on the clouds of heaven." (4) God the Father, himself, swore an oath. "When God desired to show even more clearly to the heirs of the promise the unchanging character of his purpose, he guaranteed it by an oath." (5) St. Paul used an oath, and we think that he had the Spirit of God and well understood the mind of his Master. That apostle said, "For God, whom I serve with my spirit by announcing the gospel of his Son, is my witness that without ceasing I remember you always in my prayers." He wrote to the Corinthians, "I call on God as witness against me: it was to spare you that I did not come again to Corinth." St. Paul testified to the Philippians, "God is my witness, how I long for all of you with the compassion of Christ Jesus."

From these passages, it undeniably appears that if the Apostle Paul knew the meaning of his Lord's words, they do not forbid swearing on weighty occasions, even to one another. How much less do they forbid affirming the truth before a magistrate! Finally, we have another instance of using an oath in the assertion of the great apostle. (It is impossible that he could have avoided a sense of guilt if his Lord had completely forbidden all vows.) "Human beings, of course, swear by someone greater than themselves, and an oath given as confirmation puts an end to all dispute."

11. The important lesson that our blessed Lord imparts here, and illustrates by example, is that God is in everything and that we are to see the Creator mirrored in everyone. We should use and regard nothing as existing independently of God. To regard anything apart from God is indeed a kind of practical atheism. Rather, we should see everything with a true grandeur of thought. We should view heaven and earth and everything in them as being in the hollow of God's hand. By his personal presence, he sustains all things and he pervades and guides the entire created order. In a true sense, God is "the soul of the universe."[8]

II. Purity in action

1. To this point in the Sermon on the Mount, our Lord has been more directly engaged in teaching the religion of the heart. He has shown what Christians are *to be*, and then he proceeds to show what they are *to do*. Jesus explains how inward holiness is to show itself in our outward manner of life. "Blessed are the peacemakers, for they will be called children of God."

2. It is well known that in the sacred writings the word *peace* refers to all manner of good—every blessing that pertains to the soul or the body in time or eternity. Accordingly, in his epistles St. Paul bestows "grace and peace" to the Christians at Rome and Corinth. It is as if he had said, "As a fruit of the free and undeserved love and favor of God, may you enjoy all spiritual and temporal blessings—all the good things that God has prepared for those who love him."

3. From this truth, we may freely learn in what a broad sense we are to understand the term *peacemakers.* In its literal meaning peacemakers are those who love God and others. They utterly detest and abhor all strife, debate, disagreement, and contention.

Accordingly, they labor with all their might to prevent this fire of hell from starting. Or, when it is ignited, they work to keep it from spreading any farther. They strive to calm the stormy spirits of people, quiet their turbulent passions, and soften the minds of squabbling parties. If possible, they reconcile people with each other. Peacemakers use all their virtuous skills, and employ all the strength and talents that God has given them to preserve peace where it exists, and to restore it where it does not. The joy of peacemakers' hearts is to promote, confirm, and increase joint goodwill among everyone.

However, peacemakers are also marked by lesser virtues: they are especially distinguished by their efforts to maintain harmony among the children of God. All Christians have "one Lord, one faith," and they are all "called to the one hope of their calling," so they may all "lead a life worthy of the calling to which they have been called." They are to walk "with all humility and gentleness, with patience, bearing with one another in love, making every effort to maintain the unity of the Spirit in the bond of peace."

4. In the fullest extent of the word, as opportunities arise, peacemakers "work for the good of all." Those who are filled with the love of God and of all humankind cannot confine their expressions of love just to family, friends, acquaintances, ethnic groups, or those who hold their own beliefs. The peacemakers' love is not confined to those who "have received a faith as precious as theirs." Peacemakers step over all these narrow bounds in order to do good to everyone. They strive in some way or other to express love to neighbors, strangers, friends, and enemies. Peacemakers work for the good of all, as they have opportunity. That is, on every possible occasion they "make the most of the time" in order to redeem every opportunity and improve every hour, losing no instant to benefit others.

Peacemakers do not confine "working for good" to only one particular kind of good. They work overall good in every possible way, by engaging all their abilities, powers, and capacities of body and soul. Peacemakers expend all their fortunes, advantages, and reputations, desiring only that when their Lord comes he may say, "Well done, good and trustworthy servant."

5. To the utmost of their abilities, peacemakers work for the good of people's physical bodies. They rejoice to "give bread to the hungry and cover the naked with a garment." Is anyone a stranger? The peacemaker takes him in and alleviates his needs. Are any sick or in prison? Peacemakers visit them and administer the help they need the most. Peacemakers do not minister to others in order to be seen or recognized. Instead, they remember him who said, "just as you did it to one of the least of these who are members of my family, you did it to me."

6. How much more do peacemakers rejoice in ministering good to anyone's *soul!* Of course, the power to minister belongs to God. He alone can change the heart, without which every other alteration is "lighter than a breath." Nevertheless, it pleases God who "activates all of them in everyone" to help people mainly through other people. Ordinarily, God works to convey his own power, blessing, and love through one person to another.

Of course, it is certain that "the help that is done upon earth, God does it himself."[9] Even so, no one should stand idle in God's vineyard. Peacemakers cannot remain inactive. They always labor in God's work as instruments in his hand, preparing the ground for their master's use, sowing the seed of the kingdom, or watering what is already sown, so that if possible God will give the increase. According to the measure of grace received from God, peacemakers exercise all diligence to reprove the flagrant sinner and to reclaim those that run impetuously upon the broad way of destruction. Peacemakers labor "to give light to those who sit in darkness," and are about to be "destroyed for lack of knowledge." They work to "support the weak," to "lift drooping hands and strengthen weak knees," "so that what is lame may not be put out of joint, but rather be healed."

Peacemakers are no less zealous to confirm those who are already "striving to enter through the narrow door," and to strengthen those who stand so that they may "run with perseverance the race that is set before them." They labor to "build up in the most holy faith" those that "know the one in whom they have put their trust." Peacemakers exhort others to "rekindle the gift of God that is within them," so that daily "growing in grace," "entry into the eternal kingdom of our Lord and Savior Jesus Christ will be richly provided for them."

7. Blessed are those who are continually employed in this work of faith and labor of love, "for they will be called children of God." (According to a common Hebrew saying, they will *become* the children of God.) God will continue giving them the Spirit of adoption. Yes, he will pour it more abundantly into their hearts. He will bless them with all the blessings of his children. He will acknowledge them as sons and daughters before angels and humankind. "If children, then heirs, heirs of God and joint heirs with Christ."

III. The persecuted and the persecutors

1. One would imagine that the kind of people described above would be highly regarded on the earth. They are truly humble, genuinely serious, kind and gentle, free from all selfish intentions, devoted to God, and practical lovers of others. One would assume that such people would be greatly beloved. However, our Lord was more knowledgeable about the present state of human nature. Accordingly, he closes his summary of the character of peacemakers by explaining the kind of treatment they can expect in the world. Jesus said, "Blessed are those who are persecuted for righteousness' sake, for theirs is the kingdom of heaven."

2. In order thoroughly to understand this reality, first let us ask the question, "Who are those that are persecuted?" We may easily learn the answer from St. Paul: "Just as at that time the child who was born according to the flesh persecuted the child who was born according to the Spirit, so it is now also." Paul also said, "Indeed, all who want to live a godly life in Christ Jesus will be persecuted." St. John teaches us the same truth: "Do not be astonished, brothers and sisters, that the world hates you. We know that we have passed from death to life because we love one another. Whoever does not love abides in death." It is as if John had said that only those who have passed from death to life could love Christians. Our Lord said most explicitly:

90

"If the world hates you, be aware that it hated me before it hated you. If you belonged to the world, the world would love you as its own. Because you do not belong to the world, but I have chosen you out of the world—therefore the world hates you. Remember the word that I said to you, 'Servants are not greater than their master.' If they persecuted me, they will persecute you." (John 15:18-20)

All these scriptures clearly explain who they are that are persecuted—they are the righteous. Those whom the world persecutes are those that are "born according to the Spirit." The world persecutes "all who want to live a godly life in Christ Jesus," those who have "passed from death to life," those who are "not of the world," all those that are meek and lowly of heart, who long for God, who hunger after his likeness, who love God and their neighbors and who therefore, as they have opportunity, do good unto all people. The world hates them.

3. Second, if we ask *why* the world persecutes them, the answer is equally plain and obvious. They are persecuted "for righteousness' sake." The world persecutes them because they are righteous, because they are born according to the Spirit, because they "want to live a godly life in Christ Jesus," and because they "do not belong to the world." Whatever additional cause may be alleged, righteousness is the real cause of persecution. If they have greater or lesser infirmities, if it were not for their righteousness, the world would tolerate them. "The world would love them as its own." The world persecutes Christians because they are poor in spirit.

Those who persecute Christians regard them as people who mourn and as "weak-spirited, inferior, cowardly souls that are good for nothing and not fit to live in the world." Because Christians mourn, others allege that they are stupid, burdensome, boorish creatures who depress the spirits of those that see them! Because Christians are meek, allegedly they are mere idiots who quench innocent merriment and spoil fellowship wherever they go. Because they are humble, the world considers them to be uninteresting, passive fools, fit only to be trampled underfoot.

Because Christians hunger and thirst after righteousness, the world regards them as a collection of hot-brained fanatics, gawking at what they do not understand. Others say that they are not content with rational religion, but run crazily after ecstasies and inner emotions. Because Christians are merciful and lovers of everyone, including evil and ungrateful people, the world regards them as "encouraging all kinds of wickedness, enticing people to do evil with impunity."

The world even loves those without religion, who, it is feared, have loose morals. Because Christians are pure in heart, they are assumed to be "uncharitable creatures that damn the entire world, with the exception of those of their own kind!" Christians are blasphemous scoundrels who pretend to live without sin and make God a liar!

Above all, the world hates Christians because they are peacemakers who pretend to take every opportunity to do good to everyone. The main reason Christians have been persecuted in all ages is because of who they are and what they do. They are, and will continue to be, persecuted until the final restitution of all things.

The world says, "If Christians would only keep their religion to themselves, it would be tolerable. However, we cannot endure their dispersing their errors and infecting so many others. They do so much evil in the world that they ought not to be tolerated any longer." Critics also say, "It is true, Christians do some things well enough, such as relieving some of the poor. But even this work is done only to win more people to their religion. In effect, their good works produce all the more evil!" Worldly people sincerely think and speak in this way. And the more the kingdom of God succeeds, the more the peacemakers are enabled to propagate humility, meekness, and all other divine qualities. In the estimation of the world, the more Christianity grows the more evil it propagates. Consequently, the people of the world all the more vent anger against Christians and vehemently persecute them.

4. Third, let us ask, "Who are those that persecute Christians?" St. Paul answers that they are those who are "born according to the flesh." They are not "born of the Spirit," nor do they desire to

be. Those who persecute are those that do not try in the least to "live a godly life in Christ Jesus." They have not "passed from death to life" and consequently they do not love others. According to Jesus, the world does not know God who sent his son into the world. Citizens of the world do not know God, the loving, pardoning Lord whom we can know only through the teaching of the Holy Spirit.

The reason is obvious: The spirit that is in the world is directly opposed to the Spirit that is from God. It necessarily follows, therefore, that those who belong to the world will be opposed to those who belong to God. There is the utmost antithesis between them in all their opinions, desires, plans, and attitudes. The leopard and the lamb cannot lie down together in peace. Because arrogant people are proud, they cannot do anything other than persecute those who are humble. Those who are frivolous and rude cannot help persecuting those who mourn. In every other way the contrast of character constitutes a perpetual basis for hatred (even if there were no other causes). Therefore, if it were on this account alone, all the servants of the devil will continue to persecute the children of God.

5. Fourth, the question may arise as to *how* unbelievers will persecute believers. The general answer is that persecution will occur in the manner and measure that the wise Sovereign over everything knows will work best for his glory, tend most to his children's growth in grace, and best serve the advancement of his kingdom. There is no other aspect of God's government of the world that is more to be admired than this. God's ear is never deaf to the threats of the persecutor or the cry of the persecuted. His eye is ever open and his hand stretched out to direct even the smallest circumstance. God's unerring wisdom determines when the storm will begin, how high it shall rise, which way it moves, and when and how it shall end. The ungodly are only God's sword, an instrument that he uses as it pleases him. And when the gracious goals of God's providence are satisfied, he casts the evil swords into the fire.

God has permitted the storm to rise high at some rare times, such as when Christianity was first planted and while it was taking root upon the earth. Persecution was severe when the pure doctrine of Christ began to be planted again in our nation, and his children were called to resist evil to the point of shedding their blood. There was a particular reason why God allowed persecution to fall upon the apostles—that their example might be all the more beyond reproach.

But from the history of the Church we learn another and a far different reason why God allowed the heavy persecutions that arose in the second and third centuries. Persecutions were severe because the "mystery of lawlessness was already at work" so strongly and because of the monstrous corruptions that even then reigned in the Church. God chastised this corruption and worked to heal it by those severe but necessary circumstances.

Perhaps we can make the same observation with regard to the great persecution in England. God had dealt very graciously with our nation. He had poured out various blessings upon us; he had given us peace abroad and at home; and God gave us King Edward VI who was wise and good beyond his age. Above all, God had caused the pure light of his gospel to arise and shine among us. However, what results did he see? "He expected righteousness, but heard a cry."[10] It was the cry of oppression, vice, ambition, injustice, malice, fraud, and covetousness. Yes, the cry of those who even then expired in the flames entered into the ears of the Lord of hosts.

God then arose to sustain his own cause against those "who by their wickedness suppressed the truth." Then he sold them into the hands of their persecutors, by a judgment mixed with mercy. It was an affliction whose aim was to punish, and yet a medicine to heal the grievous backslidings of his people.

6. However, God seldom allows the storm to rise as high as torture, death, chains, or imprisonments. God's children are frequently called to endure lighter kinds of persecution. They frequently undergo the estrangement of relatives, the loss of their most intimate friends. They find the truth of their Lord's word (concerning the event, although not the purpose of his coming): "Do you think that I have come to bring peace to the earth? No, I tell you, but rather division." This division naturally can lead to

the loss of business or employment, and consequently of material things. Still, all these circumstances are also under the wise direction of God who apportions to everyone what is most appropriate for each of them.

7. But the persecution that accompanies all God's children is what our Lord describes in the following words: "Blessed are you when people revile you and persecute you and utter all kinds of evil against you falsely on my account." This persecution cannot fail to happen, and it is the very badge of our discipleship. Persecution is one of the marks of our calling; it is a sure allotment required of each of God's children. If we receive no persecution, we are not God's true children. The only way to the kingdom lies through evil reports about us, as well as good reports. The meek, serious, humble, and zealous people who love God and others have a good report among their sisters and brothers. However, they receive an evil report from the world. The world judges them and treats them "like the rubbish of the world, the dregs of all things."

8. Some have supposed that before the "full number of the Gentiles has come in," the scandal of the cross will cease and God will cause even those who are still in their sins to love and esteem Christians. Indeed, it is true that even now God sometimes restrains the contempt and fierceness of others. For a time, God "causes even their enemies to be at peace with them" and gives them favor with their bitterest persecutors. However, setting aside these particular cases, the scandal of the cross has not yet ceased. One must still say, "If I were still pleasing people, I would not be a servant of Christ."

Let no one therefore pay attention to the pleasant suggestion (pleasing doubtless to flesh and blood) that bad men only *pretend* to hate and despise those who are good; actually they love and value them in their hearts. That notion is not true. They may hire them sometimes, but for their own profit. They may put confidence in Christians because they know that their ways are not like the ways of others. Nevertheless, they do not love them, unless they love to the extent that the Spirit of God may be striving within them. Our Savior's words are explicit: "If you belonged to the world, the world would love you as its own. Because you do not belong to the world . . . therefore the world hates you." Yes, the world hates Christians as earnestly and sincerely as it ever hated their master (setting aside the exceptions that can be made due to the prevenient grace of God or his unusual providence).

9. It remains only for us to ask, "How are the children of God to behave with regard to persecution?" First, Christians should not knowingly or intentionally bring persecution upon themselves. To do so is contrary to the example and advice of our Lord and all his apostles. They teach us not to seek persecution and to avoid it as far as possible, without injuring our consciences or giving up any part of the righteousness which we are to prefer over life itself. Our Lord explicitly said, "When they persecute you in one town, flee to the next." This advice (when taken) is indeed the most ordinary way of avoiding persecution.

10. Still, do not think that you can always avoid it by fleeing or by any other means. If that useless fantasy ever creeps into your heart put it to flight. Bear in mind the ardent caution of Jesus: "Remember the word that I said to you, 'Servants are not greater than their master.' If they persecuted me, they will persecute you. Be wise as serpents and innocent as doves." But will this precaution screen you from persecution? Not unless you have more wisdom than your Master, or more purity of heart than the Lamb of God.

Do not wish entirely to avoid persecution. If you do, you do not belong to Christ. If you escape persecution, you escape the blessing of those who are persecuted for righteousness' sake. If you are not persecuted for righteousness' sake, you cannot enter into the kingdom of heaven. "If we endure, we will also reign with him; if we deny him, he will also deny us."

11. "Rejoice and be glad" when others persecute you for Christ's sake. Be glad when they persecute you by "reviling you and uttering all kinds of evil against you falsely." Evil words spoken against you will always be a part of every kind of persecution, because persecutors must slander you to excuse themselves. Jesus continued, "In the same way they persecuted the prophets who were before you." Ungodly people persecuted those who were the

most exceptionally holy in heart and life. They persecuted all the righteous people who ever have existed from the beginning of the world.

Rejoice. By the mark of persecution you also know to whom you belong. Rejoice also because "your reward is great in heaven." The blood of the covenant has purchased this reward and it is freely bestowed in proportion to your sufferings and your holiness of heart and life. "Rejoice and be glad," knowing that "this slight momentary affliction is preparing us for an eternal weight of glory beyond all measure."

12. Meanwhile, allow no persecution to turn you aside from the way of humility, meekness, love, and generosity. Jesus declared,

> "You have heard that it was said, 'An eye for an eye and a tooth for a tooth.' But I say to you, do not resist an evildoer. But if anyone strikes you on the right cheek, turn the other also; and if anyone wants to sue you and take your coat, give your cloak as well; and if anyone forces you to go one mile, go also the second mile. Give to everyone who begs from you, and do not refuse anyone who wants to borrow from you." (Matt. 5:38-42)

False teachers permit us to avenge ourselves and return evil for evil. But Jesus forbade our retaliation for evils done to us.

Let your meekness be unconquerable. And let your love correspond to your meekness. However, do not give away what belongs to another, because it is not yours to give. Keep these principles in mind: (i) Take care to owe no one anything, because what you owe does not belong to you, but to another. (ii) Provide for your own family members. God requires this faithfulness of you. Therefore, what is necessary to sustain the members of your household in life and godliness does not belong to you. (iii) You may give or lend everything that remains, from day to day or from year to year. Because you cannot give or lend to everyone, remember first those of the family of faith.

13. In the verses that follow, our blessed Lord further describes the meekness and love that we are to feel and the kindness we are to show toward those who persecute us for righteousness' sake. O, that these verses were engraved upon our hearts! Jesus

proclaimed, "You have heard that it was said, 'You shall love your neighbor and hate your enemy.'" God indeed had said only the first part—"You shall love your neighbor." The children of the devil had added the latter part—"and hate your enemy." Jesus clarified the matter: "But I say to you," (i) "Love your enemies." See that you hold compassionate goodwill for those that are the most bitter of spirit against you and who wish you all kinds of evil. (ii) "Pray for those that persecute you."

Are there any whose bitter spirits break forth in harsh words and continually revile you and persecute you when you are present, and "say all kinds of evil against you" in your absence? So much the more should you bless them. In talking with them, always be gentle and use kind language. Reprove them by demonstrating a better example before them, by illustrating how they should have spoken. When speaking about them, say all the good you can, without violating the rules of truth and fairness. (iii) "Do good to them that hate you." Let your actions show that you are as genuine in love as they are in hatred. Return good for evil. "Do not be overcome by evil, but overcome evil with good." (iv) If you can do nothing more, at least "pray for those that persecute you." You can never be stopped from acting this way, nor can all the hostility and violence of others keep you from praying for them.

Pour out your souls to God for those who once persecuted you, but now have repented. It is a little thing to forgive and pray for them. However, Jesus said, "And if the same person sins against you seven times a day, and turns back to you seven times and says, 'I repent,' you must forgive." That is, if after ever so many relapses others give you reason to believe that they are truly and fully changed, forgive them. Trust them, put them in your heart as though they had never sinned against you at all. Pray for and wrestle with God for those that do not repent and scornfully use and persecute you. Forgive them, "Not seven times, but, I tell you, seventy-seven times." Whether or not they repent and even if they appear further and further from it, still show them this type of kindness. Do so in order that "you may be children of your Father in heaven" (proving that you are genuine sons and daughters).

God demonstrates his goodness by giving his most stubborn enemies all the blessings they are capable of receiving. "He makes his sun rise on the evil and on the good, and sends rain on the righteous and on the unrighteous. For if you love those who love you, what reward do you have? Do not even the tax collectors do the same?" (They profess no religion, and you yourselves acknowledge that they are without God in the world.) And if you greet (show kindness in word or deed) only your brothers and sisters (friends or relatives) what more are you doing than others (those that have no religion at all)? Do not even the Gentiles do the same?" Be Christians by showing every kind of patience, endurance, mercy, and generosity. Demonstrate these things to your bitterest persecutors. "Be perfect" (in kind, although not in degree) "as your heavenly Father is perfect."

IV. The religion of Jesus

Observe Christianity in its original form, as its great Author gave it! This is the genuine religion of Jesus Christ! He offers this religion to those whose eyes are opened. See a picture of God, insofar as humankind comprehends him! This picture is drawn by God's own hand. "Look, you scoffers! Be amazed and perish." Or, rather, wonder and adore! Cry out, "Is this the religion of Jesus of Nazareth? The religion which I persecuted? Let me no more be found fighting against God. Lord, what would you have me to do?"

What beauty appears in the whole! How true a symmetry! What exact proportion in every part! How desirable is the happiness described in the Sermon on the Mount! How time-honored and beautiful is this holiness! This sermon of Jesus contains the spirit and essence of religion. These principles comprise the fundamentals of Christianity. O that we may not be merely hearers "like those who look at themselves in a mirror; for they look at themselves and, on going away, immediately forget what they were like!"

Rather, let us steadily "look into the perfect law, the law of liberty, and persevere." Let us not rest until every line of this religion is transcribed into our hearts. Let us pay attention, pray, believe, love, and "exercise self-control in all things" until every part of it appears in our souls, graven there by the finger of God. Let us persevere until we are "holy as he who calls us is holy," and we are "perfect as our heavenly Father is perfect."

Notes

1. Ward and Heitzenrater, *Wesley's Journals and Diaries,* August 28, 1748, 20:245.
2. Telford, *Wesley's Letters,* April 10, 1761, 4:147-48.
3. *Explanatory Notes upon the New Testament,* Matt. 5:8.
4. Telford, *Wesley's Letters,* March 1, 1775, 6:142. In using the word "jar," Wesley is referring to the content of another person's teaching or doctrine.
5. Outler, *Wesley's Sermons,* "Sermon on the Mount," Discourse 3 (III, 3), 1:522.
6. *Explanatory Notes upon the New Testament,* Matt. 5:9.
7. Wisdom of Solomon 12:18.
8. The phrase "soul of the universe" *(anima mundi)* was often used by Platonic philosophers.
9. *Book of Common Prayer,* Ps. 74:13.
10. Isa. 5:7.

UPON OUR LORD'S SERMON ON THE MOUNT

Discourse 4

In addition to Antinomianism, John Wesley had to deal with another aberrant view of Christianity—mysticism. To be sure, he did not see mysticism as entirely in error. However, he opposed its excesses. He disagreed with the kind of mysticism that sets aside the use of the means of grace and posits a direct, unmediated knowledge of God attained through personal religious experience. Furthermore, Wesley contested mysticism's tendency to minimize the importance of our involvement in the world.

During Wesley's early years of spiritual struggle, he had found some solace in mysticism. Certain mystical writers had helped him to understand that his rigid legalism must give way to a personal relationship with God. In 1738 Wesley wrote in his journal, "A contemplative man convinced me still more than I was convinced before, that outward works are nothing, being alone; and in several conversations instructed me, how to pursue inward holiness, or a union of the soul with God."[1] Moreover, the mystics taught Wesley to respect the genuine spiritual insights and experiences of uneducated people, some of whom are more spiritually wise and mature than certain educated scholars. The mystics also helped

Wesley to become aware of the possibility of one's being completely given over to God. Wesley's reading of Jeremy Taylor's *Holy Living and Holy Dying* and William Law's *A Serious Call to a Devout and Holy Life* pointed him to Christian freedom. These writers underscored the possibility of resting in God and living in holiness before him.

Wesley's early appreciation for elements of mysticism prompted him to translate some of the hymns of the German mystic Gerhard Tersteegen (1697–1769), one of which Wesley rendered:

> *Thou hidden love of God, whose height,*
> *whose depth unfathomed no man knows,*
> *I see from far Thy beauteous light,*
> *Inly I sigh for Thy repose;*
> *My heart is pained, nor can it be*
> *At rest, till it finds rest in Thee.*[2]

In time, Wesley came to see serious flaws in mysticism. Concerning a mystic teacher, he wrote, "I cannot but now observe, 1. That he spoke so incautiously against trusting in outward works, that he discouraged me from doing them at all. 2. That he recommended (as it were, to supply what was wanting in them) mental prayer, and the like exercises, as the most effectual means of purifying the soul, and uniting it with God."[3]

Mysticism's errors became increasingly apparent to Wesley, and he was forced to oppose it. He even came to regard mysticism as a pernicious leaven among Christian believers. After a visit to the society at Birmingham, he wrote, "I spoke to each member of the society. What havoc have the two opposite extremes, Mysticism and Antinomianism, made among this once earnest and simple people! Had it not been good for those men not to have been born, by whom these little ones have been offended?"[4] In 1772, he wrote a letter to Ann Bolton:[5]

You cannot imagine what trouble I have had for many years to prevent our friends from *refining* upon religion. Therefore, I have industriously guarded them from meddling with the Mystic writers, as they are usually called; because these are the most artful refiners of it that ever appeared in the Christian world, and the most bewitching. There is something like enchantment in them. When you get into them, you know not how to get out. . . . Aim at nothing higher, nothing deeper, than the religion described at large in our Lord's Sermon upon the Mount, and briefly summed up by St. Paul in the 13th chapter to the Corinthians. . . . Believe me, you can find nothing higher than this till mortality is swallowed up of life.[6]

We can summarize seven excesses that Wesley found in the mystical tradition. (1) The doctrine of stillness, which many mystics tended to advocate. This approach to religion dismissed all use of the means of grace. (2) The propensity of some mystics to drift into Antinomianism. (3) The teaching that union with God robs one of his or her individual personality. (4) The view that one must set aside reason in favor of feelings. (5) The use of "fondling" language and symbolism in some mystical writings, which at times had erotic overtones. (6) The notion that one must "choose the most disagreeable things, whether they come from God or the world." (7) The tendency to withdraw from the world. This last objection was particularly in Wesley's mind when he wrote the present discourse on the Sermon on the Mount.

Wesley's first three sermons on the Sermon on the Mount dealt with the Beatitudes, which focus on dispositions and motives. In this sermon Wesley rejects the mystical notion that Christians should retreat from engagement with the world. He writes:

Many distinguished people . . . have advised us to "cease from all outward action," completely withdraw from the world, leave the body behind us, separate ourselves from all tangible things, and have no concern at all about outward religion. They advise us that the better way is to keep all virtues in the will. To them, the religion of pure *intentions* is the best way to perfect the soul and to become more acceptable to God.

Wesley vigorously asserts that this mystical tradition of insularity from the world fails to develop poverty of spirit, purity of heart, meekness of soul, and peacemaking. These qualities can find expression only as we intentionally engage the world, which is the arena of God's concern and action. Isolation from social responsibility restricts Christian spirituality, worship, and service. It is in this sermon that Wesley stated his often-quoted thesis: "Christianity is essentially a social religion, and to turn it into a solitary one is to destroy it."

Sermon 24

UPON OUR LORD'S SERMON ON THE MOUNT

Discourse 4

"You are the salt of the earth; but if salt has lost its taste, how can its saltiness be restored? It is no longer good for anything, but is thrown out and trampled under foot. You are the light of the world. A city built on a hill cannot be hid. No one after lighting a lamp puts it under the bushel basket, but on the lampstand, and it gives light to all in the house. In the same way, let your light shine before others, so that they may see your good works and give glory to your Father in heaven." *(Matthew 5:13-16)*

1 The beauty of holiness compellingly attracts every enlightened eye and mind that God has opened. Holiness is the renewal of the heart in the image of God. At the very least, the adornment of a meek, humble, and loving spirit will arouse the admiration of all who are in any way capable of discerning spiritual good and evil. From the hour that people begin to emerge out of the darkness that covers the confused and thoughtless

world, they cannot help perceiving how desirable it is to be transformed into the likeness of him who created us.

True inward religion bears the shape of God visibly impressed upon it. One must be wholly immersed in the material body to doubt religion's divine origin. In a secondary sense, we can make this statement about the Son of God himself. In him, people may see God and live. However, in his human form Christ's incarnation moderated and veiled "the reflection of God's glory and the exact imprint of God's very being." In the incarnate Christ we see the character (the stamp, or the living impression) of his person who is the fountain of beauty and love, the original source of all excellence and perfection.

2. Even if religion were carried no further than Christ who assumed human form, people could have no doubts about it. They would have no reluctance to pursue the Christian religion with all the enthusiasm of their beings. Some say, "But why is religion complicated by other things? What is the purpose of loading it with the need to take action and to suffer?" They assert, "These things interfere with the vigor of the soul and bring it down to earth again. Is it not enough to pursue love and to rise upon the wings of love?" The questioners continue, "Is it not enough to worship God who is a Spirit with the spirit of our minds, without encumbering ourselves with outward things or even thinking about them at all? Is it not better for the entire compass of our thought to be occupied with high and heavenly contemplation? Instead of busying ourselves in any way with externals, we should only commune with God in our hearts."

3. Many distinguished people have spoken this way. They have advised us to "cease from all outward action." They suggest that we completely withdraw from the world, leave the body behind us, separate ourselves from all tangible things, and have no concern at all about outward religion. These teachers advise us that the better way is to confine all virtues within the will. To them, the religion of pure *intentions* is the best way to perfect the soul and to become more acceptable to God.

4. It was not necessary for anyone to inform our Lord about this masterpiece of "wisdom" from hell. This view of religion is the

most attractive of all the devices with which Satan has ever "perverted the right ways of the Lord!" And, from time to time, O what human instruments Satan has found through whom to promote this theory in his service! It is a grand tool of hell against some of the most important truths of God. Satan works "to lead astray, if possible, even the elect"—that is, the men and women of faith and love. Indeed, for a time Satan deceived and led away a considerable number of people in all ages into a gilded snare. Those who were deceived barely escaped by the skin of their teeth (Job 19:20).

5. Has our Lord been lacking on his part? Has he not sufficiently guarded us against this beguiling delusion? Has Christ not outfitted us here on earth with the shield of proof against Satan who sometimes "disguises himself as an angel of light"? Truly, Christ has given us what we need. Here in our text, and in the clearest and strongest manner, Jesus defends the active, self-possessed religion he had just described:

> "You are the salt of the earth; but if salt has lost its taste, how can its saltiness be restored? It is no longer good for anything, but is thrown out and trampled under foot. You are the light of the world. A city built on a hill cannot be hid. No one after lighting a lamp puts it under the bushel basket, but on the lampstand, and it gives light to all in the house. In the same way, let your light shine before others, so that they may see your good works and give glory to your Father in heaven." (Matt. 5:13-16)

In order fully to explain and apply these important words, first I will endeavor to explain that Christianity is essentially a social religion, and to turn it into a solitary one is to destroy it. Second, I will demonstrate that it is impossible to conceal the Christian religion, and that it is completely contrary to the plan of its author to try to do so. Third, I will answer some objections and then conclude the sermon with a practical application.

I. Christianity is a social religion

1. First, I will endeavor to show that Christianity is essentially a social religion, and that to turn it into a solitary religion is

indeed to destroy it. By Christianity, I mean the way of worshipping God that Jesus Christ reveals in the statements I just quoted. When I say that Christianity is fundamentally a social religion, I mean that it cannot exist very well without our living among, and interacting with, others. Indeed, without human associations Christianity cannot exist at all. In explaining this truth, I will confine myself to the considerations that arise from the Sermon on the Mount here before us. If I make my case, then, without doubt, to turn Christianity into a solitary religion is to destroy it.

By no means do we censure the blending of solitude (or times of separation) with life in the company of others. Times of seclusion are not only allowable, but also advisable. As daily experience shows, periods of withdrawal are necessary for everyone who already is a real Christian, or desires to be such. We cannot spend the entire day in constant communication with others. If we were to do so, we would suffer loss in our soul, and in some measure we would grieve the Holy Spirit of God. Daily, we need to retreat from the world, at least morning and evening, to converse with God, to commune more freely with our Father who is in secret. Nor indeed can a person of experience condemn even longer periods of religious retreat. These times of solitude do not imply any neglect of the worldly employment in which the providence of God has placed us.

2. Yet such withdrawal must not swallow up *all* our time. Such isolation would destroy true religion, not advance it. The religion described by our Lord, in the words of our text just quoted, cannot exist without our living and conversing with others. The words of Jesus reveal that several of the most fundamental aspects of true religion require our involvement with the world.

3. For instance, there is no endowment more essential to Christianity than meekness. Of course, meekness, as it pertains to our submission to God or endurance in pain and sickness, may exist in a desert, in a hermit's cell, or in complete solitude. But when it implies (which it often does) the virtues of kindness, gentleness, and patience, it cannot possibly exist without associating with other people. Hence, to attempt to turn meekness into a solitary virtue is to destroy it from the face of the earth.

4. Another necessary aspect of true Christianity is peacemaking, or doing good to others. This quality is equally essential to any of the other parts of the religion of Jesus Christ. The strongest argument for this point (and it would be absurd to allege otherwise) is that in the Sermon on the Mount peacemaking is included in the original plan that Jesus has laid down with regard to the fundamentals of his religion. Therefore, to set aside peacemaking constitutes as impudent an insult to the authority of our Great Master as to set aside mercy, purity of heart, or any other aspect of the religion that he established.

However, peacemaking is apparently set aside by all who call for us to retire to the wilderness. They recommend complete solitude either to newborn Christians, or young men, or fathers in Christ. Will anyone affirm that a solitary Christian (so called, though it is little less than a contradiction in terms) can be a merciful person? In isolation from others, how can we take every opportunity to "work for the good of all"? What can be more obvious than that this fundamental aspect of the religion of Jesus Christ cannot possibly exist apart from our living and conversing with other people?

5. One might naturally raise the question, "Is it not advisable, however, to converse exclusively with good people, only with those whom we know to be meek, merciful, and holy in heart and holy of life?" The questioner might continue, "Is it not advisable to refrain from any conversation or interchange with people of opposite character? Should we not avoid those who do not obey, or perhaps do not believe, the gospel of our Lord Jesus Christ?"

The advice of St. Paul to the Christians at Corinth may *seem* to promote that notion. He said, "I wrote to you in my letter not to associate with sexually immoral persons." And it is certainly not advisable to keep company with them or with any of the workers of iniquity for the purpose of having any special intimacy or deep friendship with them. To covenant with or continue an emotional closeness with any of them is not in any way appropriate for a Christian. Such friendships would necessarily expose Christians to a multitude of dangers and snares, from which they can have no reasonable hope of deliverance.

However, the apostle does not forbid us to have any dealings at all with those that do not know God. St. Paul said that to avoid *all* contact with unbelievers would require us "to go out of the world." He would never advise such a course of action. St. Paul then adds, "Anyone who bears the name of brother or sister (one who professes to be a Christian) and is "sexually immoral or greedy, or is an idolater, reviler, drunkard, or robber—do not keep company with them or even eat with such a one." This advice necessarily implies that we break off all intimacy and closeness with such people. Elsewhere, St. Paul said, "Do not regard them as enemies, but warn them as brothers." This scripture clearly reveals that even in such a case as we are discussing we are not to renounce all fellowship with sinners. There is no advice in these verses that we should entirely separate from wicked people. Indeed, these scriptures teach us quite the opposite.

6. Even more so, the words of our Lord are far from instructing us to break off all dealings with the world. According to his account of Christianity, we cannot be Christians at all if we do not relate to people in the world. It is easy to demonstrate that some interchange even with ungodly and unholy people is absolutely required for the full use of every characteristic that Christ has described as belonging to his kingdom. Dealing with other people is indispensably necessary for the full exercise of poverty of spirit, mourning, and of every other disposition that has a place in the genuine religion of Jesus Christ.

Yes, commerce with the world is necessary for the very existence of these virtues. For example, Christ calls us to meekness instead of demanding "an eye for an eye, or a tooth for a tooth." We are not to "resist an evildoer." Instead, meekness causes us when struck "on the right cheek, to turn the other also." If we are merciful, we will "love our enemies and pray for those who persecute us." Dealing with others is necessary to develop that complexity of love and all holy attitudes that are part of suffering for righteousness' sake. It is clear that all these qualities could not exist if we had no dealings with anyone but genuine Christians.

7. Indeed, if we completely separated ourselves from sinners, how could we possibly personify the quality of character that our

Lord gives us in his own words—"You are the salt of the earth"?
He is addressing those who are humble, serious, and meek. He
directs his teaching to those who hunger for righteousness, love
God and humankind, do good to everyone, and therefore receive
evil treatment from others. It is your very nature to season (as salt)
whatever is around you. It is the nature of the divine savor in you
to spread to whatever you touch. This salt diffuses itself into every
relationship with all those that you contact.

The inner change that has taken place within you is the central
reason that the providence of God has joined you together with
others. It is God's plan that whatever grace you have received may
be communicated through you to them. God desires that all your
holy attitudes, words, and deeds may have an influence on their
lives. By this means, in some measure you serve as a barrier to the
corruption that is in the world. And at least a small part of the
world will be saved from its general corruption and be made holy
and pure before God.

8. So that we may more diligently labor to season all we can
with every holy and heavenly quality, our Lord proceeds to clarify the dangerous state of those who do not impart the religion
they have received. Indeed, as long as real religion remains in the
heart, one cannot possibly fail to communicate it to others. If salt
has lost its taste, how can its saltiness be restored? It is no longer
good for anything, but is thrown out and trampled underfoot.

Jesus is speaking to those who are holy and heavenly minded
and consequently zealous of good works. Yet, they no longer have
that savor in themselves and therefore they no longer season others. He is saying that if you have become flat, tasteless, dead, careless of your own souls, and useless to the souls of others, how can
your saltiness be restored? How will you be reclaimed? What help
is there for you? What hope? Can tasteless salt ever recover its
flavor?

No, it cannot be restored. "It is no longer good for anything,
but is thrown out," just as the mire in the streets, "and trampled
under foot" to be buried with everlasting scorn. If you had never
known the Lord, if you had never been "found in him," there
might have been hope. But what now can you say to Christ's

solemn declaration that parallels the one spoken here? He declared, "God removes every branch in me that bears no fruit. Those who abide in me and I in them bear much fruit.... Whoever does not abide in me (or does not bear fruit) is thrown away like a branch and withers; such branches are gathered, thrown into the fire, and burned."

9. God is indeed full of pity and tender mercy toward those that have never tasted of the good word. However, he fulfills justice toward those that have tasted the goodness of the word that the Lord is gracious, but have afterward "turned back from the holy commandment that was passed on to them. "For it is impossible to restore again to repentance those who have once been enlightened," those in whose hearts God had once shined, "to give the light of the knowledge of the glory of God in the face of Jesus Christ." Christ cannot renew those "who have tasted of the heavenly gift" of redemption in his blood, the forgiveness of sins, and "have shared in the Holy Spirit" (humility, meekness, and the love of God and humankind) and then have fallen away. (This statement is not a supposition, but a clear declaration of fact.) Given these circumstances, "it is impossible to restore again...since on their own they are crucifying again the Son of God and are holding him up to contempt."

So that no one will misunderstand these fearful words, we need carefully to observe the following points. (1) We will look at those spoken about here who were once "enlightened" and "have tasted the heavenly gift, and have shared in the Holy Spirit." All that have not experienced these things are completely unconcerned about this scripture. (2) We will examine the meaning of "falling away" that is spoken about here. It is an absolute and final apostasy. A believer may stumble, and not "fall away." One may fall and rise again. Even "if anyone does sin," as dreadful as it is, it is not hopeless. "We have an advocate with the Father, Jesus Christ the righteous; and he is the atoning sacrifice for our sins."

However, above all things, let us beware that our hearts are not "hardened by the deceitfulness of sin." Let us guard against sinking lower and lower until we completely fall away. Let us not become like salt that has lost its taste. "For if we willfully persist in sin after having received the knowledge of the truth, there no longer remains a sacrifice for sins, but a fearful prospect of judgment, and a fury of fire that will consume the adversaries."

II. Genuine Christianity cannot remain hidden

1. Someone may say, "Although we cannot completely separate ourselves from other people, and while we grant that we ought to season them with the religion that God has worked in our hearts, yet can we not do this work unawares? Can we not secretly convey a savor into others almost imperceptibly, so that hardly any one will be able to observe how or when it is done? Can we not work as salt conveys its own flavor into that which it seasons, without any sound and without being subject to any outward observation? And although we do not leave the world, yet we may rest hidden within it. In this way, we can keep our religion to ourselves and not offend those that we cannot help."

2. Our Lord was well aware of this deceptive human reasoning. And he has given a complete answer to it in words that we will now consider. In explaining them, I will endeavor to show that as long as true religion remains in our hearts, it is impossible to conceal it. Any attempt to do so is completely contrary to the plan of its great Creator.

To begin with, it is impossible for any that have the religion of Jesus Christ to hide it. By using a twofold comparison, our Lord makes this clear beyond all contradiction. "You are the light of the world. A city built on a hill cannot be hid." You Christians are "the light of the world," both with regard to your attitudes and your actions. Your holiness makes you as conspicuous as the sun in the midst of heaven. As you cannot "go out of the world," neither can you stay in it without being apparent to everyone. You cannot flee from contact with people. And while you are among others, it is impossible to hide your humility and meekness and those other traits by which you aspire to be perfect, as your Father who is in heaven is perfect.

Love cannot be hidden any more than light—least of all, when it radiates outwardly in action, as you engage yourselves in the work of love and in every kind of generosity. People might as well try to hide a city as to hide a Christian. Indeed we can no more conceal a city set upon a hill, as hide a holy, devoted, and active lover of God and humankind.

3. It is true that those who love darkness rather than light, because their deeds are evil, will take all possible pains to prove that the light that is in you is darkness. Concerning the good that is in you, they will utter all kinds of evil against you falsely. They will charge you with things that are farthest from your thoughts, things that are the very opposite of all that you are and do. Your patient continuation in doing good, your meek suffering all things for the Lord's sake, your calm and humble joy in the midst of persecution, your tireless labor to overcome evil with good will all make you still more visible and conspicuous than you ever were.

4. It is futile to think that we can hide the light, unless we extinguish it. It is impossible to keep our religion from being seen, unless we thrust it away! It is certain that a secret, unobserved religion cannot be the religion of Jesus Christ. Any religion that can be concealed is not genuine Christianity. If Christians could be hidden, they could not be compared to a city set upon a hill, or to the light of the world, or to the sun shining from heaven and seen by the entire world below. Therefore, never let it enter the hearts of those whom God has renewed in the spirit of their minds to hide that light or to keep their religion a private matter. This caution is especially important because it is impossible to conceal true Christianity. To attempt to do so is absolutely contrary to the design of its great creator.

5. This truth clearly appears from the following words: "No one after lighting a lamp puts it under the bushel basket." It is as though Jesus said that people do not light a candle in order to cloak and conceal it. Neither does God enlighten any soul with his glorious knowledge and love in order to have that soul covered or obscured. Genuine Christianity cannot be hidden behind "prudence" (falsely so called), embarrassment, or self-abasement that attempts to hide it in a wilderness. Your faith cannot be covered up either by avoiding people or by conversing with them. Rather, we put a light "on the lampstand, and it gives light to all in the

house." In like manner, it is God's plan that all Christians be clearly seen by others so that they can give light to everyone. In this way they visibly bear witness to the religion of Jesus Christ.

6. In all ages, God has spoken to the world through the precepts and examples of believers. In every nation where the sound of the gospel has gone forth, God has "not left himself without witness." There have always been at least a few that have witnessed to his truth by their lives and words. These witnesses have been "as lamps shining in a dark place." And from time to time, these witnesses have been the means of enlightening some and of preserving a remnant or a seed so that "future generations will be told about the Lord." They have led a few poor sheep out of the darkness of the world, and "guided their feet into the way of peace."

7. One might imagine that where both Scripture and logic speak so clearly and explicitly, there could be little argument from the opposing side, at least not with any semblance of truth. However, those who remain hidden from the world know little about the depths of Satan. After all that Scripture and logic have said, still many deceptive wiles support the notion of solitary religion. This deception is the cause of some Christians' retreating from the world or concealing themselves from the world. Because of these deceptions, we need all the wisdom of God to see through these snares. We need all of God's power to escape them. We must contend against the many strong objections against our being social, open, and active Christians.

III. Answering objections to Christianity as a social religion

1. Third, in this sermon I propose to answer objections to the declaration that Christianity is a social religion. First, it has often been objected that religion does not lie in outward things but in the heart, the inmost soul. Objectors point out that real religion is the union of the soul with God—the life of God in the soul of man. These people argue that outward religion has no value because God "does not delight in burnt offerings" (that is, outward observances), but "a broken and contrite heart God will not despise."

115

I answer that it is certainly true that the root of religion lies in the heart, the inmost soul. This union of our souls with God means that his life is within us. But if this root of true religion really is in the heart, it must send out branches. And these branches are the diverse instances of outward obedience that share the same characteristics of the root. Consequently, outward actions are not only *signs* of religion, but also religion's substantial *components*.

It is of course true that mere outer religion that has no root in the heart is worth nothing. God does not delight in empty external observances any more than he now delights in Jewish burnt offerings. It is true that a pure and holy heart is a sacrifice with which God is always well pleased. But God is also well pleased with all the outward service that arises from the heart. He takes delight in the sacrifice of our prayers (whether public or private), the sacrifice of our praises and thanksgivings, and the sacrifice of our possessions humbly devoted to him and used entirely for his glory. He delights in the presentation of our *bodies* to him, which he uniquely requires. The Apostle Paul appeals to us "to present our bodies as a living sacrifice, holy and acceptable to God."

2. A second objection to Christianity as a social religion is closely related to the first one. This criticism is that love is all that is required. Only love is "the fulfilling of the law," "the aim of the commandments." Unless we have love, all the things that we do and suffer gain us nothing. Therefore, the Apostle Paul directs us to "pursue love," which he calls "a more excellent way." In short, some say, "If we have love, we do not need good works."

I answer this objection by granting that the love of God and others, arising from sincere faith, is the sum of religion. Love is "the fulfilling of the law" and the aim of every commandment of God. It is true that without love, whatever we do or suffer gains us nothing. However, from these truths about the importance of love, it does not follow that love replaces either faith or good works. Love fulfills the law not by *releasing* us from the law, but by compelling us to *obey* it. Love is "the aim of the commandments," in the sense that every commandment leads to, and centers in, love. We acknowledge that whatever we do or suffer without love gains us nothing. But still, whatever we do or suffer in love (even if it is only the suffering of some indignity for Christ or giving a cup of cold water in his name), it shall in no way lose its reward.

3. Some may reply, "But does not the Apostle Paul direct us to 'pursue love'? And does he not call it 'a more excellent way'?" I answer that God does indeed instruct us to "pursue love," but not to seek love *alone*. Paul's words are, "Pursue love and strive for the spiritual gifts." Yes, pursue love. But also seek to spend and be spent for your sisters and brothers. "Pursue love," and "whenever you have an opportunity, work for the good of all."

In the same verse where St. Paul calls the way of love "a more excellent way," in addition to love he instructs the Corinthians to strive for other gifts. Yes, strive for them earnestly. He told us to "strive for the greater gifts." To what greater gifts does he refer? He is referring to gifts that are greater than the gifts of healing, speaking with tongues, and interpreting tongues, which he mentioned in the preceding verse. These abilities are not greater than the way of obedience. The Apostle Paul is not referring to obedience or to outward religion at all. This text does not pertain to the present question of Christianity as a social religion.

Suppose, however, that St. Paul had been speaking of both outward and inward religion and comparing them with each other. Assume that in comparing the two, he had given a slight preference to inward religion. Assume that he had preferred (as he properly might have done) a loving heart above all kinds of outward works. Still, it would not follow that we were rejecting either one or the other. Not at all. From the beginning of the world, God has joined inward and outward religion together. Let no one separate them.

4. Critics might object, "'God is spirit, and those who worship him must worship in spirit and truth.' Is this worship not enough? Ought we not to engage the entire strength of our mind in worship? Does not giving time and attention to outward things clog the soul so that it cannot soar heavenward in holy contemplation? Does not giving ourselves to outward things dampen the vitality of our thought? Do not outward concerns have a natural tendency to encumber and distract the mind? Instead of outward works,

St. Paul would have us to 'be free from anxieties and give unhindered devotion to the Lord.'"

To this contention for Christianity without social responsibilities, I answer that "God is spirit, and those who worship him must worship in spirit and truth."

Some might allege, "Yes, and this kind of worship is all we need. We should engage our entire strength of mind in worshiping God."

In response, I would ask what it means to worship God (who is Spirit) in spirit and in truth. In fact, it is to worship him with our spirits, in the way in which only human spirits are capable. It is to believe in God as a wise, just, and holy being, whose "eyes are too pure to behold evil." Yet God is merciful, gracious, and longsuffering. He forgives evil, transgression, and sin; he casts all our iniquities behind his back and accepts us in his beloved son. To worship him in spirit and truth is to love him, delight in him, and desire him with all your heart, and with all your soul, and with all your mind, and with all your strength. It is to imitate him, whom we love by purifying ourselves, just as he is pure. In thought, and word, and deed, it is to obey him whom we love and trust.

Accordingly, one aspect of worshiping God in spirit and in truth is keeping his outward commandments. True worship is to glorify God in our bodies as well as in our spirits. It means that we do outward work with hearts lifted up to him. True worship makes our daily activity a sacrifice to God, through which we buy, sell, eat, and drink to his glory. As much as praying to God in remote isolation, these outward activities are part of worshiping God in spirit and in truth.

5. If true worship includes outward activities in the world, quiet contemplation is only *one* way to worship God in spirit and in truth. To give yourselves up entirely to contemplation would be to destroy many aspects of spiritual worship, all of which are acceptable to God and beneficial (not harmful) to the soul. It is a great mistake to imagine that in any way attention to those outward things to which the providence of God has called us obstructs Christian worship. Our practical obligations by no means keep us from always seeing him who is invisible. Outward duties do not

at all dampen the devotion of our thought; they do not obstruct or distract our minds. They do not produce unsettled or harmful worry in those who perform outward works for the Lord. Outward duties do not unsettle those who "in word or deed, do everything in the name of the Lord Jesus." One eye of the soul looks toward outward things, and the other eye of the soul is resolutely fixed on God. You fruitless solitary people, learn what this balance means, so that you can clearly discern your own smallness of faith. Learn, so that you will no longer use yourselves as standards to judge others. Discover the meaning of these lines:

> Thou, O Lord, in tender love
> Dost all my burdens bear;
> Lift my heart to things above,
> And fix it ever there.
> Calm on tumult's wheel I sit;
> Midst busy multitudes alone;
> Sweetly waiting at thy feet
> Till all thy will be done.[7]

6. But the main objection to Christianity as a social religion still shadows us. Objectors say, "We appeal to experience. Our light did shine, and we engaged in outward activities for many years. Yet, they gained nothing. We used all the means of grace, but we are no better for it, nor indeed is anyone else who engaged in good works and used the means of grace. No, we were the *worse* for it, because we imagined ourselves Christians based on our outward works. All the time, we did not know the meaning of Christianity."

I acknowledge that what you say may be true. I concede that you and ten thousand more people have abused the means of grace in this way, mistaking the means for the end. The error lies in presuming that using them or doing some other outward works constitutes the religion of Jesus Christ or that they will be accepted in the place of it. However, take away the *abuse* and keep the *use*. Use all outward forms of religion, but use them for the constant purpose of renewing your souls "in true righteousness and holiness."

7. This objection raises still another one. Those teachers who deny that Christianity is a social religion say, "Experience also shows that trying to do good is only wasted work. What good does it do to feed or clothe peoples' bodies if they are about to drop into the fire of everlasting hell? Moreover, what good can anyone do to their souls? If souls are to be changed, God himself does it. Furthermore, all people are either good (or wanting to be good) or they are stubbornly evil. Those who are good or wanting to be good do not need us. They have only to ask God to help them, he will do so. The stubbornly evil people will not receive help from us. Indeed, our Lord forbids us to 'throw our pearls before swine.'"

I answer the objection in this way: (1) Whether or not people will finally be lost or saved, God specifically commands you to feed the hungry and clothe the naked. If you can help others but fail to do so, whatever may become of them you will go away into everlasting fire. (2) Although God alone changes people's hearts, he ordinarily does so through human instruments. It is our responsibility diligently to do everything we can, as though we could change them ourselves. Then, we leave it to God to change them. (3) In answer to his children's prayers, God uses their gifts to build up others, nourishing and strengthening the whole body "by every ligament with which it is equipped." Therefore, "the eye cannot say to the hand, 'I have no need of you,' nor again the head to the feet, 'I have no need of you.'"

Finally, how can you be certain which persons you meet are dogs or swine? Do not judge them until first you have tried to work with them. How do you know that you will not win your brothers or sisters and save their souls from death? When someone rejects your love and blasphemes the good word of God, only then is it time to give him or her up to God.

8. The critic may complain, "We have tried; we have labored to reform sinners. And what good did it do? On many people we could make no impression at all. And if some were changed for a while, their goodness was only like the morning dew. They were soon as bad as ever; no, they were worse than ever. So, we only hurt them and ourselves as well. Our minds were agitated and

unsettled, perhaps filled with anger instead of love. Therefore, it would have been better for us to have kept our religion to ourselves."

I reply that it is very possible what you say may be true. You have tried to do good, and have not succeeded. Some whose lives seemed to have been reformed lapsed back into sin, and "their last state is worse than the first." And why is that surprising? "Servants are not greater than their master." How often did Jesus strive to save sinners, and they would not hear him. And when some had followed him awhile, they turned back "like a dog that returns to its vomit."

Nevertheless, Jesus did not cease striving to do good. Neither should you, whatever your successes may be. Your part is to do as God commands you. The change in others lies in *his* hands. You are not accountable for the results, so leave the results with God, who does everything well. "In the morning sow your seed, and at evening do not let your hands be idle; for you do not know which will prosper, this or that."

The burden, however, agitates and frets your soul. Perhaps it does so because you thought *you* were responsible for the outcome, which no one is or can be. Perhaps you became unsettled because you were caught off your guard; you were not vigilant over your own spirit. But this fact is no reason to disobey God. Try again. And next time try more carefully than previously. Do good (even as you forgive others) "not seven times, but seventy-seven times." Only become wiser by experience. Begin your work each time more cautiously than previously. Become more humbled before God, more deeply convinced that apart from Christ you can do nothing. Be more watchful over your own spirit. Be more gentle and vigilant in prayer. Send out your bread upon the waters, for after many days you will get it back.

IV. Encouragement to bear witness to the world

1. Set aside all these deceptive pretenses for hiding your light. "Let your light shine before others, so that they may see your good works and give glory to your Father in heaven." Our

Lord himself makes practical applications from the preceding considerations.

The command "Let your light so shine" refers to your humility, gentleness, and modesty concerning your knowledge. Letting your light shine pertains to your serious and significant concern for the things of eternity, your sorrow for the sins and miseries of people, your earnest desire for universal holiness, and your complete happiness in God. It includes your compassionate goodwill toward all humankind and your ardent love for your supreme benefactor—God himself. Do not try to conceal the light with which God has enlightened your soul. In the entire scope of your conduct, let your light shine in the world before all people that you encounter. Let it shine still more abundantly in your actions by "working for the good of all." Let it shine in your suffering for righteousness' sake. "Rejoice and be glad, for your reward is great in heaven."

2. "Let your light shine before others, so that they may see your good works." Let it be very far from any Christians to plan or desire to hide their religion! On the contrary, let it be your desire not to hide it or put your lamp under a basket. Let it be your responsibility to place it on the lampstand, so that it will give light to all in the house. Only be careful not to seek your own praise or yearn for any glory for yourselves. Let it be your single aim that all who "see your good works may give glory to your Father in heaven."

3. In all things, let the practice of seeking God's glory become your one ultimate aim. With this goal in view, be simple, open, and transparent. Let your love be genuine. Why should you conceal impartial and unbiased love? Let there be no "deceit found in your mouth." Let your words echo the genuine image of your heart. Let there be no disguise or reticence in your conversation, no masquerade in your behavior. Leave these things to those who have other schemes in view, schemes that will not bear the light of truth. Be genuine and open with everyone so that they can see the grace of God within you. Although some will harden their hearts, others will know that you have been with Jesus. And by turning to the great overseer of their souls, they will "give glory to your Father in heaven."

4. With the single aim that others will give glory to the God who is within you, go forth in his name and in the strength of his power. Do not be ashamed even to stand alone, if it is in the way that God leads you. Let the light in your heart shine in all good works, in works of piety and works of mercy.

And in order to increase your ability to do good, renounce all needless accumulation. Cut off all unnecessary expense in food, furniture, and clothing. Be a good steward of every gift that God has given you, even of the lowest of his gifts. Cut off unnecessary expenditures of time and needless or useless activities. "Whatever your hand finds to do, do with your might." In a word, be full of faith and love, while doing good and enduring evil. "Be steadfast, immovable, always excelling in the work of the Lord, because you know that in the Lord your labor is not in vain."

Notes

1. Jackson, *Wesley's Works*, 1:100.
2. "Divine Love," trans. from the German, George Osborn, ed., *The Poetical Works of John and Charles Wesley*, 13 vols. (London: The Wesleyan Methodist Conference Office, 1868), 1:71.
3. Jackson, *Wesley's Works*, 1:100.
4. Ward and Heitzenrater, *Wesley's Journal and Diaries*, April 16, 1757, 21:92.
5. Ann Bolton was an exceptional young Christian whom Wesley called the "sister of my choice."
6. Telford, *Wesley's Letters*, 5:342.
7. Charles Wesley, "For a Believer in Worldly Business," stanza 3, *Poet. Wks.*, 4:215.

UPON OUR LORD'S SERMON ON THE MOUNT

Discourse 5

John Wesley often referred to the religious practices of the New Testament scribes and Pharisees. He did not portray them as being hypocritical or superficial, as many preachers often do. Instead, Wesley viewed them as impressive examples of *outward* righteousness. For example, prior to his conversion, St. Paul was a Pharisee. As such, he was neither hypocritical nor insincere. He used the means of grace and diligently kept the law. Wesley points out that most people fail to live up to the high religious standards of the scribes and Pharisees, although Jesus taught that our righteousness must *exceed* theirs.

Wesley's emphasis on keeping the moral law caused some of his detractors to charge him with preaching a righteousness that grows out of good works. Considered in the light of his consistent teaching on grace, that charge was both groundless and surprising. In *The Principles of a Methodist* Wesley wrote:

> Our justification comes freely, of the mere mercy of God; for whereas all the world was not able to pay any part towards their ransom, it pleased him, without any of our deserving, to prepare for us Christ's body and blood, whereby our ransom might be paid,

and his justice satisfied. Christ, therefore, is now the righteousness of all them that truly believe in him.[1]

Wesley insisted that good works do not produce righteousness, but righteousness produces good works.

In this sermon Wesley deals with the subjects of election and predestination. He reasons that if salvation is due to election, it cannot rest either on works or faith:

> If the salvation of every man that ever was, is, or shall be, finally saved, depends wholly and solely upon an absolute, irresistible, unchangeable decree of God, without any regard either to faith or works foreseen, then it is not, in any sense, by works. But neither is it by faith: For unconditional decree excludes faith as well as works; since, if it is either by faith or works foreseen, it is not by unconditional decree. Therefore, salvation by absolute decree excludes both one and the other; and, consequently, upon this supposition, salvation is neither by faith nor by works.[2]

Wesley insisted that if we accept the scriptural condition, "He that believes will be saved," we must make room for free will and responsible cooperation with God's grace.

Wesley preached often on the text for this sermon, showing that Christians must go beyond the righteousness of the scribes and Pharisees. On one occasion, he recorded in his journal, "As I was expounding in the Back-Lane, on the righteousness of the Scribes and Pharisees, many who had before been righteous in their own eyes, abhorred themselves as in dust and ashes. But two, who seemed to be more deeply convinced than the rest, did not long sorrow as men without hope; but found in that hour, that they had 'an Advocate with the Father, Jesus Christ the righteous:' As did three others in Gloucester-Lane the evening before, and three at Baldwin-Street this evening. About ten, two who after seeing a great light, had again reasoned themselves into darkness, came to us, heavy-laden. We cried to God, and they were again 'filled with peace and joy in believing.'"[3] This text and sermon often appear in Wesley's sermon log.

In this message, Wesley explains that Jesus did not come to bring a new religion. Rather, part of his earthly mission was to fulfill God's commands which were given in the law and rein-forced by the prophets. The cross of Christ took away the *cere-monial law,* but it did not abrogate the *moral law.* What the moral law requires, the gospel enables. Jesus said, "Unless your right-eousness exceeds that of the scribes and Pharisees, you will never enter the kingdom of heaven." If we would keep the moral law, our righteousness must move beyond a religion of duty; it must be a religion of the heart. Fulfilling the moral law requires inward righteousness, which is the biblical standard for all those who call themselves Christians.

UPON OUR LORD'S SERMON ON THE MOUNT

Discourse 5

"Do not think that I have come to abolish the law or the prophets; I have come not to abolish but to fulfill. For truly I tell you, until heaven and earth pass away, not one letter, not one stroke of a letter, will pass from the law until all is accomplished. Therefore, whoever breaks one of the least of these commandments, and teaches others to do the same, will be called least in the kingdom of heaven; but whoever does them and teaches them will be called great in the kingdom of heaven. For I tell you, unless your righteousness exceeds that of the scribes and Pharisees, you will never enter the kingdom of heaven." (Matthew 5:17-20)

1 Many condemnations fell upon Jesus Christ who "was despised and rejected by others." One criticism that was bound to come against him was that he was a teacher of new things, one who introduced a novel religion. He attracted even more intense opposition because he used many expressions that

were not common among the Jews. Either they did not use them at all, or not in the same sense, or not with such extensive and powerful meanings. Furthermore, the teaching of Jesus was offensive because he insisted that we are to "worship the Father in spirit and truth." This perspective was certain to seem like a new religion to those who had previously known nothing but external worship. The critics of Jesus knew only "the outward form of godliness."

2. It is probable that some of the people hoped that Jesus *was* abolishing the old religion and bringing in a new one. Some people wanted a religion that would flatter them and provide an easier way to heaven. But in our text our Lord refutes the vain hopes of the one and the groundless lies of the other.

Now, I will consider these words of Jesus line by line, using each verse as a distinct division of this sermon.

I. The gospel of Christ is the fulfillment of the law

1. First, Jesus said, "Do not think that I have come to abolish the law or the prophets; I have come not to abolish but to fulfill." Our Lord indeed came to destroy, dissolve, and utterly abolish the ritualistic (or ceremonial) law delivered by Moses to the children of Israel. This law contained all the commands and ordinances that pertained to the ancient sacrifices and ceremonies of the temple.

The apostles Barnabas and Paul, along with all the other apostles, bear witness to Christ's repeal of the Old Testament ceremonial law. They fervently opposed those who taught that Christians were obligated "to keep the law of Moses." St. Peter also disapproved of those who wanted to retain the ceremonial law. He stated that to require the Old Testament ritualistic law was "putting God to the test by placing on the neck of the disciples a yoke that neither our ancestors nor we have been able to bear."

As well, all the apostles, elders, and the faithful assembled together and concluded that to require Christians to keep the ceremonial law would "unsettle their minds." The New Testament Christian community declared, "For it has seemed good to the

Holy Spirit and to us to impose on you no further burden." Our Lord "erased the record that stood against us with its legal demands. He set this aside, nailing it to the cross."

2. However, God did not take away the *moral law*. This law was contained in the Ten Commandments and upheld by the prophets. The object of Christ's coming was not to revoke any part of the moral law. This law can never be overturned, and it shall continue forever. The moral law stands on an entirely different foundation than the ceremonial or ritual law, which was only designed for a temporary restraint upon a disobedient and stiff-necked people.

The moral law, however, has existed from the beginning of the world. It was not "written on tablets of stone," but on the hearts of all people made by the hands of the Creator. However, the letter of the moral law, which was written by the finger of God, is now in a great measure defaced by sin. Still, the moral law cannot be completely erased, so long as we have any consciousness of good and evil. Every part of this law must remain in force in all people and in all ages. The moral law does not depend on time, place, or any other changing circumstances. It rests on the nature of God, the nature of humankind, and their unchangeable relationship with each other.

3. Let us consider the phrase, "I have come not to abolish the law but to fulfill it." Some have conceived that our Lord meant that he himself came to fulfill the law by his complete and perfect obedience to it. In this sense, it cannot be doubted that he *did* fulfill every part of the law. However, it does not appear that this accomplishment was what he referred to in this scripture passage. The concern of the Sermon on the Mount is not *Christ's* obedience to the moral law. Despite all human explanations to the contrary, consistent with all that precedes and follows this verse of scripture, undoubtedly his meaning is that he came to establish in us the moral law in its entirety.

Jesus is saying that he came to reveal fully and clearly whatever was hidden or obscure regarding the law. He is saying, "I came to declare the true and full meaning of every part of the law. I will clarify the length and breadth, the full extent of every commandment contained in the moral law. I will reveal the height and depth and the incredible purity and spirituality of the law in all its aspects."

4. In the preceding and subsequent parts of the Sermon on the Mount, our Lord made known to us the complete meaning of the moral law. In doing so, he did not introduce a new religion into the world. The religion of Jesus is the same religion that God gave in the beginning. It is a religion that in its substance is unquestionably as old as the creation itself. It is as ancient as humankind, having proceeded from God at the very time when the first man and woman became "living beings." (I say, "the substance of religion," because some aspects of the law now pertain to humankind in its fallen estate.)

In all succeeding generations, both the law and the prophets witnessed to this religion. Yet the moral law was never fully explained or understood until the Great Author of the law himself condescended to give humankind his authentic commentary on all its fundamental branches. At that time, he declared that it would never be changed, but remain in force to the end of the world.

II. The symmetry between law and gospel

1. Jesus begins his explanation of the moral law with the words, "For truly I tell you." This solemn introduction to his teaching expresses both the importance and certainty of what is being spoken. He said that "until heaven and earth pass away, not one letter, not one stroke of a letter, will pass from the law until all is accomplished."

The phrase "not one letter" is literally "not one iota," not even the smallest vowel. The phrase "not one stroke of a letter" means not a single corner or point of a consonant. The proverbial expression "one jot or one tittle" means that not one commandment contained in the moral law, or the least part of any commandment, will ever be canceled, however meager it might seem.

Not a single letter or stroke of a letter "will pass from the law." In the Greek text, the double negative strengthens the sense, to allow no dispute about the meaning. And we may observe that the verb "will pass" is not merely future tense, declaring what *will be.*

It also has the force of an imperative, ordering what *shall* be. It is a word of authority, expressing the sovereign will and power of him who spoke. It is the declaration of him whose word is the law of heaven and earth, and his word stands firm forever and ever.

Jesus said, "Not one stroke of a letter, will pass from the law until all is accomplished." As it is expressed immediately following, " . . . until the consummation of all things. There is, therefore, no room here for that worthless evasion (with which some have delighted themselves greatly) that no part of the law was to pass away until all the law was fulfilled in Christ. Some people incorrectly allege that because Christ fulfilled the moral law it has now been canceled in order for the gospel to be instituted. This view is entirely wrong. The word *all* does not mean all the law; rather, it means all things in the universe. In the same way, the word *accomplished* does not refer to the law, but to all things in heaven and earth.

2. We may learn from these observations that there is no conflict whatsoever between the law and the gospel. There is no need for the moral law to pass away in order to establish the gospel. Indeed, neither one of them supplants the other, but they perfectly supplement each other. Indeed, considered in different respects, the very same words are elements of both the law and the gospel. If they are considered as commandments, they are parts of the law; if considered as promises, they are parts of the gospel.

Consequently, the precept "You shall love the Lord your God with all your heart," when considered as a commandment, is a part of the law. When it is regarded as a promise, it is a fundamental part of the gospel. The gospel is nothing more than the requirements of the law intended as a promise. Accordingly, poverty of spirit, purity of heart, and whatever else is commanded in the holy law of God, when viewed in the light of the gospel, are "precious and very great promises."

3. There is, therefore, the closest possible connection between the law and the gospel. On the one hand, the law continuously prepares us for, and points us to, the gospel. On the other hand, the gospel continually leads us to a more precise fulfilling of the law. For instance, the law requires us to love God, to love our

neighbor, to be meek, humble, and holy. We feel that we are not sufficient for these things; indeed, we know that "for mortals it is impossible." However, in the gospel we see God's promise to give us love and to make us humble, meek, and holy. We lay hold of the good news of the gospel, and according to our faith, it is done for us. "The just requirement of the law is fulfilled in us, through faith in Christ Jesus."

Also, we may further observe that every command in scripture is really a hidden promise. In the following declaration, God pledges to give what he commands:

> This is the covenant that I will make with them
>   after those days, says the Lord:
> I will put my laws in their hearts,
>   and I will write them on their minds. (Heb. 10:16)

Does God command us to "pray without ceasing," to "rejoice always," and to "be holy, for he is holy"? The command is sufficient—God will work in us these very things. It will be with us, according to his word.

4. But if these things are so, we must be astonished at those in all ages of the church that have attempted to change or replace some of God's commands, even professing to be guided by the Holy Spirit. Here, in the Sermon on the Mount Christ has given us an infallible rule by which to consider all such attempts to amend his words. If we will listen to God, we will learn that his final dispensation is Christianity, and it includes the entire moral law of God, by way of both commandments and promise.

There is no other dispensation to come after this present one. This dispensation is to endure until the fulfillment of all things. Consequently, all new "revelations" are of Satan, and not of God. All pretenses to another more perfect dispensation will of course fall to the ground. "Heaven and earth will pass away, but God's words will not pass away."

III. The continuing authority of the word of God

1. Jesus said, "Therefore, whoever breaks one of the least of these commandments, and teaches others to do the same, will be

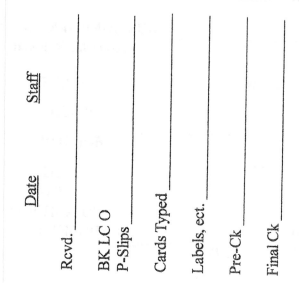

called least in the kingdom of heaven; but whoever does them and teaches them will be called great in the kingdom of heaven."

Who are the ones who make "the preaching of the law" an "object of scorn"? Do they not see on whose head their contempt must finally fall? In the end, their scorn is placed on Jesus Christ. And whoever belittles him because of his endorsement of the law belittles the one who sent him.

Although Jesus did not come to condemn the world but to save it, did anyone ever preach the law like him? He preached the law, even if it is true that he came to "bring life and immortality to light through the gospel." Can anyone preach the law more explicitly and strictly than Christ does in the words of our text? And who is the one that will amend the words of Christ? Who will instruct the Son of God on how he should preach? Who will teach him a better way to deliver the message that he received from the Father?

2. Jesus speaks to anyone who "breaks one of the least of these commandments." Let us observe that our Lord used the term "these commandments" as an equivalent to "the law"—or "the

commandments." In that statement Jesus eliminated another excuse used by many who regrettably deceive themselves, although they cannot deceive God. The sinner says, "This sin is a small one, is it not? Will the Lord not spare me in this thing? Because I do not transgress in the more important matters of the law, surely God will not be so excessively judgmental as to take note of this one transgression." This vain hope is foolish indeed!

Speaking from a human perspective, we may distinguish between large and small commandments. In reality, however, they cannot be distinguished from each other. If we speak accurately, there is no such thing as a "little sin." Every sin is a transgression of God's holy and perfect law, and each transgression is an insult to the majestic dignity of heaven.

3. To his warning against breaking the least of the commandments, Jesus adds the phrase, "...and teaches others to do the same." In some sense we can say that whoever flagrantly breaks any commandment, at the same time teaches others to do so as well. One's example speaks many times louder than one's principles. In this sense, it is evident that every public drunkard is a teacher of drunkenness. Every Sabbath-breaker is constantly teaching his neighbor to desecrate the Lord's day.

Nevertheless, there is still more. Those who regularly break the law are seldom content to stop with a mere transgression. By word and example, they teach others to transgress as well—especially when people stiffen their necks and despise correction. Such sinners soon end up as advocates of the sin. Transgressors defend what they are determined not to forsake. They excuse the sin they will not relinquish. And in this way, they openly teach every sin they commit.

Jesus said that such people "will be called least in the kingdom of heaven." In other words, they will have no part in it at all. They are aliens to the kingdom of heaven on earth. They have no portion of that inheritance—no share in "righteousness and peace and joy in the Holy Spirit." Consequently, they have no part in the glory that will be revealed to God's children.

4. It is true that "whoever breaks one of the least of these commandments, and teaches others to do the same, will be called least in the kingdom of heaven." They will have no part in the kingdom of Christ and of God. These people will be thrown into the outer

darkness, where there will be "weeping and gnashing of teeth." What, then, will be the state of those transgressors who carry the credentials of teachers sent from God? (These are the ones to which our Lord chiefly and primarily refers in these words.) What will become of the false teachers who break God's commandments and even openly teach others to do the same? What will be the end of those that are immoral in both life and teaching?

5. There are several kinds of these false teachers. First, there are those that live in some willful and habitual sin. If an ordinary sinner teaches by his or her example, how much more influential is a sinful minister of Christ? These sinners influence others, even if they do not attempt to defend, excuse, or moderate their sins! If they excuse their sin, they are murderers indeed—yes, the chief murderer of their congregations. They populate the regions of death. They are the best instruments of the Prince of Darkness. When they eventually join Satan, "hell beneath is stirred up to meet them when they come." Furthermore, they do not sink into the bottomless pit without dragging a multitude with them.

6. Next to these false teachers stand the good-natured, upright sorts of leaders that live leisurely, harmless lives. They do not concern themselves with either outward sin or inward holiness. They are not distinguished either by sin or righteousness; they are not noted either for religion or for irreligion. They are very conventional both in public and private, but they do not pretend to be any more scrupulous than their neighbors are.

Ministers of this kind break more than a few of the least of God's commandments. They break all the important and significant aspects of God's law pertaining to the power of godliness. They violate God's commands that require us to "live in reverent fear during the time of our exile" and to "work out our own salvation with fear and trembling." They do not obey the commands to be "dressed for action and have their lamps lit" and to "strive (or agonize) to enter through the narrow door."

By the entire cast of their lives and the prevailing tone of their preaching, these faithless ministers uniformly tend to soothe those in their pleasant dreams who imagine themselves to be Christians, while they are not. These false teachers persuade all that attend their ministries to take their rest and continue sleeping. Therefore, it will be no wonder at all, if both these ministers and those who follow them awaken together in everlasting flames.

7. However, above all these faithless ministers, standing in the highest order of the enemies of the gospel of Christ are those that openly and explicitly "speak evil against the law and judge the law." They teach others to break (dissolve, loose, or untie) the obligation of not just one of the laws (whether the least or the greatest), but *all* the commandments at the same time. In so many words, these false teachers say without any disguise, "What did our Lord do with the law? He abolished it. There is only one duty, and it is to believe. None of God's commandments are relevant for today. Pertaining to the requirements of the law, no one is now obligated to take one step, give away one coin, or eat or omit one bite of food."

This teaching is indeed carrying matters to a bold extreme, because it opposes our Lord face-to-face. These teachers are telling Jesus Christ that he did not understand how to deliver the message the Father sent him to deliver. O Lord, do not hold this sin against them! Father, forgive them, for they know not what they are doing!

8. The most surprising of all the circumstances that accompany this strong delusion is that these teachers especially believe that they honor Christ by destroying his law. They think that they are expanding his importance, while they are destroying his doctrine! Indeed, they honor him just as Judas did when he said, "Greetings, Rabbi!" Then he kissed him. Jesus may justly say to every one of these teachers, "Is it with a kiss that you are betraying the Son of Man?" When we talk of Christ's blood, while taking away his crown, we are betraying him with a kiss.

We betray God when under the pretext of advancing the gospel we treat any part of his law casually. Indeed, none of these teachers can escape the charge of doing exactly that. They preach faith in such a way that directly or indirectly tends to set aside any aspect of obedience. We cannot escape divine judgment if we preach Christ in a way that repeals or in any respect weakens the least of God's commandments.

9. Most certainly, it is undoubtedly impossible to have too high an esteem for "the faith of God's elect." And we must all declare, "By grace you have been saved through faith, and this is not your own doing; it is the gift of God—not the result of works, so that no one may boast." We must clearly proclaim to every penitent sinner, "Believe on the Lord Jesus, and you will be saved."

Yet, at the same time, we must diligently let everyone know that we value no faith except "faith working through love." Furthermore, we are not saved by faith, unless we are delivered from the power of sin as well as its guilt. When we say, "Have faith, and you will be saved," we do not mean, "Believe, and you will move from sin to heaven without first becoming holy." We do not allow that faith is a substitute for holiness.

Rather, we say, "Believe, and you will become holy; trust in the Lord Jesus and you will have both peace *and* power. You will receive from him, in whom you believe, the power to trample sin under your feet." Faith results in the power to love the Lord our God with all our hearts and to serve him with all our strength. "To those who by patiently doing good seek for glory and honor and immortality, he will give eternal life." In this way, you will both do and teach all God's commandments, from the least to the greatest. You will teach them by your life as well as your words, and therefore you will "be called great in the kingdom of heaven."

IV. The righteousness that is above the law

1. Those that promote any way to the kingdom of heaven other than faith working through love are teaching the way to destruction, whether one terms it "the way of faith" or gives it some other name. The way to "glory, honor, and immortality" includes holiness of heart and life. Any other way leads to ruin. Any other way cannot bring one to everlasting peace. The Lord said, "For I tell you, unless your righteousness exceeds that of the scribes and Pharisees, you will never enter the kingdom of heaven."

The scribes, whom the New Testament so often mentions as some of the most unceasing and zealous opponents of our Lord, were not just copyists or those entirely engaged in writing, as the term *scribe* might incline us to believe. Neither were they lawyers in our common sense of the word, although some translations designate them lawyers. Their occupation had no resemblance at all to lawyers as we know them. The scribes were familiar with the laws of God, but not much concerned with civil law. They studied *God's* laws.

Their proper and characteristic business was to read and explain the Old Testament law and prophets, especially in the synagogues. The scribes were the ordinary, established preachers among the Jews. Therefore, if we hold to the sense of the original term, we might call them members of the clergy or theologians. Their vocation was the study of theology. As their designation literally signifies, in the Jewish nation they were men of letters, persons with the highest reputation for learning.

2. The Pharisees were a very ancient sect, a group of Jewish men, whose name derives from the Hebrew word meaning to "separate" or to "set apart." They did not formally separate from national Judaism or form a separate cult. They were simply distinguished from other Jews by their greater strictness of life and more scrupulous conduct. They were zealous of the smallest points of the law, even tithing the mint, anise, and cumin in their gardens. Consequently, all the people honored them and generally esteemed them as the holiest of all.

Many of the scribes also belonged to the sect of the Pharisees. St. Paul himself was educated as a scribe, first at the University of Tarsus and after that in Jerusalem at the feet of Gamaliel (one of the most learned scribes or Doctors of the Law who then existed in the nation). Paul declared before the Council, "I am a Pharisee, the son of Pharisees." Standing before King Agrippa, Paul stated, "I have belonged to the strictest sect of our religion and lived as a Pharisee." In general, the entire company of scribes esteemed the Pharisees and acted in accord with their example and teaching. Because the scribes and Pharisees usually thought and acted alike, we find our Savior frequently merging them. In our text, Jesus mentions the two groups together as the most distinguished professors of religion. The scribes were considered the wisest of people, and the Pharisees were considered the holiest.

3. It is not difficult to determine what our Lord meant when he spoke of "the righteousness of the scribes and Pharisees." Our Lord has preserved an authentic account that one of them gave of himself. This scribe clearly and fully described his own righteousness, and we cannot suppose that he omitted any part of it. This man "went up to the temple to pray." Yet, he was so engrossed in his own virtues that he forgot the reason for which he came.

It is astonishing that he did not offer a proper prayer. He only told God how wise and good he was: "God, I thank you that I am not like other people: thieves, rogues, adulterers, or even like this tax collector. I fast twice a week; I give a tenth of all my income." His righteousness therefore consisted of three parts. First, he boasted, "I am not like other people. I am not a thief, rogue, adulterer," or "even like this tax collector." Second, "I fast twice a week." And, third, "I give a tenth of all my income."

It is not a small point that the Pharisee said, "I am not like other people." Not everyone can make this claim. It is as if he had said, "I do not permit myself to be carried away by the great flood of popular customs. I do not live by the standards of worldly convention, but by reason. I do not follow human examples, but the word of God. I am not a thief, an unfair man, or an adulterer, however common these sins may be even among those that are called the people of God." (Theft in particular was a legal injustice that filled every corner of the land. It was not punishable by any human law, and for personal gain the thieves took advantage of the ignorance or needs of others.) The Pharisee continued, "I am not like this tax collector; I am not guilty of any public or presumptuous sin; I am not an outward sinner. Rather, I am a fair and honest man of blameless life and conduct."

4. The Pharisee also boasted, "I fast twice a week." There is more implied in this claim than we might at first recognize. All the stricter Pharisees observed the weekly fasts, namely, every Monday and Thursday. On Mondays they fasted in memory of the tradition that on that day Moses received the two tablets of stone written by the finger of God. On Thursdays the Pharisees fasted in memory of Moses' throwing down the stone tablets when he saw the people dancing round the golden calf. On these

fast days, the Pharisees took no food until three in the afternoon, the time when they began to offer up the evening sacrifice in the temple. Until that hour, it was their custom to remain in the temple—in some of its corners, apartments, or courts—in order to be ready to assist at the sacrifices and to join in the public prayers. They spent the remaining time in private prayer, searching the scriptures, reading the law and the prophets, and in meditating on them. Consequently much is implied in saying, "I fast twice a week," which was the second part of the righteousness of a Pharisee.

5. In addition, the Pharisee said, "I give a tenth of all my income." And Pharisees did so with the utmost precision. They did not fail to tithe the slightest thing, not even the mint, anise, and cumin from their gardens. They would not hold back the smallest part of what they believed properly to belong to God. Rather, they gave a full tenth of their entire yearly income and of all their gains, whatever they were.

Indeed, as those versed in the ancient Jewish writings have often noted, the stricter Pharisees were not satisfied with giving a tenth of their income to God's Priests and Levites. They gave an *additional* tenth to God by giving to the poor, and they habitually maintained this pattern of giving. Thus, of all their substance, they gave the same portion in alms as they gave in tithes. With utmost precision, they adjusted their giving so as to hold back nothing that they considered to belong to God. From year to year, they gave away a full fifth of everything they possessed.

6. These practices (separation from the world, fasting, tithing, and alms giving) constituted "the righteousness of the scribes and Pharisees." It was a righteousness that in many respects went far beyond what many people have been accustomed to understand about their righteousness. But perhaps it will be said, "It was all false and imaginary because they were all an association of hypocrites."

I answer that some of them doubtless were frauds. And some of them actually had no religion at all, no fear of God, and no desire to please him. The insincere ones had no concern for "the glory that comes from the one who alone is God." They only wanted human praise. These are the ones that our Lord so severely condemned and so sharply censured on many occasions. However, we must not suppose that *all* the Pharisees were hypocrites, just because some of them were. Indeed, by no means is hypocrisy a necessary essential to the character of a Pharisee. Hypocrisy is not the distinguishing mark of their sect.

Rather, according to our Lord's account, the basic characteristic of the Pharisees was that they "trusted in themselves that they were righteous and regarded others with contempt." Self-righteousness was their essential mark. This kind of Pharisee cannot be a hypocrite. It is evident that the one about whom Jesus spoke must have been sincere, or else he could not have "trusted in himself that he was righteous." Without doubt, those who approved themselves to God thought of themselves as righteous. Consequently, they were not hypocrites; they were not aware of any insincerity within themselves. They said to God exactly what they thought—namely, that they were abundantly superior to other people.

If there were no other example, St. Paul is enough to put the question to rest. When he was a Christian, Paul could say, "I do my best always to have a clear conscience toward God and all people." Even when he was a Pharisee he could say, "Brothers, up to this day I have lived my life with a clear conscience before God." He was therefore sincere when he was a Pharisee as well as when he was a Christian. Paul was no more a hypocrite when he persecuted the church than when he preached the faith that he once persecuted. Let it be added to "the righteousness of the scribes and Pharisees" that they had a sincere belief that they were righteous and in all things "they were offering worship to God."

7. And yet our Lord said, "unless your righteousness exceeds that of the scribes and Pharisees, you will never enter the kingdom of heaven." All who are called by the name of Christ should ponder this solemn and weighty declaration. However, before we inquire into how our righteousness can exceed that of the scribes and Pharisees, let us examine whether we presently meet even their standard.

First, Pharisees were "not like other people." In externals, they were exceedingly good. Are we likewise? Do we dare to be at all unique? Do we not prefer to swim with the stream? Do we not many times dispense with religion and reason together because we do not want to appear unusual? Are we not often more afraid of being out of fashion, than being out of the way of salvation? Do we have the courage to stem the tide? Do we dare to run counter to the world's customs? Do we want to "obey God rather than any human authority?" If not, the Pharisee leaves us behind at the very first step. It is good if we exceed the Pharisee's zeal.

But examine the Pharisee more closely. Can we use his first appeal to God? In substance, the Pharisee claims, "I do no harm to others. I live in no outward sin. I do nothing for which my own heart condemns me." Can you say the same? Are you sure that you can? Do you do nothing for which your own heart condemns you?

If you are not an adulterer or impure in word or deed, are you not unfair? The main measure of justice and mercy is, "In everything do to others as you would have them do to you." Do you walk by this rule? Do you never do to anyone what you would not want them to do to you? Are you not flagrantly unfair? Are you not a thief? Do you not make a profit from anyone's ignorance or need, neither in buying nor selling? Suppose you are engaged in business. Do you ask and receive no more than the real value of what you sell? Do you ask and receive no more from those that are uninformed than from those who are? Do you make more profit from a novice than from an experienced businessman? If you do, why does your heart not condemn you? You are a blatant thief! Do you ask more than the usual price for goods from those who have a pressing need and who immediately must have the things that only you can supply them? If you do, this also is plain thievery. Indeed, you do not come up to the Pharisee's standard of righteousness.

8. Second, a Pharisee used all the means of grace (to express things in today's language). He fasted often and much—twice each week. As well, he often attended all the ritual sacrifices. He was consistent in public and private prayer and in reading and hearing

the scriptures. Does your faithfulness go this far? Do you fast much and often? Twice each week? I fear that you do not. Do you fast at least once a week, on all Fridays in the year? (Our church clearly and emphatically commands all her members to use these days as well as the vigils and the forty days of Lent, as days of fasting or abstinence.) Do you fast even twice in the year? I am afraid some among us cannot claim even this level of fasting!

Do you neglect no opportunity to attend and partake of the Christian service of Holy Communion? How many call themselves Christians and yet completely disregard the sacrament. They do not eat of that bread or drink of that cup for months, perhaps years, at a time! Do you daily either hear the scriptures, or read them and meditate on them? Do you join in prayer with the great congregation, daily if you have opportunity? If not, do you attend church whenever you can, especially on that day which you remember to keep holy? Do you strive to create opportunities to attend public worship services? Are you glad when they say to you, "Let us go to the house of the Lord"?

Are you zealous of private prayer and diligent in this discipline? Do you allow no day to pass without praying? Instead, are not some of you so far from spending several hours in daily prayer (as the Pharisees did) that you think one hour of prayer quite enough, if not too much? Do you spend an hour a day, or a week, in praying to your Father who is in secret? Indeed, do you pray an hour in a month? Have you spent one sustained hour in private prayer since you were born? Ah, poor Christian! Will the Pharisee not rise up in the judgment against you and condemn you? His righteousness is as far above yours as heaven is above the earth!

9. Third, the Pharisees paid tithes and gave alms from all that they possessed. And in how abundant a manner! As we sometimes say, "He was a man that did much good." In this regard, do we come up to his standard? Who among us is as abounding in good works as the Pharisee? Who among us gives a fifth of our entire substance to God, both of the principal and of the gains? Out of a hundred pounds a year, who of us gives twenty pounds to God and the poor? Who are those among us that give ten pounds out of fifty, and proportionally as we have more or less? When will

our righteousness in using all the means of grace, in attending all the ordinances of God, and in avoiding evil and doing good at least equal the righteousness of the scribes and Pharisees?

10. Even so, if our righteousness only equaled that of the Pharisees, what would that gain us? Jesus said, "Unless your righteousness *exceeds* that of the scribes and Pharisees, you will never enter the kingdom of heaven." How can the Christian's righteousness exceed theirs? In what way does the righteousness of a Christian exceed that of a scribe or Pharisee?

First, Christian righteousness exceeds theirs in its scope. Most of the Pharisees, though they were rigorously exact in many things, were prodded by the traditions of the elders to dispense with other matters of equal importance. For instance, they were extremely careful to keep the fourth commandment about keeping the Sabbath day. They would not so much as rub together a head of grain on the Sabbath day. Yet, they did not keep the third commandment about making wrongful use of the name of the Lord. They paid little heed to casual or even false swearing. Thus, their righteousness was partial.

By contrast, the righteousness of a genuine Christian is comprehensive. The genuine Christian does not observe just one or some parts of God's law, while neglecting the rest. Instead the Christian keeps all God's commandments, loves them all, and values them above gold or precious stones.

11. Of course, it may be that some of the scribes and Pharisees attempted to keep all God's commandments. As to righteousness under the law (the letter of the law), they were blameless. Nevertheless, the righteousness of a Christian exceeds all the righteousness of a scribe or Pharisee, by fulfilling not only its letter, but also its *spirit*. Christians have both inward and outward obedience to God's law. In keeping the spirit of the law, there is no resemblance between Pharisees and Christians. Throughout the entire tenor of the Sermon on the Mount, our Lord amply proved this point.

The Pharisee's righteousness was entirely external. Christian righteousness involves the inner self. The Pharisee "cleansed the outside of the cup and of the plate." The Christian is clean within. The Pharisee labored to present God with an upright life; the Christian is concerned with a holy heart. The Pharisee shook off the leaves and perhaps the fruits of sin; the Christian "lays the ax to the root" of sin. The Christian is not content with only the outward form of godliness, however precise it is. In addition to outward righteousness, the life, Spirit, and "the power of God for salvation" must be experienced in the soul.

Therefore, to do no harm, to do good, to attend the ordinances of God are all internal matters. The righteousness of a Pharisee is all external. By contrast, poverty of spirit, mourning, meekness, hunger and thirst for righteousness, the love of our neighbor, and purity of heart (the righteousness of a Christian) are internal. Even peacemaking, doing good, and suffering for righteousness' sake qualify for the blessings attached to them only as they arise from, work through, and witness to inward attitudes. Inasmuch as the righteousness of the scribes and Pharisees was only external, in some sense it may be said that the righteousness of a Christian is only internal. God appraises all our actions and sufferings based on the motives from which they rise.

12. Therefore, whoever you are that bear the holy and revered name of *Christian,* see first that your righteousness does not fall short of the righteousness of the scribes and Pharisees. Do not be like other people. Dare to stand alone. Contrary to the example of others, be resolutely good. If in any way you "follow the majority," it will inevitably be "in wrongdoing." Do not allow custom or fashion to be your guide. Instead, follow reason and religion. The practice of others should mean nothing to you. "Each of us will be accountable to God." Indeed, if you can save the soul of another, do so; but at least give attention to saving your own soul. Do not walk in the path of death, "for the gate is wide and the road is easy that leads to destruction, and there are many who take it."

The way you can know that a path is wrong is that many travel it. Is the path you now walk a broad, crowded, fashionable path? If so, it unfailingly leads to destruction. Do not be damned for the company you keep! "Cease to do evil" (Isa. 1:16). Flee from sin as from the face of a serpent! At the very least, do no harm. "Everyone who commits sin is a child of the devil." Do not be found among that number. Concerning outward sins, surely the grace of God is even now adequate for you to overcome. In this regard, strive "always to have a clear conscience toward God and all people."

Second, concerning the ordinances of God do not allow your righteousness to fall short of the righteousness of the scribes and Pharisees. If your work or physical strength do not allow you to fast each week, deal faithfully with your own soul and fast as often as your strength will allow. Omit no public or private opportunity to pour out your soul in prayer. Neglect no opportunity to eat of the bread and drink of the cup that is the communion of the body and blood of Christ.

Be diligent in searching the scriptures; read them as you can, and meditate on them day and night. Rejoice to embrace every opportunity to hear "the word of reconciliation" declared by the "servants of Christ and stewards of God's mysteries." Live up to "the righteousness of the scribes and Pharisees" by using all the means of grace and by a consistent and careful participation in every ordinance of God. Persist in these things, at least until you go beyond the standards of the scribes and Pharisees.

Third, do not fall short of a Pharisee in doing good. Give alms from everything you possess. Are others hungry? Feed them. Are people thirsty? Give them drink. Are they without clothing? Cover them with garments. If you have this world's goods, do not limit your liberality to a small percentage of what you possess. Be merciful to the utmost of your ability. Why not provide for others in the same way that the Pharisees did? Now, when you have time and opportunity, "make friends" by your generosity. When your wealth is gone and your body is in the grave, others "may welcome you into the eternal homes."

13. However, do not be content only with these actions. Let your righteousness *exceed* that of the scribes and Pharisees. Do not be content to "keep the whole law, but fail in one point." Keep *all* God's commandments and "hate every false way." Do all the things that God has commanded, and do them with all your might. You "can do all things through Christ who strengthens you." "Apart from him you can do nothing."

Above all, let your righteousness exceed the righteousness of the scribes and Pharisees in its *spirituality*. What do you think is the most exacting form of religion? The most perfect expression of outward righteousness? Go higher and deeper than all these things! Let your religion be the religion of the heart. Be poor in spirit. And in your estimation of yourself, become small, wretched, inferior, and debased. Be amazed and humbled to the dust by "the love of God in Christ Jesus your Lord!" Become serious. Let the whole stream of your thoughts, words, and actions flow from the deepest conviction that you stand on the edge of the great gulf of infinity.

You and everyone else are just ready to drop into eternity, either into everlasting glory or everlasting flames! Become meek. Let your soul be filled with kindness, gentleness, endurance, and patience toward everyone. At the same time, let everything within you thirst for the living God, longing to awaken in his likeness and to be satisfied with it. Become a lover of God, and of all humankind. In this spirit, do and endure all things. In this way, you will "exceed the righteousness of the scribes and Pharisees," and you will be "called great in the kingdom of heaven."

Notes

1 Rupert E. Davis, ed., *The Works of John Wesley,* Bicentennial ed., "The Methodist Societies: History, Nature, and Design" (Nashville: Abingdon Press, 1989), "The Principles of a Methodist, 9:51."

2. Jackson, *Wesley's Works,* "Thoughts on Salvation by Faith," 11:494.

3. Ward and Heitzenrater, *Wesley's Journal and Diaries,* May 15, 1739, 19:57-58.

UPON OUR LORD'S SERMON ON THE MOUNT

Discourse 6

Wesley's sermons 21-25, based on Matthew 5, describe the attitudes and affections that constitute a genuine religion of the heart. In this sermon, Wesley moves into Matthew 6, which explains how right attitudes and affections lead to right actions. Commenting on the structure of the Sermon on the Mount, Wesley said, "In the foregoing chapter [chapter 5] our Lord particularly described the nature of inward holiness. In this [chapter 6] He describes that purity of intention without which none of our outward actions are holy."[1] The present sermon stresses that the deeds we do apart from pure and holy intentions are of no worth in the sight of God. However, when holy affections and attitudes purify our deeds, God accounts them of great value.

Wesley states that there are two essential kinds of religious expressions—*works of piety* and *works of charity* (or mercy). Works of piety pertain to one's relationship with God, which is demonstrated in activities such as prayer and fasting. Works of charity concern one's relationships with others, which are revealed in such public activities as almsgiving, serving, and showing mercy. It is interesting to note that these religious expressions parallel the three main religious duties of Judaism—prayer, fasting, and giving alms. This sermon asserts that the instructions that Jesus gave with respect to the manner in which we perform works of piety and works of charity should apply to all aspects of our lives.

The first division of this discourse discusses the Lord's mandate to perform good works in ways that do not draw attention to ourselves. Jesus specifically forbids our performing religious duties with an eye to winning human applause. Wesley says that to look for public acclaim for our good works is to undermine our purity of intention. He maintains that God does not approve our works if we are seeking recognition or personal glory in our praying, attending public worship, or assisting the poor.

The sermon's second division discusses how our good works please God. In doing good works, we should seek God's praise, not our own. Jesus told us to look for eternal rewards, not temporal ones. In doing works of charity we should speak directly and sincerely, not using empty words and insincere talk. Elsewhere, Wesley explained, "Barely the being seen, while we are doing any of these things, is a circumstance purely indifferent. But the doing them with this view, to be seen and admired, this is what our Lord condemns."[2] The key to pleasing God is sincerity in what we do, while seeking *his* honor and glory in all things. Those works done with pure and holy intentions please God, regardless of how exalted or how menial. Thus, right motives must remain central in our works of piety and of mercy.

The final section of this sermon discusses the Lord's Prayer. Wesley contends that this model prayer contains everything we need to pray for or should pray for. In this sermon he says, "There is nothing that we *need* to ask from God and nothing that we *can* ask (without offending him) which directly or indirectly is not included in this comprehensive prayer of Jesus. Second, this prayer contains everything that we can really want. The prayer speaks to whatever works for the glory of God and whatever is needed or beneficial for us and for every person in heaven and earth.... Third, the Lord's Prayer contains a summary of all our obligations to God and to humankind."

Following the sermon, Wesley added a poetic paraphrase of the Lord's Prayer, which appeared in Wesley's 1742 collection, *Hymns and Sacred Poems*.[3] It contains nine stanzas, with eight lines per stanza, in long meter. This sublime paraphrase is generally regarded to be from the pen of John Wesley, because its style is more his than Charles Wesley's.[4] The rhythm and rhyme of Charles Wesley's hymns is uncomplicated and fluid, whereas John Wesley's hymns have more grandeur and condensed power.[5] "A Paraphrase on the Lord's Prayer" is a fitting addition and inspiring epilogue to this timeless sermon.

Sermon 26

UPON OUR LORD'S SERMON ON THE MOUNT

Discourse 6

"Beware of practicing your piety before others in order to be seen by them; for then you have no reward from your Father in heaven. So whenever you give alms, do not sound a trumpet before you, as the hypocrites do in the synagogues and in the streets, so that they may be praised by others. Truly I tell you, they have received their reward. But when you give alms, do not let your left hand know what your right hand is doing, so that your alms may be done in secret; and your Father who sees in secret will reward you. And whenever you pray, do not be like the hypocrites; for they love to stand and pray in the synagogues and at the street corners, so that they may be seen by others. Truly I tell you, they have received their reward. But whenever you pray, go into your room and shut the door and pray to your Father who is in secret; and your Father who sees in secret will reward you. When you are praying, do not heap up empty phrases as the Gentiles do; for they think that they will be heard because of their many words. Do not be like them, for your Father

knows what you need before you ask him. Pray then in this way:

> *Our Father in heaven,*
>   *hallowed be your name.*
> *Your kingdom come.*
> *Your will be done,*
>   *on earth as it is in heaven.*
> *Give us this day our daily bread.*
> *And forgive us our debts,*
>   *as we also have forgiven our debtors.*
> *And do not bring us to the time of trial,*
>   *but rescue us from the evil one.*

For if you forgive others their trespasses, your heavenly Father will also forgive you; but if you do not forgive others, neither will your Father forgive your trespasses."
(Matthew 6:1-15)

1 In the preceding chapter, our Lord described inward religion in its various aspects. He laid before us those dispositions of the soul that constitute genuine Christianity. He discussed the inward properties contained in "the holiness without which no one will see the Lord." He described the affections that flow from the only true fountain, which is a living faith in God through Christ Jesus. These dispositions are intrinsically and essentially good, and they are acceptable to God.

Now, in chapter 6 Jesus proceeds to clarify how all our actions (even morally neutral ones) can be made holy and good. These actions are acceptable to God because they flow from pure and righteous intentions. Jesus declared that whatever we do apart from a pure and holy intent is of no value before God. At the same time, whatever outward works are consecrated to God by our chaste and holy intentions are of great worth in his sight.

2. At the outset, Jesus explains the necessity of pure intentions in what we usually regard as religious works. Indeed, these works become truly religious only when performed with right intentions. Some of these religious works we ordinarily refer to as works of piety; and the rest we commonly call works of charity or mercy. When discussing works of charity or mercy, Jesus especially names almsgiving. When discussing works of piety, he refers to prayer and fasting. Yet, the guidance that Jesus gives for these works can properly be applied to all good works, whether works of charity or works of mercy.

I. How our actions become holy and good

1. First, Jesus gave instructions about works of mercy: "Beware of practicing your piety before others in order to be seen by them; for then you have no reward from your Father in heaven." Although in the scripture passage Jesus only mentions giving alms, his remarks apply to every work of charity. He is referring to everything that we give, speak, or do to uplift our neighbors in body or soul. The teaching of Jesus pertains to feeding the hungry, clothing the unclothed, hosting or assisting strangers, visiting those who are sick or in prison, comforting the ill, instructing the ignorant, reproving the wicked, exhorting and encouraging those who do good works, and any other work of mercy that we might do.

2. Jesus cautioned against our giving alms with a view that others will acknowledge our good deeds. Here, Jesus is not forbidding our doing good deeds in the sight of others. The fact that others may see what we do does not make an action good or bad. What Jesus forbids is our doing good works for the *sole purpose* of being seen by others. I say, for this purpose *only*. In some instances, allowing others to see our good works may be a part of our plan. Others may see our good works and yet the works still may be acceptable to God. We may intend for our light to shine before others, when our conscience bears us witness in the Holy Spirit that our ultimate aim is "that they may give glory to our Father in heaven."

However, be careful that you do not do the slightest thing with a view to your own praise. Exercise caution that the praise of others is of no concern to you in any of your works of mercy. If you seek your own renown or have any aim at gaining human praise, your works earn you no advantage. When you do not do your good deeds for the Lord, he does not accept them. They will bring you no reward from our Father who is in heaven.

3. Therefore, Jesus advised, "Whenever you give alms, do not sound a trumpet before you, as the hypocrites do in the synagogues and on the streets, so that they may be praised by others." Here, the word "synagogue" does not mean a place of worship. Rather, it means any place for public gatherings, such as the marketplace or business district.

Among the Jews, it was common for persons of wealth, particularly the Pharisees, to order a trumpet to be sounded before them in the most public parts of the city when they were about to give away substantial alms. The purported reason for this outward display was to call the poor people together to receive the alms. However, the real reason for the trumpets was so that the almsgivers could receive the acclamation of others. Jesus cautioned against being like those ancient almsgivers. When he said, "do not sound a trumpet before you," he was telling us not to use any public display when doing good works. Rather, we should strive only for the honor that comes from God. Those who seek human praise will have their human reward. However, they will receive no praise from God.

4. Jesus added, "When you give alms, do not let your left hand know what your right hand is doing." This is a proverbial expression, which means to give alms as secretly and quietly as possible. You must not fail to do good works or omit any opportunity to do good, whether secretly or openly. We are to do good works in the most effective manner possible. On this point, there is an exception to be made. Do not conceal your good works if you are fully persuaded in your own mind that in doing them publicly you yourself or others will be enabled or inspired to do still more good works. In that case, let your light be seen and "it will give light to all in the house."

When the glory of God and the good of humankind require you to act otherwise, do your good works in as private and inconspicuous a manner as circumstances will allow. Give in such a way "that your alms may be done in secret; and your Father who sees in secret will reward you." Perhaps God will repay you in the present world. In all ages, there are many instances of his doing so. Yet, unfailingly God will repay you in the world to come before the general assembly of humankind and angels.

II. How religious works become pleasing to God

1. From his teaching about works of charity or mercy, our Lord proceeds to teach about what we call "works of piety." He said, "And whenever you pray, do not be like the hypocrites; for they love to stand and pray in the synagogues and at the street corners, so that they may be seen by others." Jesus added, "Do not be like the hypocrites." We learn that the first thing we are to guard against in prayer is hypocrisy and insincerity. Beware of saying what you do not mean.

Prayer is lifting up your hearts to God. All the words of our prayers that do not expose our true selves to God are sheer hypocrisy. Therefore, whenever you attempt to pray, see that your single purpose is to commune with God. Lift up your heart to him and pour out your soul before him. Do not pray as the hypocrites who love "to stand and pray in the synagogues and at the street corners." (And the Pharisees did so often.) They prayed wherever the most people gathered "so that they may be seen by others." Public recognition was their single intent. It was the motive and aim of the prayers they publicly repeated. Jesus said, "Truly I tell you, they have received their reward." Hypocrites can expect no reward from our Father who is in heaven.

2. There is more than having an eye to the praise of others which cuts us off from any reward in heaven. Other things also leave us no room to expect the blessing of God upon our deeds of piety and mercy. Looking for any temporal reward is equally destructive of our purity of intention. If we pray, attend public worship, or aid the poor for the purpose of material gain, our

works are not acceptable to God. They are no more pleasing to him than if we did them to win human praise. Unless the aim of our works is to promote God's glory and to work for human happiness, they are all an abomination to him. Any temporal aim, however good it may seem to others, makes every action detestable to God.

3. Jesus said, "Whenever you pray, go into your room and shut the door and pray to your Father who is in secret." There is a time when you are openly to glorify God by praying and praising him in the great congregation. However, when you desire more extensively and precisely to "make requests known to God" (whether it be evening, morning, or noon), "go into your room and shut the door." Utilize all the privacy you can. Do not neglect to pray, whether or not you have any privacy. But, if possible, pray to God when no one sees you. If circumstances do not allow privacy, pray anyway. "Pray to your Father who is in secret" (pour out your heart before him), "and your Father who sees in secret will reward you."

4. However, when you pray, even in secret, do not "heap up empty phrases" as the heathen do. In praying, do not use an abundance of words that have no meaning. Do not repeat the same things over and over again. Never think, as the heathen do, that the fruit of your prayers depends on their length. The heathen "think that they will be heard because of their many words."

Here, Jesus is not condemning the length of our prayers any more than their brevity. First, Jesus denounced lengthy prayers that lack purpose and use many words that are only empty phrases. However, our Lord does not condemn *all* repetitions, because he himself prayed three times, repeating the same words. He denounced only *empty* repetitions, such as those used by the heathen, who recited the names of their gods over and over again. Some Christians (commonly so called), not only among the Papists but also among other groups, also repeat phrases over and over without ever feeling what they speak.

Second, Jesus warned against our thinking that our prayers will be heard because we use many words. God does not measure prayers by their length, nor is he necessarily most pleased with

156

prayers that contain the most words and sound the longest in his ears. All who are called by the name of Christ should leave to the heathen (those on whom the glorious light of the gospel has never shined) these kinds of superstitions and absurdities.

5. Jesus said, "Do not be like them." You who have tasted the grace of God in Christ Jesus are thoroughly convinced that "our Father knows what we need before we ask him." Therefore, the aim of your praying is not to inform God, as though he did not already know your needs. Instead, pray to clarify to yourself your needs and fix them more deeply in your hearts. In prayer, we sense our continual dependence on him who alone is able to satisfy all our needs. We pray not to move God, who is always more ready to give than we are to ask. Rather, we pray to arouse ourselves, that we may be willing and ready to receive the good things that he has prepared for us.

III. The Lord's Prayer

1. After having taught the true nature and aims of prayer, our Lord adds an example of a divine form of prayer. This prayer seems to be proposed here chiefly as a pattern, model, and standard for all our prayers. Jesus said, "Pray then in this way." Elsewhere, he prescribed the use of these very words. He said to use them when we pray.

2. First, we may observe in general that the Lord's Prayer contains everything that we can reasonably or honestly pray for. There is nothing that we *need* to ask from God and nothing that we *can* ask (without offending him) that directly or indirectly is not included in this comprehensive prayer of Jesus.

Second, this prayer contains everything that we can reasonably or honestly want. The prayer speaks to whatever promotes the glory of God and whatever is needed or beneficial for us and for every person in heaven and earth. Indeed, our prayers are the proper gauges of our desires. Nothing deserves a proper home in our desires that does not have an appropriate place in our prayers. We ought not to desire what we cannot pray for.

Third, the Lord's Prayer contains all our obligations to God and to humankind. This prayer expresses whatever is pure and holy, whatever God requires of us all, whatever is acceptable to him, and whatever will benefit our neighbors.

3. The Lord's Prayer consists of three parts—the preface, the petitions, and the doxology (or conclusion). The preface—"our Father in heaven"—establishes a comprehensive foundation for prayer. It consists of what we must first know about God before we can pray with the confidence that he hears us. The preface also points out to us all the attitudes with which we are to approach God. If we want him to accept our prayers and our lives, these dispositions are absolutely crucial.

4. The prayer begins with the words, "Our Father." As a father, God is good and loving toward his children. The very nature of God constitutes the first and supreme basis for prayer. God is willing to bless us; therefore let us ask for his blessing. The term "Our Father" also signifies that God is our *creator,* the author of our existence. Because God formed us from the dust of the earth and breathed into us the breath of life, we became living souls. If God made us, let us pray to him who is our Creator. He will not withhold any good thing from the work of his own hands.

The term "Our Father" also refers to God who is our *preserver.* Day by day, he sustains the life he has given. Because of his continuing love, now and in every moment, we receive "life and breath and all things." Therefore, let us all the more boldly come to him, and we will receive mercy and find grace to help in time of need.

Above all, God is the Father of our Lord Jesus Christ and of all who believe in him. He "justifies us by his grace as a gift, through the redemption that is in Christ Jesus." He has "blotted out all our iniquities" and "healed all our diseases." By adoption and grace, God has accepted us as his own children. Also, "because we are children, God has sent the Spirit of his Son into our hearts, crying, 'Abba! Father!'" God has "given us a new birth" through "imperishable seed" and "created us anew in Christ Jesus." For this reason, we know that God always hears us. And we can pray to him without ceasing. We pray, because we love him, and "we love, because he first loved us."

158

5. The phrase "Our Father" means that God is not mine alone. In the greater sense, God is *our* Father. He is "the God of the spirits of all flesh"—the father of angels and humankind. Even the heathen acknowledge God to be "the father of men and gods." God is the Father of the universe and of all the families both in heaven and earth. Accordingly, he shows no partiality regarding people. He loves everyone that he has made. "The Lord is good to all, and his compassion is over all that he has made."

Furthermore, "the Lord takes pleasure in those who fear him, in those who hope in his steadfast love." He delights in those who trust in him through his beloved son, and they know that they are accepted in him. Therefore, "since God loved us so much, we also ought to love one another." Yes, we should love all humankind, because "God so loved the world that he gave his only Son," even to die for us so that we "may not perish but may have eternal life."

6. In the Lord's Prayer, Jesus adds to the name "Our Father" the phrase "in heaven." God is high and lofty, "Lord over all, blessed forever." God sits on "the circle of the stars,"[6] observing everything in heaven and earth. His eye penetrates the whole sphere of things created and things not yet created. He knows all his works. "Known to God from old are all his works." The phrase means "from all eternity" or "from everlasting to everlasting." God also knows all the works of everything that he has created. He constrains the hosts of heaven as well as all humankind to cry out with wonder and amazement, "O the depth of the riches and wisdom and knowledge of God!"

The phrase "in heaven" implies that God is the Lord and Ruler over all, the one who administers and arranges everything. He is the blessed and "only Sovereign, the King of kings and Lord of lords."

> God, you are strong and girded with might, doing whatever pleases you! You are the Almighty One, and you command and work your will. (Ps. 65:6; Phil. 2:13)

The phrase "in heaven" means that God is particularly there, because heaven is his throne:

Heaven is thy throne, the place where thine honour particularly dwelleth. But not there alone; for thou fillest heaven and earth, the whole expanse of space. Heaven and earth are full of thy glory. Glory be to thee, O Lord most high![6]

Therefore we should serve the Lord with godly awe and rejoice in him with reverence. We should think, speak, and act as being constantly under the eye of the Lord and King, always remaining conscious of living in his immediate presence.

7. Jesus continues the prayer with the phrase "hallowed be your name." This entreaty is the first of the six petitions in this prayer. The name of God is *Yahweh,* "God who is God," which is the nature of God, so far as we can understand it. God's name and very existence contain all his attributes and perfections. His name includes his infinity, particularly expressed by his great and unfathomable name—*Yahweh.* The apostle John translates God's name as "The Alpha and the Omega, the Beginning and the End—the one who is, and was, and is to come." God's fullness of being is also denoted by his other great name, *I am that I am.* This name denotes God's omnipresence and omnipotence.

Indeed, God is the only agent in the material world. All matter is inherently inert and inactive, and it moves only as the finger of God moves it. God is the fountainhead of action in every creature, visible and invisible. Nothing could exist or act without the continual inflow and agency of God's almighty power. God's wisdom is clearly deduced from the things that are seen and from the impressive order of the universe.

God's Trinity in unity and unity in Trinity are disclosed to us in the very first line of his written word. This phrase translates literally, "the Gods created"—a plural noun joined with a singular verb. The Trinitarian God is also revealed in every part of the subsequent biblical revelation, given by the mouth of all God's holy prophets and apostles. God's name implies his basic purity and holiness and, above all, his love, which is the very reflection of his glory.

In praying that God (or God's name) may be hallowed or glorified, we pray that he may be known as he truly is, by all who are capable of knowing him. To hallow God's name is to pray that all

160

intelligent beings with inclinations suitable to that knowledge may come to know him. To hallow his name is to pray that he may be properly honored, revered, and loved by everyone "in heaven above and on earth below," by all angels and people that God has made capable of knowing and loving him forever.

8. The next petition is, "Your kingdom come." This supplication has a close link to the preceding petition. In order for God's name to be hallowed, we pray that his kingdom, the kingdom of Christ, may come. God's kingdom comes to a particular person when he or she "repents and believes the good news." We enter God's kingdom when God enlightens us to know ourselves and to "know Jesus Christ and him crucified." Our Lord said, "This is eternal life, to know the only true God, and Jesus Christ whom he has sent."

When believers know Christ Jesus and when the Lord God Almighty reigns in their hearts, the kingdom of God begins here below. At that point, God shows his mighty power and "makes all things subject to himself." God establishes himself in the soul "conquering and to conquer" until he has "put all things under his feet" and made "every thought captive to obey Christ."

God's kingdom will come to earth when the Lord who is sovereign and robed in majesty will appear to all as "King of kings and Lord of lords." In that day, God will "give his Son the nations as his heritage, and the ends of the earth for his possession." Then, "all kingdoms will fall down before him and all nations give him service." "The mountain of the LORD's house" (the church of Christ) "shall be established as the highest of the mountains." "The full number of the Gentiles will come in, and all Israel will be saved."

It is fitting for all those who "long for his appearing" to pray that God will hasten the time of his coming, so that his kingdom of grace will come quickly and swallow up all the kingdoms of the earth. It is good to pray that all humankind will receive him as king, truly believing in his name. To pray "Your kingdom come" is to petition that everyone will be filled with righteousness, and peace, and joy. This prayer asks God to fill others with holiness and happiness until he removes them from earth into his heavenly kingdom. There, they will reign with him forever and ever.

We also pray "Your kingdom come" for still more blessings from God. This petition asks for the coming of God's everlasting kingdom (the kingdom of glory in heaven), which is the continuation and perfection of the kingdom of grace on earth. Consequently, we pray this petition as well as the preceding petition, "hallowed be your name," for the entire intelligent creation, which has an interest in this grand event. It will mark the final renovation of all things. By taking all things into his own hands and setting up his kingdom that will endure throughout all ages, God will put an end to misery, sin, infirmity, and death.

In agreement with this petition are the profoundly impressive words in our church's prayer used in the liturgy for the Burial of the Dead:

> Beseeching thee, that it may please thee of thy gracious goodness, shortly to accomplish the number of thine elect, and to hasten thy kingdom: That we, with all those that are departed in the true faith of thy holy name, may have our perfect consummation and bliss, both in body and soul, in thy everlasting glory.[8]

9. The Lord's Prayer continues, "Your will be done, on earth as it is in heaven." This state of affairs follows as the necessary and immediate consequence wherever the kingdom of God comes. God's kingdom comes to us wherever God dwells in the soul by faith and Christ reigns in the heart by love.

At first glance, it is probable that many, if not most, people are inclined to assume that this petition is only an expression of (or petition for) a passive acceptance of life's events. Many regard this petition as a prayer for the readiness merely to endure the will of God concerning us, whatever it might be. To be sure, this attitude is godly, excellent, and a most precious gift from God. However, this petition is not a prayer for passive resignation—at least, that idea is not the main and fundamental sense of this prayer. In praying, "Your will be done on earth as it is in heaven," we pray not so much for a *passive*, as for an *active* conformity to God's will.

How is God's will done in heaven by his angels, those beings that circle his throne continually rejoicing? They do God's bidding *willingly.* They love his commandments and gladly attend his

162

words. It is their food to do his will; it is their highest glory and joy.

They do God's will *continually*. There is no pause in their willing service. Day and night, they do not rest, but they employ every hour in fulfilling God's commands (speaking after the manner of human time, although our measure of days, nights, and hours has no place in eternity). Constantly, the angels carry out God's plans in fulfilling the counsel of his will.

They do God's will *perfectly*. Angelic minds are not clouded with any sin or defect. It is true that "the stars"—the angels—"are not pure in his sight," even the morning stars that sing together before him. The phrase "in his sight" means that, compared to God, even the very angels are not pure. Of course, this fact does not mean that the angels are not pure in themselves. Doubtless they are. They are without spot or blemish. They are altogether devoted to God's will, and in all things they are perfectly obedient to him.

If we view this matter in another light, we may observe that the angels of God in heaven do the complete will of God. And they do nothing else but what they are certain is his will. They do all the will of God *as* he wills it to be done. They obey him in the manner that pleases him, and no other. Yes, they do God's bidding, only because it is his will, and for no other reason.

10. Therefore, when we pray that the will of God "will be done on earth as it is in heaven," the meaning of the prayer is that all the inhabitants of the earth will do the will of their Father in heaven just as willingly as the holy angels. It is a prayer that all people will continuously do God's will, even as the angels do their willing service without any interruption. It is a prayer that all people will perfectly do God's will. The petition is that "the God of peace . . . by the blood of the eternal covenant, will make everyone complete in everything good so that they may do his will, working among them that which is pleasing in his sight."

In other words, we pray that we and all humankind will do the whole will of God in all things and that everyone does nothing else, not the slightest thing except what is the holy and acceptable will of God. We pray that we may do the entire will of God as he wishes it and in the manner that pleases him. Finally, we pray that the will of God shall be done for the singular reason that it is his will. God's will forms the sole reason and motive for whatever we think, speak, or do.

11. Jesus then continues with the next petition: "Give us this day our daily bread." In the three previous petitions we have been praying for all humankind. Now, we come more particularly to praying for our own needs. Of course, this petition does not teach us to confine our prayers entirely to our individual selves. This petition and the following petitions can be used for the whole Church of Christ upon the earth.

The term "bread" stands for everything that we need, either for our souls or bodies—"everything needed for life and godliness." We understand this petition to mean not just the outward bread, which our Lord terms "the food that perishes." This prayer also refers to *spiritual* bread—that is, the grace of God which is "the food that endures for eternal life."

It was the understanding of many of the ancient Church Fathers that this scripture passage also refers to the sacramental bread. In the beginning, the entire Church of Christ received the Eucharist daily. Until the love of many grew cold, the Eucharist was highly esteemed as the principal channel through which God conveyed the grace of his Spirit to humankind.

Concerning the phrase "our daily bread," different commentators explain the word *daily* in different ways. However, the most obvious and natural meaning of the word seems to be retained in almost all translations, ancient and modern—"what is sufficient for this day; and for each day as follows."

12. The petition "give us . . . " implies that we can rightly claim nothing, except as a gift of God's free mercy. We do not deserve the air we breathe, the earth that yields food, or the sun that shines upon us. The only thing that we deserve is hell. But God loves us without restraint. Therefore, we ask God to give us what we can neither obtain for ourselves nor merit from his hands.

Of course, the goodness and power of God are not reasons for us to stand idle. It is God's will that we exercise full diligence in all things. He wants us to engage our utmost endeavors as though our success is the normal output of our own wisdom and strength. Yet, after working diligently, we are to depend on God as though we had done nothing. He is the giver of every good and perfect gift.

When we pray for daily bread for *this* day, we are "not to worry about tomorrow." So that we would look on every day as a fresh gift of God, our wise Creator has divided life into these small portions of time. Each new day is clearly separated from the others, providing us with another period that we can devote to God's glory. Every evening can be regarded as the close of the period. Beyond each new day, we are to see nothing but eternity.

13. First, Jesus taught us to pray, "Forgive us our debts, as we also have forgiven our debtors." Nothing but sin can impede God's bounty from flowing forth to every person, so this petition naturally follows the former. When all hindrances are removed (especially sin), we can more clearly trust in the God of love for everything that is good.

The phrase *our trespasses* properly signifies our debts. In scripture, our transgressions are frequently termed *sins*. Every sin puts us under a new debt to God, to whom we already owe, as it were, ten thousand talents. What, then, can we say to God when he says, "Pay what you owe"? We are totally bankrupt; we have nothing to pay; we have squandered all we had. Therefore, if God deals with us according to the strictness of his law and extracts what he justly could, he must order us to be "bound hand and foot" and "handed over to be tortured."

Indeed, we are bound hand and foot by the shackles of our own sins. Considered individually, our sins are chains of iron and fetters of brass. They are wounds where the world, the flesh, and the devil have mutilated and disabled us entirely. Our sins are diseases that consume our bodies and spirits. Sin brings us "down to the chambers of death." Considered in the sight of God, our sins are debts that are immense and numberless. Therefore, because we have nothing to pay, it is good for us to cry unto God for him freely to forgive us of them all!

The word translated as *forgive* implies either to forgive a debt, or to unloose a chain. And if we acquire forgiveness, freedom naturally follows. When our debts are forgiven, the chains fall off our hands. As soon as we "receive forgiveness of sins" through the free grace of God in Christ, we also receive "a place among those who are sanctified by faith in him." Sin has lost its power. It has no dominion over those who are under grace and in favor with God. "There is therefore now no condemnation for those who are in Christ Jesus." Those who are forgiven are freed from sin and guilt. "The just requirement of the law" is fulfilled in them, and they "walk not according to the flesh but according to the Spirit."

14. To the petition "forgive us our debts," Jesus added, "as we also have forgiven our debtors." In these words, our Lord clearly declares the condition, degree, and manner by which we may expect God to forgive us. God forgives our trespasses and sins *if* we forgive others, and *as* we forgive them. This point is of the utmost importance. Our blessed Lord is so concerned to prevent our forgetting the importance of forgiving others that he inserts it in this prayer. Soon afterward, he repeats his admonition a second time. He said, "For if you forgive others their trespasses, your heavenly Father will also forgive you; but if you do not forgive others, neither will your Father forgive your trespasses."

Second, God forgives us in the same way that we forgive others. Therefore, if any malice, bitterness, taint of unkindness or anger toward others remains in our hearts, God cannot completely and fully forgive us. God does not forgive us if we do not absolutely, wholly, and from the heart forgive all others their trespasses. To the extent that we do not forgive, we are not forgiven. God may show us some degree of mercy, but by our refusing to forgive, we do not allow him to blot out all our sins and forgive all our iniquities.

In the meantime, if from our hearts we do not forgive our neighbors their trespasses, what sort of prayer are we offering to God when we pray, "Forgive us our debts, as we also have forgiven our debtors"? We are indeed openly defying God and daring him to do his worst: "Forgive us our debts, as we also have forgiven our debtors."

In reality, we are saying to God, "Do not forgive us at all. We do not seek your favor. We pray that you will continue to remember our sins and that your wrath will rest upon us." However, can you seriously offer such a prayer to God? He has not yet cast you alive into hell. O, do not any longer tempt the Lord! This very instant, by his grace forgive as you want to be forgiven! Even now, have the same compassion upon your fellow servants that God has had, and will have, upon you!

15. Next, Jesus teaches us to pray, "And do not bring us to the time of trial" (or into temptation), "but rescue us from the evil one." The word translated *temptation,* means any kind of trial. In addition, the English word was once used in a neutral sense, to refer to trials. Now, however, the word is usually understood to mean an inducement to sin. St. James uses the word in both ways—first in its general sense and then in its specific reference to sin.

He uses the word in its general sense when he says, "Blessed is anyone who endures temptation. Such a one has stood the test of trials and will receive the crown of life." Using the word in the other sense, the apostle immediately adds, "No one, when tempted, should say, 'I am being tempted by God;' for God cannot be tempted by evil and he himself tempts no one. But one is tempted by one's own desire."

For the word "desire," James uses the word *lust* to signify that which draws us away from God (in whom alone we are safe), as a fish is attracted to bait. When we are drawn away from God and enticed, we enter into temptation. Afterward, temptation covers us as a cloud and envelops the entire soul. Then, how difficult it is to escape out of the snare! Therefore, Jesus teaches us to plead with God, "Do not bring us to the time of trial, but rescue us from the evil one." Because God does not tempt anyone, we pray that we will not be drawn into temptation.

The term *evil one* refers undoubtedly to the one who is pointedly called the prince and god of this world. And he works powerfully in the children of disobedience. Even so, all those who are the children of God by faith are delivered out of his hands. The evil one can and will fight against them. However, he cannot overcome them, unless they betray their own souls. For a time he may torment, but he cannot destroy, because God is on the side of his children. And, in the end, God will not fail to "grant justice to his chosen ones who cry to him day and night."

Lord, when we are tempted, do not permit us to enter into temptation! Make a way for us to escape so that the wicked one does not touch us!

16. The conclusion of this divine prayer, commonly called the Doxology, is a solemn thanksgiving and a summary acknowledgment of God's attributes and works. "For the kingdom and the power and the glory are yours forever." God, you have sovereign authority over all things that exist or that ever have been created. Yours is an everlasting kingdom, and your dominion endures throughout all ages. Your power is the governing power whereby you rule all things in your everlasting kingdom. Through your sovereign power, you do whatever pleases you throughout your entire kingdom. Every creature owes you glory and praise for your power, for the invincibility of your kingdom, and for all your wondrous works, which you work from everlasting and will continue to work world without end, forever and ever! Amen! So be it!

* * * * * * * *

I believe that it will not be unacceptable to the serious reader for me to add:

A Paraphrase on the Lord's Prayer[9]

I

Father of all, whose powerful voice
Call'd forth this universal frame;
Whose mercies over all rejoice,
Through endless ages still the same:
Thou, by thy word, upholdest all;
Thy bounteous love to all is show'd;
Thou hear'st thy every creature's call,
And fillest every mouth with good.

168

II

In heaven thou reign'st, enthroned in light,
  Nature's expanse beneath thee spread;
Earth, air, and sea, before thy sight,
  And hell's deep gloom, are open laid.
Wisdom, and might, and love are thine:
  Prostrate before thy face we fall,
Confess thine attributes divine,
  And hail thee Sovereign Lord of All!

III

Thee Sovereign Lord let all confess,
  That moves in earth, or air, or sky;
Revere thy power, thy goodness bless,
  Tremble before thy piercing eye.
All ye who owe to Him your birth,
  In praise your every hour employ:
Jehovah reigns! Be glad, O earth!
  And shout, ye morning stars, for joy!

IV

Son of thy Sire's eternal love,
  Take to thyself thy mighty power;
Let all earth's sons thy mercy prove,
  Let all thy bleeding grace adore.
The triumphs of thy love display;
  In every heart reign thou alone;
Till all thy foes confess thy sway,
  And glory ends what grace begun.

V

Spirit of grace, and health, and power,
  Fountain of light and love below;
Abroad thine healing influence shower,

O'er all the nations let it flow.
    Inflame our hearts with perfect love;
In us the work of faith fulfill;
So not heaven's host shall swifter move
    Than we on earth to do thy will.

VI

Father, 'tis thine each day to yield
    Thy children's wants a fresh supply:
Thou cloth'st the lilies of the field,
    And hearest the young ravens cry.
On thee we cast our care; we live
Through thee who know'st our every need;
    O feed us with thy grace, and give
Our souls this day the living bread!

VII

Eternal, spotless Lamb of God,
    Before the world's foundation slain,
Sprinkle us ever with thy blood;
    O cleanse and keep us ever clean!
To every soul (all praise to Thee!)
    Our bowels of compassion move:
And all mankind by this may see
    God is in us; for God is love.

VIII

Giver and Lord of life, whose power
    And guardian care for all are free;
To thee, in fierce temptation's hour,
    From sin and Satan let us flee.
Thine, Lord, we are, and ours thou art;
    In us be all thy goodness show'd;
Renew, enlarge, and fill our heart
    With peace, and joy, and heaven, and God.

IX

Blessing and honor, praise and love,
Co-equal, co-eternal Three,
In earth below, in heaven above,
By all thy works be paid to thee.
Thrice Holy! Thine the kingdom is,
The power omnipotent is thine;
And when created nature dies,
Thy never-ceasing glories shine.

Notes

1. *Explanatory Notes upon the New Testament*, Matt. 6:1.
2. *Explanatory Notes upon the New Testament*, Matt. 6:1.
3. John and Charles Wesley, *Hymns and Sacred Poems* (Bristol: Printed and sold by F. Farley, 1742, pp. 277-78.
4. John Lawson, *Notes on Wesley's Forty-Four Sermons* (London: The Epworth Press, 1946), p. 161.
5. John Telford, *The New Methodist Hymn-Book Illustrated in History and Experience* (London: The Epworth Press, 1934), p. 40.
6. Wisdom of Solomon 13:2.
7. *Book of Common Prayer*, Communion Service, Sanctus.
8. *Book of Common Prayer*, The Order for the Burial of the Dead.
9. *Hymns and Sacred Poems*, 1742, "The Lord's Prayer Paraphrased." Also, Franz Hilderbrandt, Oliver A. Beckerlegge, and James Dale, *The Bicentennial Edition of the Works of John Wesley*, A Collection of Hymns for the use of the People called Methodists (Nashville: Abingdon Press, 1983), Hymns #225, #226, and #227, 7:363-66.

UPON OUR LORD'S SERMON ON THE MOUNT

Discourse 7

This sermon contains John Wesley's most definitive discourse on the subject of fasting. He points out that the ancient church practiced this religious discipline, through the ages countless Christians fasted, and the Church of England gave official recognition to its value. John Wesley and the members of the Holy Club at Oxford fasted twice weekly. The length of these twice-weekly fasts was from rising in the morning to about 3:00 in the afternoon. After his evangelical conversion, Wesley continued this practice until the end of his life. He urged all Methodists to observe a fast every Friday.[1] Wesley believed that the failure to fast and pray was "one general occasion of deadness among Christians." In a letter to George Cussons, he wrote, "When you seek God with fasting added to prayer, you cannot seek His face in vain. This has been exceedingly blessed in various parts, and the revival of God's work has begun at the very time."[2] Wesley asked, "Can any one willingly neglect it, and be guiltless?"[3] According to Wesley, the aim of fasting is to disengage the soul from its natural attachment to earthly things in order to bring spiritual matters into clearer focus.

Wesley explained that some people made too much of fasting, while others disregarded it altogether. Thus, he sought to steer a path between fanatical asceticism on one hand and the complete neglect of fasting on the other hand. He disapproved of extreme ascetic practices that could injure one's health. He wrote, "Some in London carried [fasting] to excess, and fasted so as to impair their health. It was not long before others made this a pretence for not fasting at all."[4] Used as a means of grace, this spiritual discipline helps us to become more aware of those realities that are truly important. Wesley saw prayer and fasting as important means of denying self in order to gain a proper perspective on both earthly and eternal considerations.

Many of the early Methodists heeded Wesley's advice to observe personal fasts. For example, the Methodist saint, Hanna Ball, wrote in her journal, "This is a fast-day to my body, but a feast-day to my soul."[5] John and Charles Wesley regarded fasting as being so valuable that they included it as one of the means of grace in Methodism's General Rules.

The Methodists in Wesley's day fasted when burdened about particular situations or circumstances. One such occasion was Methodism's practice of prayer and fasting in conjunction with the solemn business of the annual conferences. The following entry in Wesley's journal is typical.

> On Wednesday and Thursday we had our little Conference, at which most of the [Methodist] Preachers...were present. We agreed to set apart Friday, the 21st, for a day of fasting and prayer. At every meeting, particularly the last, our Lord refreshed us in an uncommon manner. About ten [PM] I was a little tired; but before it struck twelve, my weariness was all gone. It seemed to be the same with all the congregation; and prayer was swallowed up in praise.[6]

In 1779, one of Wesley's preachers, Thomas Taylor, wrote in his diary an account of a conference fast: "This day [July 30] was observed as a fast on account of public affairs. We met in the morning at five; and, after the sermon, we continued in prayer till nine o'clock [AM]. At one, we met again, and received the sacrament. In the evening, we kept a watchnight, and I gave an exhortation."[7]

John Wesley also called the Methodists to observe National Fasts. The journal of Charles Wesley contains the following entry: "My brother writes, that I should give notice to all our Society to spend Wednesday, July 11th, in fasting and prayer, that God may be entreated for the land."[8] On one such occasion, Wesley observed, "The National Fast was observed all over London with great solemnity. Surely God is well pleased even with this acknowledgment that He governs the world; and even the outward humiliation of a nation may be rewarded with outward blessings."[9] With the "appointment" of these days for prayer and fasting, Wesley and his followers exerted a powerful spiritual influence across the United Kingdom.

This sermon points out that one of "Satan's devices" is to separate outward religion from inward religion. Wesley explains that Satan works to disconnect the *act* of fasting from the *goal* of fasting. To do so is to make fasting an end rather than a means. Here, we are reminded that, although the New Testament does not give specific directions for fasting, Jesus and the apostles assumed that Christians would exercise this spiritual discipline. Wesley makes a compelling case for the close link between fasting and the blessings of God. In the judgment of many, this discourse ranks among the best primers ever written on the subject of fasting.

Sermon 27

UPON OUR LORD'S SERMON ON THE MOUNT

Discourse 7

*"And whenever you fast, do not look dismal, like the hyp-
ocrites, for they disfigure their faces so as to show others
that they are fasting. Truly I tell you, they have received their
reward. But when you fast, put oil on your head and wash
your face, so that your fasting may be seen not by others but
by your Father who is in secret; and your Father who sees in
secret will reward you."* (Matthew 6:16-18)

1 From the beginning of the world, Satan has worked to separate what God has joined together. The enemy seeks to
detach inward religion from outward religion and to set one
of these against the other. And in this endeavor Satan has achieved
a good amount of success among those who have been "ignorant
of his designs."

In all ages, many have had a zeal for God, but their zeal was
not enlightened. They have strictly committed themselves to the
"just requirements of the law," and they concentrated their efforts

on the performance of outward duties. In the meantime, they completely disregard inward righteousness—"the righteousness from God based on faith." Also, many have veered to the opposite extreme. They ignored all outward duties and perhaps even "spoke evil against the law and judged the law" as it applied to them personally.

2. It is by this device of Satan (separating what God has joined together) that faith and works have so often been placed in opposition to each other. And many that have had a genuine zeal for God have for a time fallen into a snare on one extreme or the other. Some have elevated faith to the point of utterly excluding good works. They reject good works as being neither the cause nor the fruit of our justification. Of course, we know it is true that we are "justified by God's grace as a gift, through the redemption that is in Christ Jesus."

Other people who are eager to avoid the dangerous mistake of rejecting the importance of good works have swerved too far in the opposite direction. They have contended that good works are the *cause* of justification, at least the condition for justification. They speak of good works as though they constitute the sum total of the religion of Jesus Christ.

3. Making the same kind of mistake of separating what God has united, others have separated religion's *means* from its *end*. Certain well-meaning people seem to regard the totality of religion as consisting of attending the prayers of the church, receiving the Lord's Supper, hearing sermons, and reading books on piety. In the meantime, they neglect the objective of all these means of grace—to promote the love of God and neighbor.

Others, in their concern for the love of God and neighbor have settled into a neglect (if not contempt) of the ordinances of God. These people so shamefully disregard the means of grace that they weaken and overturn the very end these means were intended to promote.

4. Of all the means of grace, however, there is hardly any that people have taken to greater extremes than that of which our Lord speaks in this text—religious fasting. How tragically have some exalted fasting beyond all scripture and reason! At the same time,

others have utterly disregarded fasting. It is as though they under-valued fasting to the same extent that others have overvalued it.

Those who overvalue fasting have spoken of it as if it were everything. They believe that if fasting is not the end of religion, it is necessarily connected with it. Then, others have no regard for fasting. They treat it as if it were nothing or as if it were a fruit-less labor completely unrelated to religion. Certainly, the truth lies between these two extremes. Fasting is not the whole of religion, nor is it completely unrelated to religion. It is not the *end* of reli-gion, but it is a valuable *means*. Fasting is a practice that God him-self has ordained, and when we properly use it, he will surely give us his blessing.

In order to set fasting in the clearest light, first, I will attempt to explain the nature and types of fasting. Second, I will clarify the reasons, grounds, and purposes for fasting. Third, I will answer the most misleading objections to fasting. And fourth, I will dis-cuss how we should fast.

I. The nature and types of fasting

First, I will attempt to explain the nature of fasting and its dif-ferent kinds and degrees. As to the nature of fasting, all the inspired writers in both the Old and New Testaments use the phrase *to fast* in only one sense, which is not to eat—to abstain from food. This interpretation is so clear that it would be lost labor to quote the words of David, Nehemiah, Isaiah, and the prophets that came after them. As well, our Lord and his apostles all agreed that fasting means to refrain from eating for a pre-scribed length of time.

2. To this understanding of fasting, people in earlier times have added certain other conditions that have no essential connection with it at all. For instance, people affixed such practices as neglecting their clothing, laying aside the ornaments they usually wore, assuming the look of one in mourning, scattering ashes on their heads, or wearing sackcloth next to their skin. However, the New Testament contains little mention of any of these unrelated additions. Also, Christians in purer times did not lay any

emphasis on these irrelevant things, although some penitents might have voluntarily used them as outward signs of inward abasement.

By no means did the apostles or the Christians of that era ever beat or mutilate their own flesh. One could expect such "discipline" as befitting the priests or worshipers of Baal. The gods of the heathen were only demons. And self-mutilation was doubtless acceptable to their demon-god when his priests "cried aloud and . . . cut themselves with swords and lances until the blood gushed out over them." However, such behavior cannot be pleasing to him who did not come to destroy people's lives, but to save them. This kind of behavior does not become those who follow Jesus Christ.

3. As to the degrees or lengths of fasting, we have instances of some who have fasted many days on end. Moses, Elijah, and our blessed Lord, who were endued with supernatural strength for that purpose, are recorded to have fasted continuously for "forty days and forty nights." However, scripture records the most frequent length of fasting as one day—from morning until evening. This length of fast was commonly observed among the ancient Christians. In addition to these fasts, the early Christians also observed half-fasts (as Tertullian called them). These fasts were on the fourth and sixth days of the week (Wednesdays and Fridays) throughout the year. On these fast days the Christians took no food until three in the afternoon, the time when they returned from the public service of worship.

4. Closely related to this fast is what our Church seems particularly to mean by the term *abstinence,* which may be observed when we cannot fast entirely, because of sickness or physical weakness. This practice is partial abstinence, or eating only a smaller amount of food than usual. I do not think of any scriptural example of this kind of fasting. Yet, neither can I condemn it, for the scripture does not. It may have its use, and it may receive a blessing from God.

5. The least kind of fasting, if it can be called by that name, is to abstain from pleasing food. In scripture we have several instances of this practice. Daniel and his associates fasted in this way, in order not to "defile themselves with the royal rations of

food and wine" (a "daily portion that the king assigned to
them"). They asked and received from the palace master his per-
mission to eat only vegetables and water. It is possible that this
practice of Daniel and his friends gave rise to the mistaken practice of abstaining from meat and wine during stated times. The
example of Daniel and his friends may lie behind this practice. It
is also possible that the practice is based on the speculation that
meat and wine were the most pleasant food and that it was proper to consume what is least pleasing when we solemnly approach
God.

6. The ancient Jewish community observed certain required
fasts. One such fast was the Fast of the Seventh Month, appointed
by God to be observed by all Israel. Failure to observe this fast
resulted in the severest penalty. In Leviticus we read,

> The LORD spoke to Moses, saying: Now, the tenth day of this
> seventh month is the day of atonement; it shall be a holy convoca-
> tion for you: you shall deny yourselves and present the LORD'S
> offering by fire; and you shall do no work during that entire day;
> for it is a day of atonement, to make atonement on your behalf
> before the LORD your God. For anyone who does not practice self-
> denial during that entire day shall be cut off from the people. (Lev.
> 23:26-29)

In later ages, several other stated fasts were added to these fasts.
The prophet Zechariah mentions not only the Fast of the Seventh
Month but also fasts of the fourth, fifth, and tenth months.

The ancient Christian church likewise observed stated fasts,
both annual and weekly. Annually, some in the church fasted
forty-eight hours before Easter. Others fasted for an entire week;
many fasted for two weeks, each day taking no food until the
evening of each day.[10] Epiphanius (c. 315–403) wrote as though it
was an undeniable fact that Christians fasted on Wednesdays and
Saturdays throughout "the entire habitable earth." If this fast was
not observed "in all the earth," at least it was observed wherever
Christians lived. The annual fasts in our Anglican Church are the
forty days of Lent, the Ember days at the four seasons, the
Rogation days, the Vigils or evenings before several solemn

festivals, and the weekly fasts, which are to be observed "all Fridays in the year, except Christmas Day."[11]

In addition to these established fasts, in every nation that honored God, from time to time, there have always been occasional fasts appointed as the particular circumstances and occasions required. For instance, King Jehoshaphat proclaimed a fast: "[When] the Moabites and Ammonites...came against Jehoshaphat for battle...Jehoshaphat...set himself to seek the Lord, and proclaimed a fast throughout all Judah." We read of another similar kind of fast:[12] "In the fifth year of King Jehoiakim son of Josiah of Judah, in the ninth month all the people in Jerusalem and all the people who came from the towns of Judah to Jerusalem proclaimed a fast before the LORD."

Similarly, individuals who examine their ways and desire to walk humbly and closely with God will set aside frequent occasions for private fasts and penitence before their Father. And it is to this kind of fasting that the directions here in the Lord's teaching mainly and essentially refer.

II. The reasons, grounds, and purposes for fasting

1. In the second place, I move on to explain the basis, reasons, and aims of fasting. First, those who are deeply stirred up and impressed with any strong emotion such as sorrow or fear are often so completely occupied with their thoughts that they are "too wasted to eat their bread." At such times, they have little regard for food, not even what is necessary to sustain themselves. Even less do they desire any delicacy or varieties of food. They are engrossed with quite different thoughts.

When Saul said, "I am in great distress, for the Philistines are warring against me," it is recorded that "he had eaten nothing all day and all night." Similarly, those in the storm-tossed ship with St. Paul did not eat. "No small tempest raged, and all hope of their being saved was at last abandoned." They fasted for fourteen days, "having been in suspense and remaining without food, having eaten nothing." We also read that "David...and all the men who were with him" heard the report that "the army fled from the battle, but also many of the army fell and died; and Saul and his son Jonathan also died." We learn that others "mourned and wept, and fasted until evening for Saul and for his son Jonathan, and for the army of the LORD and for the house of Israel."

Often, when people's minds are deeply absorbed, they are impatient with interruptions; they even refuse to eat essential food. Food only diverts their thoughts from those things to which they want to give undivided attention. When Saul, on the occasion mentioned above, had "fallen full length on the ground...there was no strength in him. Nevertheless, he would not eat until his servants urged him to eat."

2. Here, then, is the natural incentive for fasting. Those who are under deep affliction, overwhelmed with sorrow for sin, and filled with a strong anxiety about the wrath of God are "too wasted to eat their bread." Without any rule and without knowing or considering whether or not it is a command of God, they abstain from pleasant food and from necessary nourishment. They are like St. Paul after he was brought into Damascus. "For three days he was without sight, and neither ate nor drank."

Yes, when the storm rises high and "fear and trembling comes, and horror overwhelms" those that have been without the conscious presence of God will "loathe any kind of food." Eating would be unpleasant and annoying to them. They would be impatient with anything that might interrupt their ceaseless cry, "Lord, save us! We are perishing!"

How strongly does our church in the first part of the homily on fasting express this mood!

When people feel in themselves the heavy burden of sin, see damnation to be the reward of it, and behold with the eye of their mind the horror of hell, they tremble, they quake, and are inwardly touched with sorrowfulness of heart, and cannot help accusing themselves, and opening their grief unto Almighty God, and call unto him for mercy. This being done seriously, their mind is so occupied (taken up) partly with sorrow and heaviness and partly with an earnest desire to be delivered from this danger of hell and damnation, that all desire for food and drink is set aside, and loathing of all worldly things and pleasure come in place; so that they want nothing more than to weep, to lament, to mourn, and both with words and behavior of body to show themselves weary of life.[13]

3. Another reason or motive for fasting is that many who now fear God are deeply aware of how often they have sinned against him by the abuse of lawful things. They know how much they have sinned by excess eating and how long they have transgressed the holy law of God with regard to moderation, if not sobriety as well. God's people are aware of how they have indulged their sensual appetites, perhaps even to the impairment of their physical health, and certainly to the considerable hurt of their souls.

No less than by excess of wine or strong drink, they have also become spiritually intoxicated by lighthearted folly, merriment, shallowness, careless neglect of things of the gravest importance, flightiness, and carelessness of spirit. These things stupefy all their noblest abilities. Therefore, to remove the effect, they remove the cause. They avoid all excesses. As far as possible, they abstain from what had almost plunged them into everlasting perdition. In some things, they refrain entirely, and in all things they take care to be sparing and temperate.

4. Those who fast also well remember how excess of food has increased their spiritual carelessness and shallowness as well as their foolish and unholy desires. Yes, these things even lead to impure and evil inclinations. Experience absolutely confirms this chain of cause and effect.

Even a conventional, regular appetite continually debases the soul and lowers it to a level with the animals that perish. One cannot adequately express what an effect a variety and delicacy of food has on the mind and body. Undisciplined eating makes us hunger for every sensual pleasure as soon as the opportunity arises. Therefore, this danger provides a reason for every prudent person to discipline and subdue the soul, and to keep it in check.

Fasting will wean us more and more from all those indulgences of the lower appetites that naturally tend to chain the soul to earth, polluting and debasing us. So, here is another enduring reason for fasting: it removes the incitement toward lust and sensuality; it abolishes the incentives of foolish and hurtful lusts and of evil and vain inclinations.

5. Perhaps we should not omit another reason for fasting, which some good people have strongly urged (although I do not know if we should appropriately lay any great stress upon it). Some advise fasting as a means of punishing ourselves for having abused the blessings of God. They sometimes completely refrain from using any of them, thereby exercising a kind of "holy revenge" upon themselves for their past folly. Once, through ingratitude, they used the things that were intended for their health as an occasion of falling. They conjecture that David had this purpose in mind when he said, "I humbled my soul with fasting." Also, St. Paul spoke about the "punishment" that "godly grief" produced in the Corinthians.

6. A fifth and more important reason for fasting is that it helps us to pray, particularly when we set apart longer amounts of time for private prayer. In these times, especially, God is often pleased to lift up the souls of his servants above all the things of earth and sometimes draw them up, as it were, into heaven. Mainly, fasting is a support to the kind of prayer that people so often find a means by which God confirms and increases virtue. By prayer and fasting, we grow in chastity. (Some have improperly imagined that this growth was the only benefit of prayer and fasting. However, there is no basis for this assumption in scripture, reason, or experience.) We also grow in earnestness, sincerity, discernment, tenderness of conscience, and deadness to the world. Consequently, we grow in love for God and in every holy and heavenly affection.

7. Of course, there is no intrinsic or automatic connection between fasting and God's blessings. "He has mercy on whomever he chooses." He will convey whatever seems good, by whatever means he is pleased to select. In all ages, however, God has chosen fasting as a means of averting his wrath and our obtaining whatever blessings from time to time we need.

We can see how powerful a means is fasting to avert the wrath of God in the remarkable example of Ahab:

> There was no one like Ahab, who sold himself to do what was evil in the sight of the LORD.... He acted most abominably in going

after idols.... [Yet] he tore his clothes and put sackcloth over his bare flesh; he fasted, lay in the sackcloth, and went about dejectedly. Then the word of the LORD came to Elijah the Tishbite: "Have you seen how Ahab has humbled himself before me? Because he has humbled himself before me, I will not bring the disaster in his days." (1 Kings 21:25-29)

In order to avert the wrath of God, Daniel sought God "by prayer and supplication with fasting and sackcloth and ashes." Preventing God's wrath seems to be the entire focus of his prayer, especially his solemn conclusion:

O Lord, in view of all your righteous acts, let your anger and wrath, we pray, turn away from your city Jerusalem, your holy mountain.... Listen to the prayer of your servant and to his supplication, and for your own sake, Lord, let your face shine upon your desolated sanctuary.... O Lord, hear; O Lord, forgive; O Lord, listen and act and do not delay! For your own sake.... (Dan. 9:16-19)

8. It is not only from the people of God that we learn to seek God by fasting and prayer when his anger is kindled. Also, from the heathen we learn to fast and pray.

[Jonah declared,] "Forty days more, and Nineveh shall be overthrown!" And the people of Nineveh believed God; they proclaimed a fast, and everyone, great and small, put on sackcloth.
When the news reached the king of Nineveh, he rose from his throne, removed his robe, covered himself with sackcloth, and sat in ashes. Then he had a proclamation made in Nineveh: "By the decree of the king and his nobles: No human being or animal, no herd or flock, shall taste anything. They shall not feed, nor shall they drink water." (Of course, the animals had not sinned, nor could they repent. Their example, however, was a lesson to the people, because God's anger threatened all living things.) . . . "Who knows? God may relent and change his mind; he may turn from his fierce anger, so that we do not perish." (Their labor was not in vain. God turned his fierce anger away from them.)
When God saw what they did (the fruits of their repentance and faith brought about by Jonah), how they turned from their evil

ways, God changed his mind about the calamity that he had said he would bring upon them; and he did not do it. (Jonah 3:4-10)

9. Fasting is a means of turning away the wrath of God and also of obtaining whatever blessings we need. When the other tribes of Israel were defeated by the Benjamites, "all the Israelites, the whole army, went back to Bethel and wept, sitting there before the LORD; they fasted that day until evening." And then the Lord answered, "Go up, for tomorrow I will give them into your hand." Then Samuel gathered all Israel together, when they were in bondage to the Philistines. "They fasted that day, and said, 'We have sinned against the LORD. . . .' The Philistines drew near to attack Israel; but the LORD thundered with a mighty voice that day against the Philistines and threw them into confusion; and they were routed before Israel" (1 Sam 7:5, 6, 10).

We also read in Ezra, "Then I proclaimed a fast there, at the river Ahava, that we might deny ourselves before our God, to seek from him a safe journey for ourselves, our children, and all our possessions . . . and he listened to our entreaty" (Ezra 8:21-23).

Nehemiah declared, "I sat down and wept, and mourned for days, fasting and praying before the God of heaven. . . . 'Give success to your servant today, and grant him mercy in the sight of this man'"(Neh. 1:4, 11). And God granted him mercy in the sight of the king.

10. In the same way, the apostles always joined fasting with prayer when they desired the blessing of God on any important undertaking. In Acts we read,

Now in the church at Antioch there were prophets and teachers. . . . While they were worshiping the Lord and fasting (doubtless, for guidance), the Holy Spirit said, "Set apart for me Barnabas and Saul for the work to which I have called them." Then after fasting and praying they laid their hands on them and sent them off. (Acts 13:1-3)

As we read in the next chapter of Acts, Paul and Barnabas themselves "returned to Lystra, then on to Iconium and Antioch. There, they strengthened the souls of the disciples and encouraged them to continue in the faith, saying, 'It is through many persecutions that we must enter the kingdom of God.' And after they had appointed elders for them in each church, with prayer and fasting they entrusted them to the Lord."

Indeed, there are blessings that can be obtained only through prayer and fasting. Our Lord expressly taught this truth to his disciples who asked why they were unable to cast out a demon. Jesus replied to their question, "Because of your little faith. For truly I tell you, if you have faith the size of a mustard seed, you will say to this mountain, 'Move from here to there,' and it will move; and nothing will be impossible for you. But this kind [of demon] does not come out except by prayer and fasting." Prayer and fasting are the appointed means of obtaining the faith to which even demons are subject.

11. It was not merely by the insights of reason or natural conscience (so-called) that in all ages the people of God have been directed to use fasting as a means to the ends that we have been enumerating. Prayer and fasting are means that God has appointed. And from time to time God himself has taught about them through clear and open revelations of his will. One such instance is found in the prophet Joel:

> Yet even now, says the LORD, return to me with all your heart, with fasting, with weeping, and with mourning. . . . Who knows whether he will not turn and relent, and leave a blessing behind him. . . . Blow the trumpet in Zion; sanctify a fast; call a solemn assembly. . . . Then the LORD became jealous for his land, and had pity on his people. In response to his people the LORD said: I am sending you grain, wine, and oil . . . and I will no more make you a mockery among the nations. (Joel 2:12-19)

Temporal blessings are not all that God directs his people to expect through prayer and fasting. On the one hand, to those who seek God with fasting, weeping, and mourning, he promised, "I will repay you for the years that the swarming locust has eaten, the hopper, the destroyer, and the cutter, my great army." On the other hand, God added, "You shall eat in plenty and be satisfied, and praise the name of the Lord your God. . . . You shall know that

I am in the midst of Israel, and that I, the Lord, am your God."
Then, immediately, God gave the great gospel promise:

> I will pour out my spirit on all flesh; your sons and your daughters
> shall prophesy, your old men shall dream dreams, and your young
> men shall see visions. Even on the male and female slaves, in those
> days, I will pour out my spirit. (Joel 2:28, 29)

12. The same reasons for fasting and prayer that enlivened
ancient people in their zealous and constant use are equally strong
to enliven us today. Even above these motivations, we have an
extraordinary reason for frequent fasting—the command of him
by whose name we are called.

It is true that in this part of the Lord's teaching, he did not
specifically command fasting, alms giving, or prayer. However, his
instructions on how to fast, give alms, and pray carry the equivalent weight of specific commands. A command for us to do anything in a certain way is without doubt a command to do it.
Obviously, it is impossible to do something in a certain way if we
do not do it at all. Accordingly, the Lord's telling us to give alms,
pray, and fast in a certain way is in fact a clear command to do
these things as duties. By performing them in the way that the
Lord commanded, we will certainly not lose the reward that God
gives to obedience.

Of course, the promise of a reward is a further motive and
encouragement to fast and pray. Our Lord has graciously added
the promise to reward those who obey him: "Your Father who
sees in secret will reward you openly." These purposes, then, constitute the clear grounds, reasons, and aims of fasting. We have
every encouragement to persevere, despite the many objections
that people who deem themselves wiser than their Lord have continually raised against fasting.

III. Answers to the objections to fasting

1. In considering the objections to fasting, we come now to consider the most groundless reason against it. First, it has been frequently said, "Let a Christian fast from sin and not from food.

Avoiding sin is all that God requires." Certainly, God does require us to avoid sin. However, he also directs us to fast. "It is this you ought to have practiced without neglecting the other."

View this argument against fasting in the form of a syllogism, and you can easily determine whether it is valid:

(1) If a Christian should abstain from sin, then a Christian should not abstain from food.

(2) And because Christians should abstain from sin, they should not abstain from food.

So goes the hollow argument against fasting. To be sure, it is most certainly and entirely true that a Christian *should* abstain from sin. But how does it follow that Christians ought not to fast? Let them abstain from both. By the grace of God, let Christians always abstain from sin, and let them often abstain from food. Scripture and experience give us clear reasons and aims for doing so.

2. One who objects to fasting may say, "Is it not better to abstain from pride and vanity, 'senseless and harmful desires,' peevishness, anger, and discontent than to abstain from food?" Certainly, that is so. Once again, however, we need to remind you of our Lord's words: "It is these you ought to have practiced without neglecting the other." Indeed, one fasts only as a means to the greater end of holiness of heart and life. We abstain from food for a good purpose. We fast so that by the grace of God conveyed into our souls through this outward means of fasting, in conjunction with all the other channels of his grace which he has designated, we may be enabled to abstain from every desire and disposition that does not please him. We refrain from food (being endued with power from on high) so that we may be able to refrain from everything displeasing to God.

Therefore, the argument against fasting proves just the opposite of what it was intended to prove. That argument proves that we *should* fast. If we should abstain from evil passions and desires, then at times we should also abstain from food. The small acts of self-denial are ways that God has chosen to bestow "so great a salvation."

3. Some people may offer a third objection: "We do not find fasting to be helpful. We have fasted much and often. But what did it accomplish? We are not a particle better; we found no blessing in fasting. No, we have found it a hindrance rather than help. For instance, instead of preventing anger or irritability, fasting increased them to such a level that we could tolerate neither ourselves nor others."

I acknowledge that your experience may very possibly be as you say. It is possible to fast or pray in a way that makes you much worse than you were before your fast. Fasting may cause you to become more unhappy and unholy. However, the fault does not lie in the fast, but in the *way* you fasted. Continue to fast, but in a different manner. Do *what* God commands, and do it as he commands it. Then, without doubt his promise will not fail.[14] His blessing will no longer escape you. Rather, when you fast in secret, "your Father who sees in secret will reward you."

4. There is a fourth objection given by those who oppose fasting. Some people protest, "Is it not a simple superstition to think that God regards such little things as fasts?"

We answer that if you say fasting is a simple superstition you are reproving all the generations of God's children. Are you willing to say that all who have fasted are weak and superstitious people? Can you be so bold as to affirm that Moses, Joshua, Samuel, David, Jehoshaphat, Ezra, Nehemiah, and all the prophets were weak and superstitious? Indeed, are you willing to make this charge against the one who is greater than all these people—the Son of God himself?

It is certain that our Master and all his servants did not consider fasting to be a worthless thing. Moreover, he who is "higher than the highest" regards fasting as important. It is obvious that all his apostles, after they were "full of the Spirit and of wisdom," also held the same opinion about fasting. When they had "been anointed by the Holy One" who "taught them everything," they still commended themselves as God's ministers by fasting and by "the weapons of righteousness for the right hand and for the left." When the bridegroom was taken away from them, then they fasted on that day. Without solemn fasting and prayer the apostles would not attempt anything pertaining to God's glory. For instance, they fasted before sending forth laborers into the harvest.

5. In the fifth place, some say, "If fasting is indeed so important and accompanied with such a blessing, is it not best to fast constantly? Is it not good, then, to fast not occasionally but all the time? Should we not fast as much as our physical strength will allow?"

We answer that no one should be discouraged from fasting as much as possible. By all means, use as little and plain food as you can, and exercise as much continual self-denial as your physical strength will bear. By God's blessing, this practice may promote some of the great goals mentioned above. Such self-denial may be a considerable help to chastity and also to heavenly-mindedness. This kind of living may help wean your affections from "things that are on earth" and set them on "things that are above."

However, this way of fasting is not *scriptural* fasting, and nothing in the entire Bible ever counts it as such. In some measure, severe fasting may lead to some scriptural aims, but it is still not biblical fasting. By all means, practice fasting, but not in ways that set aside a command of God. Fasting should never violate any instituted means to avert God's judgments and obtain the blessings he intends for his children.

6. Continually abstain from food as much as you please, so long as you are consistent with Christian moderation. Your abstinence must not interfere with your observing solemn times of fasting and prayer. For instance, your habitual abstinence or moderation would not prevent your fasting in secret if sudden great sorrow, remorse, fear, or dismay overwhelmed you. Such a circumstance would almost constrain you to fast. You would loathe your delectable food and you would hardly be able to eat even the food necessary for your body, until God "drew you up from the desolate pit, out of the miry bog, and set your feet upon a rock, making your steps secure." You would feel the same if you were in pangs of desire, fervently wrestling with God for his blessing. You would not need anyone to instruct you to fast until you had obtained the request you voiced.

7. Again, if you had been at Nineveh, would your regular fasts have been any reason for not participating in the general mortifi-

cation throughout the city? It was proclaimed, "No human being or animal, no herd or flock, shall taste anything. They shall not feed, nor shall they drink water. Human beings and animals shall be covered with sackcloth, and they shall cry mightily to God." Doubtless, your customary disciplines of fasting would not have interfered with the special call to a common fast. You would have been as much concerned as anyone else not to taste food on that day.

In the same way, abstinence or continual fasting would not have excused any of the children of Israel from fasting on the tenth day of the seventh month, the great annual Day of Atonement. There was no exception for these in that solemn decree, "For anyone who does not practice self-denial during that entire day shall be cut off from the people."

Finally, if you had been with the sisters and brothers in Antioch when they fasted and prayed before the sending forth of Barnabas and Saul, can you possibly imagine that your moderation or abstinence would have been a sufficient cause for not joining in the fast? Without doubt, if you had not fasted with the others you would soon have been separated from the Christian community. You would have deservedly been isolated from the others as one "bringing confusion into the church of God."[15]

IV. How Christians should fast

1. Finally, I will explain how we should fast in a way that will prove acceptable to the Lord. First, we should fast as unto the Lord, with eyes exclusively fixed on him. Let your purpose in fasting be only to glorify our Father who is in heaven, to express sorrow and shame for manifold transgressions of his holy law, to wait for additional purifying grace, and to turn your affections to things above. We should fast to add seriousness and fervor to our prayers, to avert the wrath of God, and to obtain all the "precious and very great promises" that he has made to us in Christ Jesus.

Let us beware of mocking God by mixing our fasting with any temporal intent, particularly seeking the praise of others. To do so, would turn our fasts and prayers into an abomination unto the

Lord. In the words of our sermon text, our blessed Lord peculiarly protects us from this danger:

> "And whenever you fast, do not look dismal, like the hypocrites, for they disfigure their faces so as to show others that they are fasting. Truly I tell you, they have received their reward. But when you fast, put oil on your head and wash your face, so that your fasting may be seen not by others but by your Father who is in secret; and your Father who sees in secret will reward you." (Matt. 6:16-18)

2. Second, if we desire God's reward let us beware of imagining that we earn any merit from God by our fasting. We cannot be too often warned of this truth, because deeply rooted in all our hearts is a desire to "establish our own righteousness" and to win salvation through our merit and not by God's grace. Fasting is only a *means* that God has ordained, by which we wait for his unmerited mercy. Apart from our own deserving, God has promised freely to give us his blessing.

3. We should never imagine that performing the mere outward act will gain any blessing from God. In Isaiah we read

> Is such the fast that I choose,
>   a day to humble oneself?
> Is it to bow down the head like a bulrush,
>   and to lie in sackcloth and ashes?
> Will you call this a fast,
>   a day acceptable to the LORD? (Isa. 58:5)

Are these outward acts, however strictly performed, all that is meant by one's "humbling oneself"? Surely not. If fasting were only an external act, all of it is lost labor. Such a practice may possibly afflict the body, but it has no value for the soul.

4. We may indeed afflict the body too much, making it unfit for the works of our calling. So we must also diligently guard against doing physical harm to ourselves. We must preserve our health as a good gift from God. Therefore, whenever we fast we should exercise care to adjust the fast to the needs of the body. We must not offer God murder for sacrifice or destroy our bodies in efforts to benefit our souls.

During these solemn seasons of fasting, even in great weakness of body, we may avoid the other extreme for which God condemns those in ancient times who remonstrated with him for not accepting their fasts. They complained,

> "Why do we fast, but you do not see?
> Why humble ourselves, but you do not notice?"

God answered them:

> Look, you serve your own interest on your fast day,
> and oppress all your workers. (Isa. 58:3)

If we cannot wholly abstain from all food, we can at least abstain from pleasurable food. Then, we will not seek his face in vain.

5. Let us be sure to humble our souls as well as our bodies. Let every season of fasting, either public or private, be a time of exercising all those holy affections that are implied in "a broken and contrite heart." Let your fasting be a season of devout mourning and godly sorrow for sin. Let your sorrow be like that of the Corinthians. Writing to them, St. Paul said, "Now I rejoice, not because you were grieved, but because your grief led to repentance; for you felt a godly grief, so that you were not harmed in any way by us." Paul's phrase "godly grief" means a sorrow that comes from God. It is a precious gift of his Spirit, lifting the soul to God from whom it flows. It "produces a repentance that leads to salvation and brings no regret."

Let our godly grief produce in us both inward and outward repentance. Let our repentance lead to a complete change of heart, one that is "renewed according to the image of its creator." May our godly grief produce a changed life, so that we are "holy as he who called us is holy" in all our conduct. May we "strive to be found by him, without spot or blemish," having an "eagerness to clear ourselves" by our lives rather than our words, and "to abstain from every form of evil."

Let us have the same kind of indignation against, and vehement abhorrence of, every sin. Let us fear our own deceitful hearts and desire in everything to be conformed to the holy and acceptable will of God. Let us be zealous for whatever can be a means of promoting God's glory and our growth in "the grace and knowledge of our Lord and Savior Jesus Christ." Let us set ourselves against Satan and all his works and against all filthiness of flesh and spirit.

6. Let us always link fervent prayer with our fasting, pouring out our whole souls before God. Let us confess our sins with all their heartaches. Let us humble ourselves under God's mighty hand, and lay open before him all our needs, guilt, and helplessness. Fasting is the time for increasing our prayers on behalf of ourselves and of our brothers and sisters. It is the time to bewail the sins of our people and cry aloud for the city of our God that the Lord may build up Zion and "let his face shine upon our desolated sanctuary." We can observe this kind of penitence among the people of God in ancient times who always joined together prayer and fasting. In the same way, the apostles, in all the instances cited above, fasted and prayed. Also, in the Sermon on the Mount, our Lord joined together fasting and prayer.

7. Now, for us to fast in a way that is acceptable to the Lord, it remains only for us to add almsgiving. As we are able, we should do works of mercy to the bodies and souls of others. "Do not neglect to do good and to share what you have, for such sacrifices are pleasing to God." The angel appeared to Cornelius who was fasting and praying in his house. The angel declared, "Your prayers and your alms have ascended as a memorial before God." God himself expressly and amply declares the kind of fasts we should observe:

> Is not this the fast that I choose:
>   to loose the bonds of injustice,
>   to undo the thongs of the yoke,
> to let the oppressed go free,
> and to break every yoke?
> Is it not to share your bread with the hungry,
>   and bring the homeless poor into your house;
> when you see the naked, to cover them,
>   and not to hide yourself from your own kin?

Then your light shall break forth like the dawn,
    and your healing shall spring up quickly;
your vindicator shall go before you,
    the glory of the LORD shall be your rear guard.
Then you shall call, and the LORD will answer;
    you shall cry for help, and he will say, Here I am.

If you remove the yoke from among you,
    the pointing of the finger, the speaking of evil,
if you offer your food to the hungry
    and satisfy the needs of the afflicted,
then your light shall rise in the darkness
    and your gloom be like the noonday.
The Lord will guide you continually,
    and satisfy your needs in parched places,
    and make your bones strong;
and you shall be like a watered garden,
    like a spring of water,
    whose waters never fail. (Isa. 58:6-11)

Notes

1. Jackson, *Wesley's Works,* 8:323.
2. Telford, *Wesley's Letters,* November 18, 1768, 5:112.
3. Curnock, *Wesley's Journal,* June 7, 1763, 5:17.
4. Outler, *Wesley's Sermons,* The Causes of the Inefficacy of Christianity, 4:94.
5. *Memoir of Miss Hanna Ball of High Wycombe* (London: Mason, 1839), pp. 39-40.
6. Curnock, *Wesley's Journal,* July 15, 1769, 5:329.
7. From a manuscript diary, quoted by Luke Tyerman, *The Life and Times of the Rev. John Wesley, M.A.,* 3 vols. (London: Hodder & Stoughton, 1870), 3:287.
8. Charles Wesley, *Journal,* 2 vols., ed. Thomas Jackson (London: John Mason, 1849), 2:253.
9. Ward and Heitzenrater, *Wesley's Journal and Diaries,* March 12, 1762, 21:352.
10. *The Didache,* 8; Clement of Alexandria, *Stromateis,* VII. 12; Tertullian, *Of Fasting,* chap. 2.
11. *Book of Common Prayer,* Tables and Rules.
12. The occasion was when the people feared the military threat of the King of Babylon.
13. *Sermons or Homilies Appointed to be Read in the Time of Queen Elizabeth, of Famous Memory: To Which are Added the Articles of Religion, the Constitutions and Canons Ecclesiastical and Indexes of Subjects, Scriptures and Names* (London: Ellerton and Henderson, 1817), "Of Good Works, and First of Fasting," part 1.
14. Deut. 31:6; Josh. 1:5; 1 Chron. 28:20; Judith 11:6; Sirach 2-8.
15. Council of Antioch, A.D. 341.

UPON OUR LORD'S SERMON ON THE MOUNT

Discourse 8

In the previous discourses in this series on the Sermon on the Mount, John Wesley dealt with purity of attitudes, dispositions, and motives in one's relationship to God. In this discourse, Wesley points out that these same attitudes must also motivate life's ordinary affairs. He emphasizes the importance of right intentions in both our "works of piety" toward God and in our "works of charity" toward others. Elsewhere, Wesley commented on the text for this sermon: "Our Lord here makes a transition from religious to common actions, and warns us of another snare, the love of money, as inconsistent with purity of intention as the love of praise."[1] This sermon underscores the importance of maintaining a right attitude toward our desires, concerns, and actions.

Here, Wesley expounds on the Lord's teaching that what the eye is to the body, motives are to the soul. When one's spiritual eye is "single," one views everything in the light of honoring God, whose purpose is to show his kingdom, power, and glory in and through our lives. The single eye focuses on one thing only—to know, please, serve, and delight in God. If one's motives are pure, the whole body is full of light. At this point, Wesley re-emphasizes a favorite theme of Puritanism: holiness and happiness are inseparably linked. To be truly holy is to be happy, and to be truly happy is to be holy.

This sermon emphasizes that if the "eye is evil," the entire soul is full of darkness and impurity. Satan, the god of this world, works to blind the eyes of our minds and to drape a veil over our hearts. When this blindness occurs, our lives become confused; evil desires, attitudes, and affections consume our thoughts. This darkness of soul brings unhappiness, confusion, and uncertainty. Disharmony dominates the life. Such a state of being always leads to misery, death, and eternal anguish. Wesley explains that being full of light or full of darkness is nowhere more evident than in one's attitude toward, and use of, worldly wealth.

Throughout Wesley's writings, he gives three rules about money—gain all you can, save all you can, and give all you can. (1) The axiom *gain all you can* underscores the need for industry, the proper recognition and stewardship of our abilities, and the recognition of God's divine providence in our lives. The New Testament clearly condemns laziness and sloth. God wants us to be productive and to increase our incomes. (2) The adage *save all you can* points to the truth that extravagance, improvidence, unnecessary consumption, and waste are not compatible with the Christian ethic. It is unwise, reckless, unsatisfying, and evil to spend money solely for oneself. (3) The advice *give all you can* underscores the fact that benevolence and liberal giving are clear Christian duties. Eventually, we lose what we keep and we keep what we give. One recalls the statement of Martin Luther that he had held many things in his hands, and that he had kept only those things that he had given away. This sermon constitutes one of John Wesley's most definitive statements on the use and misuse of money and material possessions.[2]

Most of the early Methodists had little money or property. Yet Wesley was aware that wrong attitudes toward money are always a clear and present possibility, even for the poor. The danger tends to grow especially as people become more prosperous. Four facts lay behind Wesley's decision to include among his Standard Sermons a message on money: (1) Jesus talked much about this important matter, and we must understand what he said. (2) Most Christians do not understand how to manage money, and there was little available instruction on this subject. (3) Our possessions are not our own. We are temporary stewards, who eventually must give an accounting for what God has entrusted to us. (4) The right and wrong uses of money have far-reaching consequences for this life and the life to come. Wesley explains that hoarding material possessions or using them selfishly and extravagantly rank among the major causes of spiritual blindness, unhappiness, and ultimate condemnation. This sermon clearly underscores the truth that one's attitudes toward the accumulation and use of money strike at the heart of one's earthly priorities, Christian character, and final destiny.

Sermon 28

UPON OUR LORD'S SERMON
ON THE MOUNT

Discourse 8

*"Do not store up for yourselves treasures on earth, where
moth and rust consume and where thieves break in and steal;
but store up for yourselves treasures in heaven, where neither moth nor rust consumes and where thieves do not break
in and steal. For where your treasure is, there your heart will
be also. The eye is the lamp of the body. So, if your eye is
healthy, your whole body will be full of light; but if your eye
is unhealthy, your whole body will be full of darkness. If
then the light in you is darkness, how great is the darkness!"*
(Matthew 6:19-23)

1 In the first part of the Sermon on the Mount, our Lord deals
with those actions that we commonly term "religious." These
spiritual disciplines constitute essential parts of true religion
and they properly express it. Next, our Lord proceeds to a discussion of the actions of daily life. He explains that the same purity
of intention attached to giving alms, fasting, and praying is also
necessary in ordinary living.

Without question, William Law correctly pointed out that the same purity of intention "which makes our alms and devotions acceptable must also make our labor or occupation a proper offering to God." Mr. Law made his point in this way:

> If a man . . . pursues his business that he may raise himself to a state of honor and riches in the world, he is no longer serving God in his employment . . . and he has no more title to a reward from God than he who gives alms that he may be seen, or prays that he may be heard of men. For vain and earthly plans are no more permissible in our occupations than in our alms and devotions. . . . They are not only evil when they mix with our good works, but they have the same evil nature . . . when they enter into the common business of our vocations. If it were permissible to pursue them in our worldly occupations, it would be permissible to pursue them in our devotions. But as our alms and devotions are not an acceptable service to God unless they proceed from a pure intention, so our common employment cannot be considered a service to God unless it is performed with the same piety of heart.[3]

2. In the sixth chapter of Matthew, in strong and comprehensive words, our Lord explains, advocates, and expands this truth in the most spirited manner. Jesus said, "The eye is the lamp of the body. So, if your eye is healthy, your whole body will be full of light; but if your eye is unhealthy, your whole body will be full of darkness."

The eye represents one's intention, and what the eye is to the body, intentions are to the soul. As one's eye guides the movements of the body, one's intentions guide the soul. The eye of the soul is said to be "single" when it focuses on one thing only. We have a single (or healthy) eye when we have no other aim but to "know God, and Jesus Christ whom he has sent." The single eye is to know God with proper affections, loving him as he has loved us. It is to please God in all things, to serve him (as we love him) with all our heart and mind and soul and strength, and to enjoy God in all and above all things, in time and in eternity.

3. Jesus said, "If your eye is healthy, your whole body will be full of light." Just as the body is guided by one's physical eye, in this context "your whole body" represents all the things that are

guided by your intentions. In sum, "your whole body" means all you are and do, including your desires, dispositions, affections, thoughts, words, and actions.

If your eye is single, your entire life "will be full of light"—that is, full of true divine knowledge. This knowledge is the first thing that we understand by "light." "In his light we see light." "For it is the God who said, 'Let light shine out of darkness,' who has shone in our hearts." He will enlighten the eyes of your understanding with the knowledge of the glory of God. His Spirit will reveal to you "even the depths of God." The inspiration of the Holy One will give you understanding and cause you to know God's hidden wisdom. Yes, the anointing that you receive from him will "abide in you" and "teach you about all things."

How is this truth confirmed by experience? Even after God has opened the eyes of our understanding, if we seek or desire anything other than God, how soon are our "senseless minds darkened!" Once again, clouds descend upon our souls. Doubts and fears return to overwhelm us. We are tossed back and forth, and we do not know what to do or which path to follow.

However, when we desire and seek nothing else but God, clouds and doubts vanish away. "We who are now in the Lord are light and live as children of light." Now, "the night is as bright as the day," and we find that "the path of the righteous is like the light of dawn." God shows us the path we should take, and he "makes the way straight before us."

4. In this scripture, the second thing that we understand by "light" is holiness. As you seek God in all things, you will find him in everything. He is the fountain of all holiness, continually filling you with his own likeness, justice, mercy, and truth. As you look to Jesus alone, you will be filled with the mind that was in him. Day by day, your soul will be renewed after the image of him that created it. If the eye of your mind remains fixed on him and if you "persevere as though seeing him who is invisible" and seek nothing else in heaven or earth, then you see the glory of the Lord. In this light you will be "transformed into the same image from one degree of glory to another; for this comes from the Lord, the Spirit."

Also, it is a matter of daily experience that "by grace we have been saved through faith." By faith the eye of the mind is opened to see the light of the glorious love of God. And as long as we are steadily fixed on God's love in Christ who reconciled the world to himself, more and more we are filled with love for God and others. We receive meekness, kindness, patience, and all the fruits of holiness, which through Christ Jesus redound to the glory of God the Father.

5. Third, in addition to holiness, the light that fills those who have a single eye for God also implies happiness. In the natural realm, "light is sweet, and it is pleasant for the eyes to see the sun." How much more pleasant it is to see the sun of righteousness continually shining upon the soul! "If then there is any encouragement in Christ, any consolation from love," if "any peace which surpasses all understanding," if any "hope of sharing the glory of God," they belong to those whose eye is single. Because of these blessings, one's "whole body will be full of light." One "rejoices always, prays without ceasing, and gives thanks in all circumstances, enjoying what is the will of God in Christ Jesus."

6. Jesus also said, "if your eye is unhealthy (or evil), your whole body will be full of darkness" (Matt. 6:23). The phrase "if your eye is evil" tells us that there is no middle ground between a single eye and an evil eye, between a healthy and an unhealthy eye. If the eye is not single, then it is *unhealthy*. If we do not intend exclusively to seek God's glory in everything we do, and if we seek anything else, then our "very minds and consciences are corrupted."

If in any matter we seek any aim apart from God, our eye is evil. Our eye is unhealthy and evil if we have any view other than to know and to love God and to please and serve him in all things. The eye is evil in those who have any intention other than to enjoy God and to be happy in him both now and forever.

7. If your eye is not singly focused on God, "your whole body will be full of darkness." A veil will continue to remain over your heart. "The God of this world" will increasingly blind your mind so that you will not benefit from "the light of the gospel of the glory of Christ." You will be full of ignorance and error. You will

not be able to receive or discern things concerning God. Even when you have some desire to serve him, you will be full of uncertainty as to how to proceed. You will encounter doubts and difficulties on every side, not discerning any way to escape from your confusion.

Indeed, if your eye is not fixed toward God and if you seek any of the things of this world, you will be full of ungodliness and unrighteousness. Your desires, dispositions, and affections will be without direction because they are entirely unenlightened, depraved, and vain. Your speech will be as corrupt as your heart; it will not be "seasoned with salt" or able "to give grace to those who hear." Instead, your speech will be trivial, profitless, corrupt, and grievous to the Holy Spirit of God.

8. Of those whose eyes are unhealthy, it can be said, "Ruin and misery are in their paths, and the way of peace they have not known." There is no settled, solid peace for those who do not know God. There is no true or lasting contentment for all who do not seek God with the whole heart. So long as you focus on any of the things that perish, "all that comes is vanity." Indeed, both in your pursuits and satisfaction, to seek after perishable things is not only vanity but also "a chasing after wind."

Most certainly, you walk in an empty shadow, and "you are in turmoil for nothing." You walk in "a darkness that can be felt." You are "still sleeping, but not taking your rest." You know well that the dreams of life can give pain but they cannot give contentment. There is no rest for you in this world or in the world to come. The only true contentment is in God, the source of all spirits.

Jesus said, "If then the light in you is darkness, how great is the darkness!" One's motives should enlighten the entire soul and fill it with knowledge, love, and peace. Indeed, it does so as long as it is single and fixed on God alone. If the eye is focused on anything besides God, it is filled with darkness. Instead of light, blackness covers the soul with ignorance, error, sin, and misery. O how great is that darkness! It is the very smoke that rises from the bottomless pit! It is the quintessential night that reigns over the lowest hell in that land of the shadow of death.

9. Therefore, Jesus said, "Do not store up for yourselves treasures on earth, where moth and rust consume and where thieves break in and steal." If you do, it is obvious that your eye is evil and not fixed completely on God.

With regard to most of God's commandments relating to the heart and life, the heathen of Africa or America stand on about the same moral level as many here that call themselves Christians. With only a few exceptions, Christians in England observe God's commandments to about the same extent as the heathen. For instance, most of England's citizens (commonly called Christians) are as serious and as self-restrained as the typical heathen near the Cape of Good Hope. Likewise, the Dutch or French Christians are as humble and as chaste as the Choctaw or Cherokee Indians. When we compare most of the nations in Europe with people in America, it is not easy to say whether moral superiority lies on one side or the other. (At the least, those in America do not have much moral advantage.) However, with regard to the commandment about storing up treasures on earth, we cannot affirm a correspondence between the heathen and the Christians of Europe and America.

On one point, the heathen are decidedly superior. They desire and seek nothing more than simple food to eat and plain clothing to wear. Furthermore, they seek these things only from day to day. The heathen store up nothing, unless it is as much grain for one season of the year as will be needed before the new season returns. Therefore, the heathen constantly and punctually observe this command not to store up treasures on earth, even though they do not know about the command. They hoard no treasures on earth—no stores of purple, fine linen, gold, or silver. Concerning these things Jesus said, "Moth and rust consume and thieves break in and steal."

How do the Christians observe what they profess to accept as a command of the highest God? They do not observe this command at all, any more than if it had never been given. Even the "good Christians" (as others deem them and as they regard themselves) pay no attention to this command. It might as well still be buried in its original Greek language. In what Christian city do you find one person among five hundred who has the least reluctance to lay up as much treasure as possible?

Of course, there are Christians who would not gather wealth unfairly. Many of them will not rob, steal, or defraud their neighbors just because they are ignorant or in need. But that virtue is another matter. Even these people do not hesitate to gain all they can; they only avoid the improper means of increasing their store of wealth. They have no qualms about "storing up treasures on earth," only they will not store them by dishonest means.

They are not afraid of disobeying Christ; they fear only the immoralities practiced by the heathen. These honest Christians do not obey Christ's command about storing up earthly treasures any more than do bandits or burglars. Indeed, many Christians never even *plan* to obey it. From the time of their youth, it never entered into their thoughts. Christian parents, teachers, and friends reared them without any instruction at all concerning this commandment. Instead, they have been taught to break it as soon and as much as they can, and to continue breaking it to the end of their lives.

10. In the entire world, there is no example of spiritual obsession that is more astonishing than the lust to store up material goods. Most of these very people read or hear the Bible read, many of them every Sunday. They have read or heard these words a hundred times. Still, they never suspect that they are themselves condemned by them, any more than the words that forbid parents to sacrifice their children to Moloch (Lev. 18:21; 20:2-5). O that God would speak to these miserable self-deceivers with his own mighty voice! May they finally "escape from the snare of the devil," and may the "scales fall from their eyes"!

11. Do you ask what it is to "store up for yourselves treasures on earth"? It is necessary to examine this matter thoroughly. So that we can clearly apprehend this command, first, let us observe what is *not* forbidden. This command does not forbid us "to do what is right in the sight of others" and to set aside what we need to "pay revenue to whom revenue is due" or whatever is justly required of us. Indeed, Paul teaches us, "Owe no one anything." Therefore, with diligence we ought to carry out our work so as to

have no debts. This obligation is nothing more than an evident law of common justice which our Lord "came not to abolish but to fulfill."

Second, this command of Jesus does not prohibit our providing for ourselves the things that are necessary for the body, including enough simple, wholesome food and clean clothing. As far as God puts it into our power, it is indeed our duty to provide these things for ourselves. When we do so, we "earn our own living" and "eat our own bread" without "burdening anyone."

Third, we are not forbidden to supply the needs of our children and for those of our own household. It is our *duty* to provide for them (even heathen morality requires us to meet the needs of our families). Every man ought to provide the simple necessities of life for his family and provide for its needs after his death. By diligent labor, we should supply our families with the simple necessities of life, but not delicacies or lavish provisions. It is not our duty to furnish our families (any more than ourselves) with the means for indulging in luxury or idleness. Yet, if we do not provide the necessities for our own children (as well as for "the widows of our own house," of whom primarily St. Paul is speaking in those well-known words to Timothy), in effect we have denied the faith and we are worse than unbelievers or heathen.

Last, this command does not forbid us from time to time storing up what we need to conduct our earthly business in the amount and degree sufficient to fulfill those purposes we have mentioned. Save an amount of money so as, (1) to "owe no one anything," (2) to acquire for yourselves the essentials of life, and (3) to supply the basic needs of the members of your own household while you live and with the means for acquiring what they need after you have gone to God.

12. Now, we can clearly discern (unless we are unwilling to discern it) what this commandment forbids. It forbids us from intentionally acquiring more of this world's goods than is consistent with the purposes listed above. We are not to toil for greater and greater measures of worldly substance and ever-larger amounts of gold and silver. This command of Jesus explicitly and absolutely

forbids our storing up any more material things than our duties require.

If the words mean what they say, they mean nothing else. Consequently, whoever owes no debts, has food and clothing for himself and his family, and possesses enough money to carry on his earthly business, but still seeks an even greater amount of wealth, is one who habitually lives in the open denial of the Lord that bought him. In effect, that one "has denied the faith and is worse than an unbeliever" (1 Tim. 5:8).

13. Listen, all you who live in the world and love the world. You may be "highly prized by others," but you are "an abomination in the sight of God" (Luke 16:15). How long will "your souls cling to the dust"? How long will you load yourselves with "thick clay"?[4] When will you awaken and see that the honest, reflective heathen are nearer the kingdom of heaven than you? When will you be persuaded to choose a better way, one that cannot be taken away from you? When will you endeavor only to "store up for yourselves treasures in heaven," and renounce, fear, and despise all other riches? If you aim at "storing up treasures on earth" you are merely wasting your time and "spending your money for that which is not bread."

What are the consequences if you succeed in attaining what you seek? You have murdered your own soul. You have extinguished the last spark of spiritual life in it. Indeed, while you are now in the midst of life, you are actually in death. You are a living person, but also a dead Christian. "For where your treasure is, there your heart will be also." Your heart has descended into the dust, and your soul clings to the ground. Your affections are not "set on things that are above," but "on things that are on earth." You seek the barren husks that can poison but cannot satisfy an everlasting spirit made for God. Your love, joy, and desire are fixed on the things that "perish with use." You have thrown away treasures in heaven. God and Christ are lost to you. You have gained riches but also the fire of hell.

14. O, "how hard it will be for those who have wealth to enter the kingdom of God!" When our Lord's disciples expressed astonishment at these words of Jesus, he did not retract them. Indeed,

he repeated them in even stronger terms: "It is easier for a camel to go through the eye of a needle than for someone who is rich to enter the kingdom of God."

How hard it is for the rich whose every word is praised not to think of themselves as wise people! It is very difficult for them to keep from imagining that they are better than the poor, inferior, uneducated masses of people! How hard it is for them not to seek happiness in their wealth or in things related to them and their money. How they are tempted to surrender to "the desire of the flesh, the desire of the eyes, or pride in riches." O you rich people, "how can you escape being sentenced to hell?" Jesus looks at us and says, "For mortals it is impossible, but for God all things are possible."

15. And even if you do not succeed in storing up earthy treasures, what would be the consequence even of *trying* to do so? The apostle Paul stated, "Those who want to be rich fall into temptation and are trapped by many senseless and harmful desires that plunge people into ruin and destruction." "Those who want to be rich" whether they succeed or not, "fall into temptation and are trapped." They are caught in a snare, a pitfall of the devil.

They also fall into "many senseless and harmful desires." These desires do not accord with the reason that properly belongs to rational and immortal beings. Rather, these desires belong to the savage beasts that lack understanding. These senseless and harmful desires "plunge people into ruin and destruction." They propel people into present and eternal misery. Let us open our eyes. Daily, we can see the sad evidence of people who desire and resolve to become rich. "For the love of money, the root of all kinds of evil," they have "pierced themselves with many pains." This present anguish is a foretaste of the hell to which they are going.

It is important to notice the care with which Paul speaks in these verses. He does not state that every rich person will invariably come to an evil end. There are those who have riches due to circumstances not of their own making. Providential conditions have made them rich, quite apart from their personal choices. However, Paul does say that an evil end will come to those who crave riches. They lust after wealth and strive to attain it.

As dangerous as riches are, they do not always "plunge people into ruin and destruction." However, the *craving* for riches is destructive. Those who deliberately set their hearts and efforts upon acquiring wealth will invariably lose their souls, whether or not they actually attain the wealth they covet. These people would sell the Christ who purchased them with his blood in order to gain a few pieces of gold or silver. They enter into a covenant with death and hell, and this agreement will remain intact. Daily, they are qualifying themselves to partake of their inheritance with the devil and his angels.

16. Who will warn this "brood of vipers" to "flee from the wrath to come"? Not those who camp at the doorstep of the wealthy or cower before them, hoping to partake of what falls from the rich persons' tables. It is not those who court the favor of the wealthy or fear their frown. Warnings against the dangers of riches will not come from those who focus on earthly things. However, we can expect more from a Christian who has overcome the world, desires nothing but God, and "fears only him who can destroy both soul and body in hell."

You, O man of God, speak out and spare no one. "Lift up your voice like a trumpet." Proclaim your message and explain to these "respectable sinners" just how desperate is their condition. It may be that one of them in a thousand will have ears to hear and will arise, and shake away the dust. Some may break loose from the chains that bind them to the earth and finally lay up treasures in heaven.

17. It might be that, by the mighty power of God, one of these who love riches will awake and ask, "What must I do to be saved?" The Bible gives an answer that is clear, adequate, and explicit. God does not say to everyone, "Sell all that you own." God, who sees into every heart, knew that in the particular case of the rich young ruler this action was necessary. However, in all succeeding generations God did not make this action a general rule for all rich people. God's prevailing instruction is, first, "Do not become proud." "God does not see as mortals see." He does not value you for your wealth or for what comes from it. God does not esteem you for your possessions, eminence, provisions,

qualifications, or accomplishments that wealth can bring. To him, all these things are as filth and trash. You, also, should regard them in the same way.

Take caution not to think that you are one bit wiser or better if you have wealth and what it brings. Weigh yourself on different scales. Evaluate yourself only by the standard of faith and love, which God has given. If you have more of the knowledge and love of God than another does, it is only on this account that you are a wiser and better person. But if you do not have the treasures of faith and love, all your achievements and possessions are more frivolous, repulsive, and truly abject than those of the lowest worker in your employment, or even the diseased beggar lying at your doorstep.

18. Second, "do not trust in uncertain riches." Do not have faith in them for support or happiness. To begin with, do not trust in riches for your well-being. You are miserably mistaken if you seek support in gold or silver. These are no more able to lift you above the world than to lift you above the devil. Understand that both the world and Satan laugh at all such shields against them. Riches will provide little support in the day of trouble, even if you manage to retain them in your hour of testing.

Moreover, it is not certain that you will retain your riches, for how often do they make themselves wings and fly away? But if your wealth does not vanish, what support will it give even in life's everyday troubles? The delight of your eyes, the desire of your eyes, the wife of your youth, your only child, or your most intimate friend may be taken away in a single stroke.

When you die, will your riches reawaken the breathless clay or call back the soul of its former inhabitant? Will riches safeguard you from sickness, disease, or pain? Do these afflictions visit only the poor? No. The one who tends your flocks or tills your ground has less sickness and pain than you do. Your servant is less often visited by these unwelcome troubles than you are. And if adversities do come to your servant, they are more easily driven away from the little cottage than from what William Shakespeare called "the cloud-capped towers and gorgeous palaces."[5] When your body is humbled with pain or wastes away with grieving sickness, how do your treasures help you? Permit the poor heathen to answer: "Such pleasures as pictures can afford to weak eyes or bounty-laden tables to a man with gout."[6]

19. However, there looms a greater tribulation than these: You will die. You will descend into the dust, return to the earth from which you were taken, and you will mix with common clay. "The dust returns to the earth as it was, and the spirit returns to God who gave it." Time moves onward and the years fade away with a swift though silent pace. Perhaps your life is far spent: the noon of life has passed and the evening shadows begin to rest upon you. You feel yourself in certain physical decline. The sources of life swiftly decline. What help now is there in your riches? Do they make death softer or sweeter? Do they charm that solemn hour? Quite the opposite: "O death, how bitter is the thought of you to the one at peace among possessions" (Sirach 41:1).

How unacceptable to such a one is that awful sentence, "This very night your life is being demanded of you!" Will riches prevent the unwelcome stroke or prolong the dreadful hour? Can riches deliver your soul from death? Can wealth restore the years that are past? Can riches add a month, a day, an hour, or a minute to your appointed time to die? Will the good things that you have chosen for your share on earth follow you over the great gulf? They will not. Naked you came into this world; naked must you depart.

> You must take leave of lands, home, beautiful wife;
> And no tree whose culture had pleased
> Will survive your brief reign
> Except those mournful cypresses.[7]

Surely, these truths are not too obvious to be observed because they are too apparent to be denied. No one who is to die could possibly "set their hopes on the uncertainty of riches" (1 Tim. 6:17).

20. Do not trust wealth to bring you happiness. Weighed on the scales, riches are "lighter than breath." Indeed, from what has already been observed, every rational person can come to the same conclusion. It follows that silver and gold cannot make us happy

if all the advantages or pleasures that they can purchase cannot prevent our being miserable. What happiness can riches provide to the one who in the midst of life is compelled to cry out the following verse?

> To my new courts sad thought does still repair,
> And round my gilded roofs hangs hovering care.[8]

Indeed, the verdict of common experience is so abundant, powerful, and certain that it makes all other arguments needless.

We appeal, therefore, to facts. Are only rich and notable people happy? Are people more or less happy in proportion to the measure of their wealth? Are wealthy people happy at all? I almost said, "Of all people they are the most to be pitied!" Rich persons, for once, speak the truth from your hearts. Speak in behalf of yourself and your peers:

> Amidst our plenty something still . . .
> To me, to thee, to him is wanting!
> That cruel something unpossessed
> Corrodes and leavens all the rest.[9]

Yes, and so it will, until your monotonous days of vanity are sealed in the darkness of death.

Surely, therefore, trusting in riches for happiness is the greatest possible absurdity under the sun! Are you not convinced that this is so? Is it possible that you still expect to find happiness in money or what it can obtain? Think! Can silver and gold, eating and drinking, horses and servants, glittering apparel, entertainment, and pleasures (as they are called) make you happy? They can just as soon make you immortal!

21. All riches are only dead fantasies. Do not value them. "Set your hope on the living God." In doing so, you will "abide in the shadow of the Almighty." "God's faithfulness is a shield and defense." "He is a very present help in trouble." When God becomes your treasure, even if all your other friends die, you will say, "The LORD lives! Blessed be my rock." He will "sustain you on your sickbed." When "human help is worthless" and when all the things of earth can give no support, he will support you. God

will make sweet your pain, and his comfort will cause you to clap your hands when you are in the flames. Even when the very earth is almost destroyed, when it is about ready to crumble into the dust, God will teach you to say, "Where, O death, is your victory? Where, O death, is your sting? Thanks be to God, who gives us the victory through our Lord Jesus Christ" (1 Cor. 15:55-57).

O, trust in God for happiness as well as for help. All the fountainheads of happiness are in him. Trust in him "who richly provides us with everything for our enjoyment." In his own rich and free mercy God extends these blessings to us in his own hand so that we may receive them as his gifts and pledges of his love. Therefore, we may enjoy each object that we have. God's love gives enjoyment to all that we taste. He puts life and sweetness into the whole. Everything leads us upward to the great Creator, and all earth becomes a step toward heaven. God injects the joys that are at his own right hand into everything he bestows upon his thankful children. They have fellowship with the Father and his Son Jesus Christ, enjoying God in all and above all.

22. Third, do not seek to increase your possessions. The command of Jesus is absolute and incontestable: "Do not store up for yourselves treasures on earth." This command is as fully clear as the mandate, "You shall not commit adultery." How, then, is it possible for rich persons to grow richer without denying the Lord who bought them? Yes, how can any of us who already have the necessities of life be without guilt if we gain more or aim at more?

Again, Jesus said, "Do not store up for yourselves treasures on earth." If you ignore the words of Jesus and desire and work to store up money or possessions (things that moth and rust consume and thieves break in and steal), and if you "join house to house and add field to field," why do you call yourself a Christian? You do not obey Jesus Christ, nor do you intend to do so. Why do you call yourself by his name? Jesus asked, "Why do you call me 'Lord, Lord,' and do not do what I tell you?"

23. If you say, "We have more possessions than we can use. If we must not store them up, what should we do with them? Must we throw them away?" I answer that if you threw them into the sea or burned them up in a fire they would be put to better use

than they are now. You cannot find as harmful a way of squandering them as storing them up for your offspring or using them for your own foolishness and excess. Of all possible methods of "throwing them away," these two are the very worst. They are the most contrary to the gospel of Christ and the most harmful to your own soul.

A late writer, William Law, has masterfully written about how destructive to one's soul it is to dissipate one's possessions in excessive consumption:

> If we waste our money, we are not only guilty of wasting a talent that God has given us...but we do ourselves a further harm. We turn this useful talent into a powerful means of corrupting ourselves; because as far as it is spent wrongly it is spent in the support of some wrong attitude, by gratifying some vain and absurd desires, which as Christians we are obligated to renounce.
>
> As intelligence and fine qualities cannot be trifled away only, they will subject those that have them to greater follies. Therefore, money cannot only be squandered, but if it is not used according to reason and religion it will make people live more silly and extravagant lives than they would have done without it. If therefore you do not use money to do good to others, you must spend it to the hurt of yourself. You act like one that refuses medicine to his sick friend which he cannot drink himself without inflaming his blood. It is this way with excess money. If you give it to those who need it, it is a medicine, but if you spend it on yourself for something that you do not need, it only inflames and disorders your mind....

Mr. Law continues:

> In spending riches where they have no authentic use or we any genuine need, we only use them to our own great harm. We create absurd desires, by nourishing evil dispositions, indulging in foolish passions, and supporting a vain mindset. Expensive eating and drinking, fine clothes and fine houses, appearances and possessions, jovial pleasures and entertainment all without a doubt damage and confuse our hearts. They are the food and nourishment of all the vices and weaknesses of our natures....They all support something that ought not to be supported. They are opposed to

that solemnity and piety of heart which prefers divine things. They act as so many weights upon our minds, and they render us less able and less inclined to elevate our thoughts and affections to things above.

Therefore, the money spent in this way is not only wasted or lost, but it is spent for bad purposes and worthless results. The misuse of money corrupts and clutters our hearts, making us unable to follow the sublime doctrines of the gospel. It is like withholding money from the poor to buy poison for ourselves.[10]

24. Equally inexcusable are those who lay up what they do not need for any reasonable purposes. Mr. Law writes,

If a man had hands and eyes and feet which he could give to those that needed them, and if he were to lock them up in a chest . . . instead of giving them to those that are blind and crippled, should we not appropriately consider him to be an inhumanly miserable creature? Might we not justly reckon him to be insane, if he chose to amuse himself with hoarding them up rather than entitle himself to an eternal reward by giving them to those that needed eyes and hands?

Now, money has very much the character of eyes and feet. If therefore we lock it up in chests . . . while the poor and distressed require it for their essential needs . . . we are not far from the cruelty of the one that chooses to hoard up the hands and eyes rather than to give them to those who need them. If we choose to store money rather than to entitle ourselves to an eternal reward by disposing of our money fittingly, we are guilty of insanity. It is the insanity of those that choose to lock up eyes and hands rather than to make themselves forever blessed by giving them to those who need them.[11]

25. May not the following cause be another reason that "it will be hard for a rich person to enter the kingdom of heaven"? Vast majorities of wealthy people are under the particular curse of God. In the general inclination of their lives, they are continually robbing God, embezzling and wasting their Lord's property, and by that very means they corrupt their own souls. Also, they are robbing the poor, hungry, and unclothed. They are mistreating the widow and the fatherless and making themselves accountable for

all the needs, afflictions, and distresses that they can, but fail to, eliminate. Yes, does not the blood of all those that perish for the lack of what the rich either store or expend needlessly cry against them from the earth? O, what explanation will the greedy give to him who is ready to judge both the living and the dead!

26. Fourth, from the words of our Lord you may learn the proper way of using what you do not need yourselves. These words are the complement of his command not to store up for yourselves treasures on earth. Jesus adds, "Store up for yourselves treasures in heaven, where neither moth nor rust consumes and where thieves do not break in and steal." Invest whatever you can spare in better security than this world can provide. Store up your treasures in the bank of heaven, and God will restore them in the Day of the Lord. "Whoever is kind to the poor lends to the LORD, and will be repaid in full." Those who give to the poor are saying to the Lord, "Place that in my account." However, in truth the Lord says to us, "You owe me even your own self." Give to the poor with a single (or healthy) eye. Give with an upright heart, and record, "I have given this amount to God." Jesus said, "Truly I tell you, just as you did it to one of the least of these who are members of my family, you did it to me."

Faithful and prudent managers act in the following way. Unless some peculiar circumstance should require it, they do not sell their houses, lands, or principal provisions—be they more or less. They do not desire or seek to become richer, any more than to squander what they possess in trivial ways. Rather, they use what they have solely for the wise and sensible purposes for which the Lord has placed it in their hands. Wise stewards provide their own households with "everything needed for life and godliness." Then, wise stewards use their money (tainted as it is) to make friends, so that when the end comes, these friends may welcome them into eternal homes. When our earthly bodies have dissolved, those who were taken to be with Abraham, after having eaten his bread, worn the fleece of his flock, and praised God for the comfort, may welcome them into paradise, God's house "not made with hands, eternal in the heavens."

27. As one who possessed authority from our great Lord and Master, Paul charged us continually to do good. Therefore, "those who in the present age are rich" are habitually "to do good, to be rich in good works, generous, and ready to share." Jesus said, "Be merciful, just as your Father is merciful." Who ceaselessly does good to others? To what extent are we to be merciful? We should show mercy according to our capacity, and with all the ability that God gives. Make this standard your only measure for doing good; do not look to any meagerly maxims or customs of the world. We command you to "be rich in good works."

Give abundantly, because you have much. "You received without payment; give without payment." Store up your treasures nowhere but in heaven. Be "ready to share" with all people according to their needs. Distribute widely, give to the poor, and "share your bread with the hungry." "Cover the naked with a garment"; "show hospitality to strangers"; carry or send relief to those in prison. Heal the sick, not by miracles, but through the blessing of God upon your appropriate support. Let the blessing of that one who is ready to perish through languishing need come upon you. Defend the oppressed, plead the cause of the fatherless, and make the widow's heart sing for joy.

28. In the name of the Lord Jesus Christ, we encourage you "to do good, to be rich in good works, generous, and ready to share." Be of the same spirit (though not in the same outward state) as believers of ancient times. They "devoted themselves to the apostles' teaching and fellowship," and "no one claimed private ownership of any possessions, but everything they owned was held in common." Be a faithful and wise steward of God and of the poor. Be unlike the ancient believers in these two circumstances only— that your needs are first supplied out of the portion of your Lord's belongings that remain in your hands and that you have the blessedness of giving. Thus "store up for yourselves the treasure of a good foundation," not in the present world, but "for the future, so that you may take hold of the life that really is life."

Indeed, the great foundation of all the blessings of God, whether temporal or eternal, is the Lord Jesus Christ, his righteousness and blood, what he has done, and what he has suffered for us. "For no one can lay any other foundation," not an apostle or an angel from heaven. Only through his merits, whatever we do in his name is a foundation for a good reward in the day when "each will receive wages according to the labor of each." Therefore, "do not work for the food that perishes, but for the food that endures for eternal life."

Whatever your hand finds to do, do with your might. Therefore allow

> No fair occasion pass unheeded by;
> Snatching the golden moments as they fly,
> Thou by few fleeting years ensure eternity![12]

"To those who by patiently doing good seek for glory and honor and immortality, God will give eternal life." In a continual, zealous performance of all good works, wait for that joyful hour when "the king will say... 'I was hungry and you gave me food, I was thirsty and you gave me something to drink, I was a stranger and you welcomed me, I was naked and you gave me clothing, I was sick and you took care of me, I was in prison and you visited me. Come, you that are blessed by my Father, inherit the kingdom prepared for you from the foundation of the world.'"

Notes

1. *Explanatory Notes upon the New Testament*, Matt. 6:19.
2. See also four additional sermons that Wesley wrote about stewardship and worldly wealth: *The Use of Money, The Good Steward, The Single Eye* (written at Bristol in 1789), and *Worldly Folly* (written at Balham in 1790).
3. William Law, *A Serious Call to a Devout and Holy Life*, 1729.
4. Hab. 2:6. This phrase means goods taken in pledge.
5. William Shakespeare, *The Tempest*, IV.1, 152.
6. Horace, *Epistles*, I. ii, 52, 53.
7. Horace, *Odes*, II, xiv, 21-24.
8. Matthew Prior, *Solomon*, ii, 53, 54.
9. Matthew Prior, *The Ladle*, ii, 53, 54.
10. William Law, *A Serious Call to a Devout and Holy Life* (1729), *Works*, 4:50, 51.
11. Ibid., 4:50.
12. Samuel Wesley, Jr., "On the Death of Mr. Morgan," in *Poems on Several Occasions* [1736] (London: J. Rogers, 1812), p. 108.

UPON OUR LORD'S SERMON ON THE MOUNT

Discourse 9

The first message that John Wesley preached after his ordination in 1725 was from Matthew 6:33, which is included in the text for this sermon. He preached often from this verse because he believed that it was central to Christian discipleship. In 1772, he wrote in his journal:

> At twelve I set out in the stage coach, and in the evening came to Norwich. Finding abundance of people were out of work, and, consequently, in the utmost want . . . I enforced, in the evening, "Seek ye first the kingdom of God, and his righteousness; and all these things shall be added unto you." For many years, I have not seen so large a congregation here, in the mornings as well as evenings. One reason of which may be this: Thousands of people, who, when they had fulness of bread, never considered whether they had any souls or not, now they are in want begin to think of God.[1]

The sermons that Mr. Wesley preached from this text proved highly effective in his evangelistic and nurturing ministries.

Wesley begins this sermon with a discussion of the verse, "No one can serve two masters; for a slave will either hate the one and love the other, or be devoted to the one and despise the other."

Quoting a passage from the Old Testament, he speaks about the foolishness of holding two religions. In ancient Samaria, certain people "worshiped the LORD but also served their own gods" (2 Kings 17:33). Wesley points out that people often attempt simultaneously to worship the true God *and* other gods. He states, "How closely the worship of most modern Christians resembles the practice of the ancient heathen! Today's Christians fear the Lord and perform outward service to him, demonstrating that they have some fear of God. Nonetheless, they also 'serve their own gods.'" Using scripture and logic, this sermon demonstrates that attempts to worship more than one deity always fail.

Jesus was culturally and racially inclusive, but he was religiously exclusive. He declared, "Worship the LORD your God, and serve only him." He spoke of *the* way, *the* truth, and *the* life (John 14:6). Wesley illustrates this point by reminding us that it is impossible to walk in opposite directions at the same time or to travel separate roads concurrently. Religious syncretism is an illogical position that Jesus exposed, and Wesley compellingly "enforces" this truth.

Wesley develops the verse, "You cannot serve God and mammon." Mammon was an Aramaic term that the ancient Jews used to refer to wealth or property. Wesley explains that mammon refers both to money and to those things that money can purchase—such as pleasure, fame, influence, or comfort. Elsewhere, he describes *mammon* as "riches, money, any thing loved or sought, without reference to God."[2] Worshiping the true God instead of mammon involves four essential things: believing and trusting God, loving God, obeying God, and becoming like God.

Wesley explains that to serve "mammon" means (1) seeking for one's happiness in riches or what they can obtain, (2) loving the present world and accepting its values, (3) following the world by adopting its standards, and (4) adopting the values of the present age by conforming to its customs and patterns. Those who live in this manner worship the false gods of mammon. Moreover, they necessarily dishonor the true God and invariably oppose those who serve him. A preoccupation with the gods of mammon causes us constant worry, and eventually destroys our lives.

This sermon explains that "taking no thought" for our lives does not mean that God wants us to be heedless of present concerns or tomorrow's needs. Wesley contends that indifference, indolence, and idleness are no more compatible with the will of God than drunkenness and adultery. God expects Christians to "do their work quietly" and to earn their own living. Jesus said, "Strive first for the kingdom of God and his righteousness, and all these things will be given to you as well" (Matt. 6:33).

Wesley declares, "How kind are these precepts! The substance of which is only this, Do thyself no harm! Let us not be so ungrateful to him nor so injurious to ourselves, as to harass and oppress our minds with that burden of anxiety, which he has so graciously taken off.... We will cheerfully repose ourselves on that heavenly Father, who knows we have need of these things; who has given us life, which is more than meat [food], and the body, which is more than raiment. And thus instructed in the philosophy of our heavenly Master, we will learn a lesson of faith and cheerfulness from every bird of the air, and every flower of the field."[3]

UPON OUR LORD'S SERMON ON THE MOUNT

Discourse 9

"No one can serve two masters; for a slave will either hate the one and love the other, or be devoted to the one and despise the other. You cannot serve God and wealth. Therefore I tell you, do not worry about your life, what you will eat or what you will drink, or about your body, what you will wear. Is not life more than food, and the body more than clothing? Look at the birds of the air; they neither sow nor reap nor gather into barns, and yet your heavenly Father feeds them. Are you not of more value than they? And can any of you by worrying add a single hour to your span of life? And why do you worry about clothing? Consider the lilies of the field, how they grow; they neither toil nor spin, yet I tell you, even Solomon in all his glory was not clothed like one of these. But if God so clothes the grass of the field, which is alive today and tomorrow is thrown into the oven, will he not much more clothe you—you of little faith? Therefore do not worry, saying, 'What will we eat?' or 'What will we drink?' or 'What will we wear?' For it is the Gentiles who strive for

*all these things; and indeed your heavenly Father knows that
you need all these things. But strive first for the kingdom of
God and his righteousness, and all these things will be given
to you as well. So do not worry about tomorrow, for tomorrow will bring worries of its own. Today's trouble is enough
for today.*   *(Matthew 6:24-34)*

1   After the King of Assyria carried Israel away into captivity,
he placed certain nations in the cities of Samaria. It is recorded that "they worshiped the LORD but also served their
own gods." The inspired biblical writer said, "These nations worshiped the Lord," that is, they gave him outward worship (clear
proof that they feared God, but lacked enlightenment). These
people "also served their carved images. To this day their children
and their children's children continue to do as their ancestors did."

How closely the worship of most modern Christians resembles
the practice of the ancient heathen! Today's Christians fear the Lord
and also perform an outward service to him, demonstrating that
they have some fear of God. Nonetheless, they also "serve their own
gods." There are those who "teach them the law of the god of the
land," just as there were those who instructed the ancient Assyrians
in pagan ways. Israel worshiped the God whose very name the
country bears to this day—Israel. Once, God was worshiped there
with a holy devotion. Nevertheless, the people did not serve him
exclusively. They did not respect him enough to worship him only.
"Every nation still made gods of its own, as did every nation in the
cities in which they lived." These nations feared the Lord, and
they did not lay aside the outward forms of worshiping him.

At the same time, they served their carved images of silver and
gold, which were all the product of human hands. Alongside the
God of Israel, money, pleasure, and applause (the gods of this
world) claimed more than their share of service. This kind of worship became the practice both of their children and their children's
children. "To this day they continue to practice their former
customs."

2. Speaking in an ordinary way, as people commonly speak, those pitiful heathen were said to "fear the Lord." Yet, speaking according to the truth and real nature of things, the Holy Spirit immediately adds,

> They do not worship the LORD and they do not follow the statutes or the ordinances or the law or the commandment that the LORD commanded the children of Jacob, whom he named Israel. The LORD had made a covenant with them and commanded them, "You shall not worship other gods or bow yourselves to them or serve them or sacrifice to them . . . but you shall worship the LORD your God; he will deliver you out of the hand of all your enemies." (2 Kings 17:34, 35, 39)

The infallible Spirit of God, and indeed all whose eyes of understanding he has opened to discern the things of God, pass the same judgment upon today's pathetic, nominal "Christians," commonly so called. If we speak according to the truth and real nature of things, "they do not worship the LORD, and they do not serve him." They do not live according to the covenant that the Lord made with them. They do not follow the law and commandment that he has dictated: "Worship the LORD your God, and serve only him." They serve other gods—and "no one can serve two masters."

3. How useless is it for anyone to attempt to serve two gods! Is it not easy to predict what must be the unavoidable consequence of such an attempt? That person "will either hate the one and love the other, or be devoted to the one and despise the other." The two parts of this sentence, although separately proposed, are to be understood in connection with each other. The second part is a consequence of the first part. We will naturally be devoted to him whom we love. We will cling to him so as to render willing, faithful, and diligent service. And, in the meantime, we will disobey the master we hate and give no regard to his commands. If we obey him at all, we will do so in an insignificant and careless way. Therefore, whatever the "wise people" of the world may assume, *You cannot serve God and wealth.*

4. "Mammon" was the name of one of the heathen gods, who was thought to preside over riches. Here, *mammon* refers to riches—gold, silver, or money. By implication, *mammon* also refers to everything that riches can buy, such as comfort, fame, and sensual pleasure. Now, what are we to understand here by "serving God" and by "serving mammon"? We cannot serve God unless we believe in him. This belief is the only true basis for serving him. Therefore, the first great aspect of God's service is believing in him as "reconciling the world to himself" through Christ Jesus. It is trusting in him as a loving, pardoning God.

And to believe in God in this way involves trusting in him as our strength, without whom we can do nothing. It is to trust that every moment God gives us power from on high, without which it is impossible to please him. It is to trust him as our only help in time of trouble, the one who surrounds us with glad cries of deliverance. God is our shield, our defender, and the one who lifts up our heads above all our enemies that surround us. To believe in God means to trust him as our happiness, the central focus of spirits, and the only rest of our souls. It is to trust him as the only good who is entirely adequate for us and sufficient to satisfy all the desires that he has given us.

Closely connected with trusting God as our center, belief in God means having faith in God as our life's aim. It is to look to him in everything, to use all things entirely as means of enjoying him, wherever we are and in whatever we do. Believing in God means seeing God, who is invisible, looking upon us with pleasure. It means referring all things to him in Christ Jesus.

5. Thus, to *believe* in God and to trust God is the first thing involved in serving God. Then, the second aspect of serving God is to *love* him. To love God in the way scripture describes and in the way God himself requires, is to love him as the one true God "with all our heart, and with all our soul, and with all our mind, and with all our strength." In requiring us to love him in this way, God commits himself to work in us. Loving God is to desire him for his own sake alone, and to love nothing else except in reference to him. It is to rejoice in God, to delight in him, and to seek and find happiness in him. Loving God means enjoying him as

"distinguished among ten thousand." It is to rest in him as our God and our all. In a word, it is to have such intimacy with God as to make us always happy.

6. A third thing we are to understand by "serving God" is to *resemble* or *imitate* God. So the ancient Church Father states: "The best service of God is to imitate him whom you worship."[4] We are speaking of imitating or resembling him "in the spirit of our minds." For here the true Christian imitation of God begins. God is a Spirit; and they that imitate or resemble him must do so in spirit and in truth.

"God is love." Therefore those who resemble him in the spirit of their minds are "being transformed into the same image." They are merciful, just as he is merciful. Their soul is full of love. They are kind, benevolent, compassionate, tenderhearted—not only to the good and gentle, but also to those that are obstinate. Yes, in accord with the nature of God they are also loving toward everyone, and their mercy extends to all that God has made.

7. We need to understand one more thing about serving and obeying God. We are to *glorify* him, which means to worship him. We glorify him in our bodies as well as in our spirits. We glorify him by keeping his outward commandments, zealously doing whatever he has commanded, and carefully avoiding whatever he has forbidden. We worship God by performing the everyday conduct of life with a single eye and a pure heart. We live in holy, ardent love, offering this worship as a sacrifice to God through Jesus Christ.

8. On the other hand, let us consider what we are to understand by serving mammon. First, worshiping this false god means trusting in riches, money, or the things they can obtain. To serve mammon is to look to money as our strength and the means by which we order our lives. Serving mammon means trusting in riches as the support by which we expect to be comforted in, or delivered from, trouble.

Serving mammon means trusting in the world for happiness and supposing that the comfort of our lives consists in "the abundance of possessions." It means looking for tranquillity in things that are seen, seeking for contentment in outward abundance, and expecting gratification in the things of the world. In truth, however, these things can never be found apart from God.

If we live to serve wealth, we cannot avoid making the world the aim and ultimate end of many or all of our endeavors, actions, and plans. In all that we do, we will aim only at increasing our wealth, obtaining pleasure or acclaim, and gaining a greater measure of temporal things—without any reference to things eternal.

9. Second, serving mammon involves loving the world and desiring it for its own sake. It means fixing our joy on the things of the world and setting our hearts upon them. Serving mammon means seeking (what indeed is impossible to find) our happiness in the world, resting the entire weight of our souls upon the staff of this broken reed. However, daily experience demonstrates that the world cannot uphold us. "That broken reed of a staff will pierce the hand of anyone who leans on it."

10. The third thing meant by serving mammon is to resemble the world or to be conformed to the world. Being conformed to the world involves having plans, desires, attitudes, and affections in harmony with those of the present age. It is to possess an earthly, sensual mind that is shackled to the things of earth. It means being persistent and excessive lovers of ourselves. It means to think highly of our own attainments, to desire and delight in the adulation of others. Serving the present world also means that we fear, shun, and abhor correction. Being conformed to this age means being impatient with reprimands, being quick to take offense, and being swift to return evil for evil.

11. Finally, serving mammon is to obey the world by outwardly conforming to its standards and customs. It is to walk on the same common road as others, traveling the world's broad, smooth, well-worn path. Serving mammon means to be in fashion, to follow the multitude, and to behave in the same way as one's neighbors. It means following the inclinations of the flesh and intellect and gratifying our appetites and inclinations. Day after day, those who live this way in word and deed cater to themselves and focus on their own comfort and pleasure. Now, what can be more undeniably obvious than that we "cannot serve God and mammon"?

12. Is it not perfectly clear that we cannot comfortably serve both? Is it not apparent that to fluctuate between God and the world is the certain way to be disappointed in both and to have no rest in either? In how unpleasant a condition must those be who fear God but do not love him. They try to serve God, but not with the whole heart. These people have only the toils of religion, but not its joys! They have enough religion to make them miserable, but not enough to make them happy. Their religion will not permit their enjoyment of the world, and the world will not allow their enjoyment of God. Therefore, by hesitating between God and the world, they lose both, and they have no peace in either.

13. Does not everyone see that we cannot serve both God and the world with inner consistency? In those who obey two masters, what more glaring discrepancy can be conceived than that which continuously surfaces in their efforts to serve God and mammon! They are indeed "sinners who walk a double path!"[5] They take one step forward and another backward. They repeatedly build up with one hand and pull down with the other, at the same time loving sin and hating it. They are always seeking God, yet always fleeing from him. They would and would not serve God. They are not consistently the same persons for a single day—no, not even for an hour.

They are miscellaneous mixtures of all sorts of contradictions, an accumulation of discrepancies muddled into one. Oh, one way or the other, be consistent with yourselves! "Turn either to the right hand or to the left." If mammon is God, serve this god; if the Lord is God, then serve him. However, do not think of serving either God, unless you serve with all your heart.

14. Does not every reasonable, thinking person see that we cannot possibly serve both God and wealth? The most absolute antithesis and irreconcilable enmity exist between the two of them. The antithesis between the most opposite things on earth (fire and water, darkness and light) vanishes into nothing when compared to the conflict between the true God and the god of mammon. Consequently, in whatever way you serve the one, you necessarily renounce the other.

Do you believe in God through Christ? Do you trust in him as your strength, your help, your shield, and your very great reward? Above all things, do you trust him for your happiness and your goal in everything? If so, you cannot trust in mammon. As long as you have complete faith in God, it is impossible for you to trust in mammon.

Do you trust in riches with absolute devotion? Then you have denied the faith. You do not trust in the living God. Do you love God, and do you seek for and find your happiness in him? If so, you cannot love the world or the things of the world. You are crucified to the world and the world is crucified to you. Do you "love the world"? Are your affections set on "things that are on earth"? Do you seek happiness in earthly things? If you do, it is impossible for you to love God. The love of the Father is not in you. Do you pattern yourself after God? Are you merciful, just as your Father is merciful? Are you transformed by the renewing of your mind into the image of him that created you? Then you cannot be conformed to the present world. You have renounced all its passions and desires.

Are you conformed to the world? Does your soul still bear the image of the earthly? If so, you are not renewed in the spirit of your mind and you do not bear the image of "the man of heaven." Do you obey God? Are you zealous to do his will on earth as do the angels in heaven? If not, it is impossible for you to avoid serving the god of mammon. If you love the true God, you set yourself defiantly against the world. You trample under foot its customs and maxims, and you will neither follow nor be led by them. Do you pursue the world? Do you live like other people? Do you seek to please people and please yourself? If so, you cannot be God's servant. "You are from your father the devil."

15. "Worship the Lord your God, and serve only him." Lay aside all thoughts of obeying two masters, of serving God and mammon. Plan for yourself no objective, help, or happiness but God. Seek nothing on earth or in heaven but him; aim at nothing but to know, love, and enjoy him. This goal constitutes your entire business on earth, the only prospect you can reasonably have, and the one intent to which you should aspire in everything. As our

Lord says, "Do not worry about your life, what you will eat or what you will drink, or about your body, what you will wear." This command of Christ is profound and important. It is therefore very important for us to study it and thoroughly understand it.

16. Our Lord's command does not require us to be completely unmindful of the concerns of this life. An unreliable and careless disposition lies at the farthest distance from the full religion of Jesus Christ. The Lord does not want us to "lag in zeal" or to be lazy and tardy in our work. Laziness is contrary to the entire spirit and genius of the religion of Jesus. Christians despise habitual idleness as much as drunkenness; they avoid laziness as much as adultery. The Christian knows well that there is one kind of thinking and responsibility with which God is well pleased. This way of life is absolutely needed for the proper performance of those outward works to which the providence of God has called us.

It is God's will that Christians should "do their work quietly and to earn their own living." Yes, all adults should provide for those of their own households. It is likewise God's will that "we owe no one anything," and that we "take thought for what is noble in the sight of all." We cannot do these things without thinking about our business and keeping our minds on our responsibilities. Indeed, we must often give long and serious thought to our work. Consequently, our blessed Lord does not condemn our responsibility to provide for our households and ourselves and to pay everyone what we owe them. Yes, this way of living "is right and acceptable in the sight of God our Savior."

It is right and acceptable to God that we should ponder and arrive at a clear understanding of whatever business is at hand and plan our work before we begin it. It is also right, from time to time, to arrange our work so as to carry it out in the most effective way. Our Lord by no means intended to denounce this attention to our work, which some call "the worry of the head."

17. What Jesus condemns here is "the worry of the heart," by which is meant the fearful, unsettled cares that torment our spirits. Jesus denounced all the worries that harm either the soul or the body. What he forbids is the kind of anxiety that unhappy experience shows will poison the blood and absorb the spirit. This

anxiety expects all the misery it fears, and the future arrives to torment before its time. Christ forbids only the sort of concerns that poison the blessings of today for fear of what may come tomorrow, the worry that keeps us from enjoying present abundance for fear of future insufficiency. This worry is not only a severe disease and sad sickness of soul, but also an atrocious offense against God. It is a sin of the deepest sort. It is an appalling affront to God who is the gracious Governor and wise Arranger of everything.

Such anxiety necessarily suggests that the Judge of all the earth does not do what is just. It clearly implies that he lacks either wisdom (if he does not know what we need) or goodness (if he does not provide for the needs of all who put their trust in him). Therefore, be on your guard that you do not become apprehensive. "Do not worry about anything." Hold no troubled thought. The following rule is clear and certain: *Uneasy concern is unlawful concern.* With a single eye to God, "take thought for what is noble in the sight of all." So, yield everything into better hands; leave everything to God.

18. Jesus said, "Do not worry about your life, what you will eat or what you will drink, or about your body, what you will wear. Is not life more than food, and the body more than clothing?" If God gave you the greater gift of life, will he not give you food to sustain it? If he has given you your body, how can you doubt that he will give you clothing to cover it? How much more is this the case if you give yourselves up to him and serve him with all your heart.

Jesus said, "Look at the birds of the air; they neither sow nor reap nor gather into barns, and yet your heavenly Father feeds them. Are you not of more value than they?" You who were created with a capacity for God, in his eyes are you not of greater value than birds? Do you not belong to a higher rank of beings than they do? Jesus said, "Can any of you by worrying add a single hour to your span of life?" What can you hope to gain by worrying? It is in every way futile and pointless.

Jesus said, "And why do you worry about clothing?" (Wherever you look, are you not daily rebuked about fretting over what you wear?)

Jesus continued:

Consider the lilies of the field, how they grow; they neither toil nor spin, yet I tell you, even Solomon in all his glory was not clothed like one of these. But if God so clothes the grass of the field, which is alive today and tomorrow is thrown into the oven, will he not much more clothe you—you of little faith? (Matt. 6:28-30)

You, whom God "made in the image of his own eternity," he made to endure forever and ever. You that worry, indeed you possess little faith. Otherwise you could not for a moment doubt his love and care.

19. If you do not store up treasures on earth, then do not ask, "What will we eat?" If you serve God with all your strength and if your eye is singly fixed on him, do not ask, "What will we drink?" If you refuse to be conformed to the world and offend those who might profit you, then you do not need to ask, "What will we wear?" Jesus said, "It is the Gentiles" (the heathen who do not know God) "who strive for all these things." But you are discerning. "Your heavenly Father knows that you need all these things." And he has shown you a dependable way of being constantly supplied with what you need: "Strive first for the kingdom of God and his righteousness, and all these things will be given to you."

20. Jesus advised, "Strive first for the kingdom of God." Before you entertain any other thought or worry, let it be your concern that the God and Father of our Lord Jesus Christ rules in your heart. "God gave his only Son, so that everyone who believes in him may not perish but may have eternal life." He wants to manifest himself in your soul and dwell and reign there. He is able to "destroy arguments and every proud obstacle raised up against the knowledge of God, and take every thought captive to obey Christ." Let God have complete dominion over you. Permit him to reign without a rival. Allow him to possess all your heart, and rule alone. Let him be your one desire, your joy, and your love. Then you can continually cry out, "For the Lord our God the Almighty reigns."

Jesus commanded, "Strive first for the kingdom of God and his righteousness." Righteousness is the fruit of God's reign in your heart. And what is righteousness other than love? Righteousness is the love of God and all humankind flowing from faith in Jesus

Christ and producing humility, meekness, gentleness, forbearance, patience, and death to the world. Love is having every right attitude of heart toward God and others. Righteousness and love produce all holy actions—"whatever is true, whatever is honorable, whatever is just, whatever is pure, whatever is pleasing, whatever is commendable." Love leads to whatever "works of faith and labors of love" are acceptable to God and profitable to others.

Jesus also commanded us to seek "God's righteousness." All righteousness remains *his* righteousness still. This righteousness is God's own free gift to us, for the sake of Jesus Christ the righteous, through whom alone it is purchased for us. And it is his work alone. He singularly works in us by the inspiration of his Holy Spirit.

21. Perhaps a careful examination of this command of Jesus can shed light on some other scriptures that we have not always clearly understood. Speaking in his epistle to the Romans concerning the unbelieving Jews, St. Paul said, "Being ignorant of the righteousness that comes from God, and seeking to establish their own, they have not submitted to God's righteousness." I believe that one meaning of the words "ignorant of the righteousness that comes from God" is that the Jews were unaware of the righteousness of Christ imputed to all believers, by which all their sins are blotted out and they are reconciled to God's favor.

These words also seem to mean that the Jews were ignorant of the inward righteousness and holiness of heart (best described as "God's righteousness") which is God's free gift through Christ, working in us by his all-powerful Spirit. And because they were ignorant of this gift, they "sought to establish their own righteousness." They labored to establish that outer righteousness, which might very properly be called "their own righteousness." It was not the result of the work of God's Spirit, and they did not own or accept it. They themselves tried to work this righteousness by their own natural strength. When they had done so, it was a stench in his nostrils. Trusting in their own righteousness, they "did not submit to God's righteousness."

Yes, they hardened themselves against the faith by which alone one can attain God's favor. "For Christ is the end of the law so that there may be righteousness for everyone who believes." When Christ said, "It is finished," he put an end to the law of external rites and ceremonies. He did so in order to introduce "a better hope" through his blood, given in the sacrifice of himself. Now, all who believe in Christ can experience the image of God in their inmost souls.

22. Closely related to these words are those of the Apostle Paul in his epistle to the Philippians:

> I regard everything as loss because of the surpassing value of know-ing Christ Jesus my Lord. For his sake I have suffered the loss of all things, and I regard them as rubbish, in order that I may gain Christ and be found in him, not having a righteousness of my own that comes from the law, but one that comes through faith in Christ, the righteousness from God based on faith. (Phil. 3:8, 9)

The righteousness that comes from the law is only an external righteousness, the outward religion by which St. Paul formerly had hoped to be accepted by God. "As to righteousness under the law," Paul was blameless.

However, the righteousness that comes from God is the righ-teousness that comes through faith in Christ. This righteousness is that holiness of heart and renewal of the soul in all its desires, dis-positions, and affections—and it comes from God. It is his work, not ours. It comes through faith in Christ, by his divine revelation to us. We acquire his blessing through his blood, and it is effective through faith. It is by faith alone that we obtain the remission of our sins and an inheritance among those that are sanctified.

23. "Strive first for the kingdom of God" in your hearts. Seek this righteousness, which is the gift and work of God, the image of God renewed in your souls. Then God will give you all things needed for the body. He apportions to us what is best for us, as well as what will best advance his kingdom. God gives us all that we need, in addition to his saving grace. In seeking the peace and the love of God, you will find both in what you most immediate-ly seek—"a kingdom that cannot be shaken." You will also receive the material things that you do not seek primarily, except as they pertain to the kingdom of God and his righteousness.

On your way to God's kingdom, you will find all the outward things that are appropriate for you. God has taken this responsibility upon himself, so "cast all your anxiety on him." He knows your needs. Whatever you lack, he will not fail to supply.

24. Jesus said, "Do not worry about tomorrow." Do not worry about

> Storing up treasures on earth,
> Increasing in worldly things,
> Procuring more food than you can eat,
> Getting more clothing than you can wear, or
> Gaining more money than is required from day to day
> for the simple, reasonable purposes of life.

Do not even worry about those things that are absolutely required for the body. Do not trouble yourself today with worry about what you will do at a time that is still far away. Perhaps that time will never come, or if it does come it may not be any concern of yours. Before that time arrives, you may have passed through the entire storm and be in eternity.

All those distant scenes do not belong to you who are only creatures of a day. More strictly speaking, what have you to do with tomorrow? Why should you trouble yourself unnecessarily? Today, God provides for you what you need to sustain the life that he has given you. It is enough. Give yourself up into his hands. If you live another day, God will provide for that day as well.

25. Above all, do not make your concern for the future an excuse for neglecting present duty. This mistake is the most fatal way of "worrying about tomorrow." How common this tendency is among us all! If we admonish people to "have a clear conscience toward God and all people" and to "abstain from every form of evil," they complain. They do not hesitate to reply, "How then are we to live? Should we not take care of ourselves and of our families?" They assume that this worry is a sufficient reason for continuing in known, willful sin.

They say (and perhaps believe) that they would serve God in the present if it were not that in doing so they would eventually go hungry. They would prepare for eternity, but they are afraid of lacking present necessities. Therefore, they serve the devil for a piece of bread, and they rush into hell for fear of going without what they need to sustain their physical lives. They forfeit their barren souls for fear that they might some time or other fall short of what they need for their bodies.

It is not strange that those who take matters out of God's hands should so often fail to receive the very things they seek. They relinquish heaven to secure the things of earth, with the result that they lose the one and fail to gain the other. The watchful God, in the wise course of his providence, frequently allows this very thing to occur. Those who refuse to cast their anxieties on God and worry about temporal things, having little concern for eternal matters, lose the very things they have chosen. There is a visible blight on all their efforts. Whatever they do, it fails to prosper. After they have forsaken God for the world, they lose what they sought, as well as what they did not seek. They fall short of the kingdom of God and his righteousness, and the other things are not added to them.

26. There is another way that we "worry about tomorrow," and it is an attitude which these words of Jesus also forbid. It is possible to concern ourselves wrongly even with spiritual things. We can be so vigilant about what may come in the future that we neglect what is required of us now. If we are not continually in prayer, how unknowingly we can slide into this mistake! How easily are we carried away in a kind of waking dream, projecting far away schemes and drawing fine pictures in our own imagination! We think about what good we will do when we are in such a place or when a certain time arrives! We dream about how useful we will be and how abundant will be our good works when we have more comfortable circumstances! We think of how earnestly we will serve God once a certain obstacle is taken out of the way!

Perhaps even now your soul is depressed. It is as though God is hiding his face from you. You see little of the radiance of his face, and you cannot sense his redeeming love. In such a state of mind it is natural to say, "O how I will praise God when the light of his countenance shall be again lifted up upon my soul! How I will exhort others to praise him when his love is again poured into my heart! Then, I will do so and so; I will speak for God in all places; I will not be ashamed of the gospel of Christ. Then, I will make the most of the time and use to the uttermost every ability I have received."

Do not believe what you are telling yourself. You will not do these things then if you do not do them now. "Whoever is faithful in a very little is faithful also in much," whether in worldly matters or in the reverence or love of God. But if you now hide one talent in the ground, you will then hide five. You assume that God will give these talents to you, but there is little reason to expect that he ever will. Indeed, "to those who have" (that is, those who *use* what they have) "more will be given, and they will have an abundance. But from those who have nothing" (that is, who do not use the grace which they have already received, whether a smaller or greater measure), "even what they have will be taken away."

27. Furthermore, do not fret about the temptations of tomorrow. To do so is also a dangerous snare. Do not ponder, "When some temptation comes, what will I do? How will I stand against it? I feel that I do not have the power to resist. I will not be able to conquer that enemy." It is entirely true that you do not *now* have the power that you do not presently need. At this time, you are not able to conquer that enemy because at this time you are not under assault. With the grace you now have, you could not withstand the temptations that you do not presently face. But when the temptation comes, the grace will come. In greater trials you will have greater strength. When sufferings abound, God's comfort will also abound in the same proportion. Therefore, in every situation the grace of God will be sufficient for you. "God will not let you be tested beyond your strength, but with the testing he will also provide the way out so that you may be able to endure it." "As your days, so is your strength."

28. Jesus said, therefore, "Do not worry about tomorrow, for tomorrow will bring worries of its own." That is, when tomorrow comes, deal with it then. Live your life today. Let it be your fervent concern to make the most of the present hour. This hour belongs to you, and it is all you have. The past is as nothing; it is

as though it had never been. The future is not your present concern. And perhaps it never will be. You cannot depend on what is yet to come, because "you do not know what a day may bring." Therefore live this present day. Do not lose an hour. Use this moment, because it is your portion. Who among us knows the things prior to our existence and what will take place after we are gone?

Where now are the generations that were from the beginning of the world? They have fled away, and they are forgotten. They once were; they had their day. Now, they are swept off the earth, as leaves from trees. They crumbled away into common dust. One group of people after another succeeded them. "They will go to the company of their ancestors, who will never again see the light." Now, it is your turn to live upon the earth.

Rejoice, young man, while you are young,
and let your heart cheer you in the days of your youth. (Eccles. 11:9)

Enjoy the very present, and delight in God whose years never fail. Here and now, let your eye be singly fixed on him "with whom there is no variation or shadow due to change." This moment, give him your heart; fix yourself on him; be holy, as he is holy. Just now, seize the blessed opportunity to do his "good and acceptable and perfect will." At this time, rejoice to suffer the loss of all things so that you will gain Christ.

29. For the sake of Christ, gladly undergo today whatever he permits to come upon you. But do not worry about the sufferings of tomorrow. "Tomorrow will bring worries of its own." "Worry" is a term commonly used to refer to tomorrow's abuse, need, pain, or sickness. However, in God's language, everything is his blessing. It is a precious ointment prepared by the wisdom of God, and variously bestowed to his children according to the different needs of their souls. God gives in one day what is adequate for that day, proportioned to our needs and strengths. Therefore, if you grasp today what belongs to tomorrow and add it to what you already have, it will become more than you can bear. This way of acting is not the way to heal your soul; it is the way to destroy it.

Therefore, take just as much as God gives you now. Today, permit God's will in your life, and do it. In the present, surrender yourself—body, soul, and spirit—to God, through Christ Jesus. Desire nothing more than for God to be glorified in all you are, do, and endure. Seek nothing except to know God and his Son Jesus Christ, through the Eternal Spirit. Pursue nothing except to love him, serve him, and enjoy him—in this hour and to all eternity!

Now unto God the Father, who has made me and all the world, unto God the Son, who has redeemed me and all humankind, unto God the Holy Spirit, who sanctifies me and all the elect people of God: be honor and praise, majesty and dominion forever and ever! Amen.

Notes

1. Ward and Heitzenrater, *Wesley's Journal and Diaries,* October 26-7, 1772, 22:350.
2. *Explanatory Notes upon the New Testament,* Matt. 6:24.
3. *Explanatory Notes upon the New Testament,* Matt. 6:31.
4. St. Augustine, *The City of God,* viii. 17.
5. Sirach 2:12.
6. Wisdom of Solomon 2:23.

UPON OUR LORD'S SERMON ON THE MOUNT

Discourse 10

According to John Wesley's analysis of the Sermon on the Mount, the fifth chapter of Matthew deals with how our attitudes affect all aspects of life. In that chapter, Jesus explains that real religion is a matter of the heart. Proper attitudes and dispositions constitute the core of true religion, and they shape everything that we say and do. The sixth chapter of Matthew deals with the way Christ's followers live in the world. That chapter shows how our attitudes express themselves in daily life. Finally, in the seventh chapter of Matthew Jesus discusses the hindrances to holiness, and he encourages us to overcome these impediments in order to secure the fullness of God's blessings and rewards.

The first hindrance to true religion is the tendency to judge others. This sin is one of the easiest to commit, and its consequences are destructive. In the *Minutes of Several Conversations between the Rev. Mr. Wesley and Others,* the British Conference of Methodist preachers identified judging as the major source of division between Christians:

> We are not Seceders [those who separate from the church], nor do
> we bear any resemblance to them. We set out upon quite opposite

principles. The Seceders laid the very foundation of their work in judging and condemning others: We laid the foundation of our work in judging and condemning ourselves. They begin everywhere with showing their hearers how fallen the Church and Ministers are: We begin everywhere with showing our hearers how fallen they are themselves.[1]

Ultimately, we must refrain from judging others because Jesus Christ is the only proper judge.

Wesley states that judging others can easily lead to condemning innocent people. We seldom know all the facts about the people and circumstances which we judge. Those who pass judgment on others often denounce the innocent and assign more blame to the guilty than they deserve. Thus, Wesley advises, "Judge not any man without full, clear, certain knowledge, without absolute necessity, without tender love."[2] In the end, judging others is thinking about them in ways that are contrary to love.

This sermon also explains the command of Jesus, "Do not give what is holy to dogs; and do not throw your pearls before swine." Wesley approaches this scripture first by cautioning us against assuming that other persons deserve to be put into the category of "dogs" or "swine." However, when it is clear that others are set against, or disobedient to, God, Wesley tells us how to deal with them. He speaks of the tendency of Christians (especially new converts) to fall into excessive zealousness. Immature Christians, in their enthusiasm, sometimes "offer what is holy" to persons who are not ready to hear their message or witness.

Wesley, of course, allows no room for compromise in sharing the gospel—Christians must declare the full truth of the scriptures. However, in working with others, Christians should remain alert to people's differing states of spiritual readiness. Wesley advises, "Christians should not press the gospel on those that are not interested; rather, Christians should guide unbelievers as far as they are able to receive the truth." Excessive and insensitive zeal injures both the one who witnesses and the one to whom the witness is given.

The sermon closes with an encouragement to Christians never to lose hope when people reject their witness or turn against them.

Prayer is the highest form of ministry to those who do not understand the gospel, neglect truth, or oppose the Christian message. Only through prayerful intercession do Christians find the wisdom, strength, and courage to do God's work. The sermon gives abundant hope to those who continue in prayer: "If you then, who are evil, know how to give good gifts to your children, how much more will your Father in heaven give good things to those who ask him!"

Wesley insists that prayer must be combined with love. And the proof of love lies in complete obedience to the command of Jesus regarding the proper way to treat others: "In everything do to others as you would have them do to you; for this is the law and the prophets." Wesley summed up this verse by saying, "The whole is comprised in one word, imitate the God of love."[3]

Sermon 30

UPON OUR LORD'S SERMON ON THE MOUNT

Discourse 10

"Do not judge, so that you may not be judged. For with the judgment you make you will be judged, and the measure you give will be the measure you get. Why do you see the speck in your neighbor's eye, but do not notice the log in your own eye? Or how can you say to your neighbor, 'Let me take the speck out of your eye,' while the log is in your own eye? You hypocrite, first take the log out of your own eye, and then you will see clearly to take the speck out of your neighbor's eye. Do not give what is holy to dogs; and do not throw your pearls before swine, or they will trample them under foot and turn and maul you. Ask, and it will be given you; search, and you will find; knock, and the door will be opened for you. For everyone who asks receives, and everyone who searches finds, and for everyone who knocks, the door will be opened. Is there anyone among you who, if your child asks for bread, will give a stone? Or if the child asks for a fish, will give a snake? If you then, who are evil, know how to give good gifts to your children, how much more will your

Father in heaven give good things to those who ask him! In everything do to others as you would have them do to you; for this is the law and the prophets."   *(Matthew 7:1-12)*

1 In Matthew chapters 6 and 7, our blessed Lord completed his principal plan for his Sermon on the Mount. First, he set forth the sum of true religion. He carefully guarded against those human commentaries that would negate the real sense of the word of God. Next, he set forth the rules that make right attitudes the only proper basis for establishing outward actions. Then, he moved on to point out the main hindrances to true religion. Finally, he concluded with an appropriate application.

2. In the fifth chapter of Matthew's Gospel our Great Teacher fully described inward religion in its various aspects. There, he laid before us those spiritual attitudes that constitute genuine Christianity. These attitudes constitute "the holiness without which no one will see the Lord." Jesus spoke about those affections that God accepts as intrinsically and essentially good when they flow from their proper source, which is an active faith in God through Christ Jesus. Likewise, in the sixth chapter of Matthew's Gospel Jesus explained how pure and holy intentions enable all our actions (even those that are morally neutral) to become holy, good, and acceptable to God. Jesus declared that God does not value anything we do apart from pure and holy intentions. However, he greatly values all works that we sincerely consecrate to God.

3. In the early part of this chapter, Jesus points out the most common and fatal hindrances to genuine holiness. In the latter part of the chapter, by various incentives, Jesus exhorts us to overcome all obstacles and secure "the goal for the prize of the heavenly call of God in Christ Jesus."

4. The first hindrance to holiness against which Jesus warns is *judging*. He said, "Do not judge, so that you may not be judged." Do not judge others, so that God will not judge you with vengeance heaped upon your heads. "For with the judgments you

make you will be judged, and the measure you give will be the measure you get." This rule is clear and fair. God permits you to determine for yourselves how he will pass judgment on you in the coming Great Day.

5. From the hour of our first repenting and believing the gospel until we are made perfect in love, there is no level of life or period of time when every child of God does not need this warning. Opportunities to judge others are never lacking, and temptations to judge are innumerable. Many of them are so shrewdly disguised that we fall into the sin of judging before we suspect any danger.

The evils produced by judging others are inexpressible. Harm always comes to those who judge others. They wound their own souls and subject themselves to the righteous judgment of God. Frequently, those who are the objects of judgment acquire "drooping hands"—that is, they are weakened and hindered in their pilgrimage. They may even be completely turned from the way and caused to draw back into damnation. Yes, how often when a "root of bitterness springs up," many "become defiled." This falling away means that "the way of truth will be maligned" and some will "blaspheme the excellent name that was invoked over them."

6. Even so, it does not appear that our Lord directed this caution only, or chiefly, to the children of God. Rather, it is intended for the children of the world who do not know God. Non-Christians cannot avoid hearing about those who are not of this world, and they cannot help knowing about those who follow after the religion described above. Those who are not Christians are aware of those who attempt to be humble, serious, gentle, merciful, and pure in heart. These Christians sincerely desire the measures of these holy virtues that they have not yet attained. They expectantly wait to have them, and they do good to all people and patiently endure evil. Any who live this way cannot remain concealed any more than can "a city built on a hill."

Is there a reason why unbelievers fail " to see Christians' good works and give glory to their Father in heaven"? What excuse do they have for not following in their steps? Why do they not imitate their example and follow them as they follow Christ? The reason is that unbelievers excuse themselves by condemning those that they ought to imitate. They spend their time searching for their neighbor's faults, instead of correcting their own. They are so engrossed about others straying from the way that Christ taught that they themselves never come into it at all. At least, they never advance beyond a paltry, dead form of godliness without its *power.*

7. Most especially, it is to these people that our Lord says, "Why do you see the speck in your neighbor's eye" (the infirmities, mistakes, carelessness, and weakness of God's children), "but do not notice the log in your own eye?" You do not think about your wicked lack of repentance, satanic pride, accursed self-will, and idolatrous love of the world in you. These things make your entire life an abomination to the Lord. Above all, with what sleepy carelessness and indifference you are dancing over the mouth of hell! With what kind of favor, decency, or modesty will you say to another, "Let me take the speck out of your eye"?

The "speck" that you criticize is excessive zeal for God, exceptional self-denial, too much detachment from worldly cares and activities, the desire to pray without ceasing, and listening to the words of eternal life. And observe that a log is in your own eye. Not just specks such as you criticize in those who are seeking after God! You hypocrite! You pretend to care for others, and you have no concern for your own soul. You make a display of zeal for God's cause, when in reality you neither love nor honor him!

First, take the log of stubbornness out of your own eye. Understand who you really are. See and feel that you are a sinner. Perceive that inwardly you are very wicked and that you are altogether corrupt and disgusting. Understand that God's wrath rests on you. Take out the log of your pride. Despise yourself. Sink down, as it were, in dust and ashes. Increasingly, become small, low, unworthy, and evil in your own eyes. Take out the log of self-will. Learn the meaning of these words: "If any want to become my followers, let them deny themselves and take up their cross daily and follow me." Let your entire soul cry out, "I have come down from heaven" (for so you did, you deathless spirit, whether or not you know it), "not to do my own will, but the will of him who sent me."

Take out the log of love for the world. "Do not love the world or the things in the world." Become crucified to the world, and let the world become crucified to you. Use the world, but *enjoy* God. Seek all your happiness in him. Above all, cast out the main log—your sleepy carelessness and indifference. Profoundly consider: "There is need of only one thing"—the one thing that you have hardly ever thought about.

Comprehend and feel that you are a poor, evil, guilty parasite, shuddering over the great gulf! What are you? You are a sinner born to die, a leaf driven before the wind, a cloud ready to vanish, just appearing and then dispersed into air where "no trace can be found!" Understand this message: "First take the log out of your own eye, and then you will see clearly to take the speck out of your neighbor's eye." Only then, if you have spare time from the concerns of your own soul, you will know how to correct your neighbor also.

8. But what is the correct meaning of this command, "Do not judge?" What kind of judging is forbidden here? It is not the same as *slander*, although the two are often joined together. Slander is saying anything evil about an absent person. Judging another, however, applies to what we say about others, whether or not they are present or absent. Furthermore, judging does not refer only to speaking; judging has to do with *thinking* evil about another person.

The judgment to which our Lord refers here does not include *every* kind of thinking evil. If I see someone commit robbery or murder or hear him revile God's name, I cannot avoid thinking evil about the robber or murderer. However, such thoughts are not to be confused with the judging that Jesus condemned. This realistic appraisal is not evil judging, and it is not sinful or contrary to sympathetic affection.

9. The judging that Jesus condemns here is thinking about another person in a way that is contrary to love. And there are various kinds of sinful judging. First, we may think that another person is guilty, when he or she is not. We may charge others (at least in our own minds) with things of which they are not guilty. We may attribute to them words that they have never spoken, or

247

actions that they have never done. We may think that the way they act is wrong, although in truth it is not wrong. We may assume that another's intention was not good (either in the act itself or in the way in which it was done), even when there is nothing that can properly be faulted. We condemn the person, while at the same time God who searches the heart sees the person's holiness and godly sincerity.

10. Second, we may not only fall into the sin of judging by our condemnation of innocent people, but also by condemning the guilty to a higher degree than they deserve. This kind of judging is an offense against justice and mercy. It is the sort of transgression that we can avoid only by the deepest and kindest affection. Without it, we quickly assume that those who are clearly at fault are more in the wrong than they really are. We underestimate the good that is within them. Indeed, we are not easily convinced that anything good can reside in those in whom we find some wrong.

11. This kind of judging reveals an obvious lack of the kind of love that is "not resentful." Such love never draws an unfair or unkind conclusion from any assumption whatever. When a person one time falls into an act of open sin, love will not infer from it that the person is habitually guilty of the sin or that he or she regularly commits it. Even if at one time others were habitually guilty of the sin, love does not conclude that they are still guilty. And most certainly, love will not assume that a person who is presently guilty of a sin is also guilty of other sins as well. These evil inferences are all examples of the sinful judging from which our Lord protects us. If we love God and our own souls, we will be preeminently concerned to avoid this kind of judging.

12. Let us suppose that we do not judge innocent people and that we judge the guilty no more than they deserve. We still may not be completely free from the snare of judging. There is a third kind of sinful judging—faulting anyone else without sufficient evidence. Even if what we assume about another is true, we are not free from guilt. The facts should not be merely assumed; they must be proved. And until they are proved, we should not form any judgment.

Even if the facts about another person are ever so strong, we must not pass sentence on him or her until we have clear proof of wrongdoing. First, we must compare this proof of guilt with the evidence of innocence. Moreover, we should not judge other people before they are allowed to speak in their self-defense.

Even Jewish law teaches us this principle—it is a simple matter of fairness drawn from mercy and fraternal love. Nicodemus asked this question: "Our law does not judge people without first giving them a hearing to find out what they are doing, does it?" Indeed, when the chief of the Jewish nation wanted a judgment against a prisoner, even a heathen could say, "Is it not the custom of the Romans to hand over anyone before the accused has met the accusers face to face and has been given an opportunity to make a defense against the charge?"

13. Indeed, we would not easily fall into sinful judging if we only observed the rule that another of those heathen Romans assert to have been their standard. Seneca said, "I am so far from easily believing every man's or any man's evidence against another, that I do not easily or immediately believe a man's evidence against himself. I always let him have second thoughts, and many times counsel as well." You who are called Christians, "go and do likewise." Otherwise, even the heathen "will rise up at the judgment and condemn you."

14. How seldom would we condemn or judge one another (at least how soon would that evil be remedied) if we followed the clear and explicit rule that our Lord has taught us himself! He said, "If another member of the church sins against you" (or if you hear or believe that he or she has) "go and point out the fault when the two of you are alone." This step is the first one you are to take.

Jesus continues, "If the member listens to you, you have regained that one. But if you are not listened to, take one or two others along with you, so that every word may be confirmed by the evidence of two or three witnesses." This step is the second one you should take. Next, Jesus concludes, "If the member refuses to listen to them, tell it to the church." Take your concern either to the leaders or to the whole congregation. Finally, you have done your part, so think no more about it. Give the entire matter to God.

15. Suppose, by the grace of God, that you have "taken the log out of your own eye," and now "see clearly the speck in your neighbor's eye." Watch that you yourself do not receive harm by trying to help him. Jesus said, "Do not give what is holy to dogs." Exercise caution that you do not fail to reckon that other persons might be among that number. If it is clear that they are, "do not throw your pearls before swine." Avoid zeal that is not enlightened. Unenlightened enthusiasm is a serious hindrance in the way of those who would be "perfect as their heavenly Father is perfect."

Those who hunger for God's fullest blessings cannot help wanting everyone else to have the same benefits. And when we ourselves first partake of God's heavenly gift—the divine "conviction of things not seen"—we are amazed that everyone does not see the things that we now see so clearly. We are confident that we will open the eyes of everyone with whom we have any association. Immediately, we want to confront all the people that we meet and compel them to open their spiritual eyes, whether they want to or not. And by the failures of our excessive zeal, we often suffer in our own souls.

To prevent our squandering our energies in vain, our Lord adds a necessary warning, needed by all, but especially by those that are aglow with their first love. Jesus cautioned, "Do not give what is holy to dogs; and do not throw your pearls before swine, or they will trample them underfoot and turn and maul you."

16. Let us examine the counsel of Jesus: "Do not give what is holy to dogs." Be careful not to think that anyone deserves to be designated a "dog" until there is full and indisputable proof of the kind that cannot be denied. However, it may be that there is clear and positive proof that they are unholy and wicked people, strangers to God, and enemies to him and to "true righteousness and holiness." In that case, you should not offer them what is holy. We are not to present to them the holy and unique doctrines of the gospel, those that were "hidden throughout the ages and generations" and "have now been revealed" by the revelation of Jesus Christ and the inspiration of his Holy Spirit. They "have not even heard that there is a Holy Spirit."

Of course, the representatives of Christ cannot refrain from declaring gospel truth when the congregation meets in church where some that oppose the truth will probably be present. We must declare the truth, whether people will hear or refrain from hearing. However, such is not the case with individual Christians. They do not bear that awful responsibility and they are not under a formal obligation to commend these great and glorious truths to those who contradict and blaspheme them and have a fixed enmity against them. No, these Christians should not press the gospel on those who are not interested. Rather, Christians should guide unbelievers as far as they are able to receive the truth.

Do not begin a dialogue with unbelievers with talk about the remission of sins and the gift of the Holy Spirit. Rather, talk with them in their own way of talking and build on their own beliefs. With the rational, honorable, unjust lover of pleasure, talk about "justice, self-control, and the coming judgment." This approach is the best possible way to make "Felix tremble." Reserve higher subjects for persons that are more spiritually advanced.

17. Let us look at our Lord's instruction: "Do not throw your pearls before swine." Be very reluctant to judge another person as being a "swine." However, if the swine do not attempt to disguise themselves, it is obvious, undeniable, and beyond question who they are. They rejoice in their shame, make no claim to purity of heart or life, and do all kinds of unclean and greedy things. Do not throw your pearls before them. Do not talk with them about the "mysteries of the kingdom" or about "what no eye has seen, nor ear heard." Because of their spiritual blindness, they have no sources of spiritual understanding; it cannot enter their hearts to conceive of God's mysteries. Do not tell them about the "precious and very great promises" that God has given us in his beloved Son.

What understanding can those have that do not even desire to "escape from the corruption that is in the world because of lust"? What grasp would they have of being made "participants of the divine nature"? They do not understand the value of God's truth any more than swine understand the value of pearls. The amount of attraction that hogs have for pearls is the amount of attraction that those immersed in the mire of this world and in worldly pleasures, desires, and worries have for the deep things of God and the mysteries of the gospel.

Do not throw your pearls before them, for fear that they will trample God's truth under their feet. They might completely despise what they cannot understand and speak evil of the things they do not grasp. It is likely that their rejection of the gospel is not the only serious problem that would follow. It would not be unusual if (true to their nature) they would "turn and maul you." It is likely that they will return evil to you for the good you offered them. They will probably return cursing for blessing and hatred for your goodwill. "The mind that is set on the flesh is hostile to God" and all the things of God. You can expect the same treatment from these worldly-minded people if you offer them the "unforgivable insult" of trying to save their souls from death and snatch them as burning sticks from the fire!

18. Still, you need not completely lose hope for those who now turn against you. Even if all your arguments and inducements fail, there yet remains another remedy, and it is often effective when no other method succeeds. This remedy is *prayer*. So the third grand hindrance of holiness is our neglect of prayer. Therefore, whatever you desire or need, either for others or for your own soul, "Ask, and it will be given you; search, and you will find; knock, and the door will be opened for you." "You do not have, because you do not ask."

O how meek and gentle, humble in heart, full of love to God and others you might have become by now if you had only asked and "persevered in prayer!" At least, starting now, "Ask, and it will be given you." Ask that you may experience in detail and perfectly practice every aspect of the religion that our Lord has so beautifully described in the Sermon on the Mount. It will be given to you in your heart and all your conduct to "be holy, as God is holy."

Seek in the way that God has established—searching the scriptures, hearing his word, meditating on it, fasting, and partaking of the Lord's Supper. Assuredly, "Seek and you will find." You will find "the one pearl of great value." You will find "the faith that conquers the world," the peace that the world cannot give, and the love that is "the pledge of our inheritance toward redemption as God's own people."

Keep on knocking. Continue in prayer and in all the ways of the Lord. Do not "grow weary in doing what is right" or "lose heart." Press on toward the goal. Accept no refusal to your requests. Do not turn loose of God until he blesses you. Continue to "ask, search, and knock," and the doors of mercy, holiness, and heaven "will be opened."

19. Out of compassion for our hard hearts that are so unprepared to believe the goodness of God, our Lord generously amplifies his point. He repeats and confirms what he has already promised: "Everyone who asks receives." No one needs to come short of the blessing. Everyone who searches will find the love and the image of God. And for everyone who knocks, the gates of righteousness will be opened.

Consequently, in view of these promises, there is no room for anyone to be discouraged. We should not even think that we might ask, or search, or knock in vain. Just remember, "You need to pray always and not to lose heart." When you pray, God's promises stand firm. They are as reliable as the pillars of heaven. Indeed, God's promises are even more unshakable, because "Heaven and earth will pass away, but God's words will not pass away."

20. To cut off every excuse for unbelief, in the verses that follow our blessed Lord illustrates still further what he said about asking, searching, and knocking. He appeals to the natural instincts of every one of us. Jesus asked, "Is there anyone among you who, if your child asks for bread, will give a stone?" Will natural affection permit you to refuse the reasonable request of a child that you love? Jesus continued, "If the child asks for a fish, will you give him a snake?" Will a parent give a child something harmful instead of something beneficial? From what you yourselves feel and do, you can gain the most abundant assurance that when you petition God he will hear your prayer and fully supply your needs.

Jesus concluded, "If you then, who are evil, know how to give good gifts to your children, how much more will your Father in heaven give good things to those who ask him!" God is pure, absolute, quintessential goodness. On another occasion, Jesus said, "If you then, who are evil, know how to give good gifts to your children, how much more will the heavenly Father give the Holy Spirit to those who ask him!" All good things are in the Holy Spirit—complete wisdom, peace, joy, love; and all the treasures of holiness and happiness—everything that God has prepared for those who love him.

21. Maintain love for all people, so that your prayer will have its full influence with God. Without love, your seeking, searching, and knocking are more likely to bring you a curse than a blessing. You cannot expect to receive any blessing from God while you do not demonstrate love for your neighbor. Therefore, without delay let the hindrance of an unloving heart be removed from you. Confirm your love toward one another and toward all people. And love them not only "in word or speech, but in truth and action." Jesus said, "In everything do to others as you would have them do to you; for this is the law and the prophets."

22. Love is the "royal law," the Golden Rule of mercy and justice. Even the heathen emperor, Alexander Severus,[4] ordered this rule to be inscribed over the gate of his palace. Many people believe that the Golden Rule naturally enlightens the mind of everyone that comes into the world. At least, this much is certain: As soon as this rule is heard, it commends itself to everyone's moral sense and discernment. We cannot knowingly break this rule without bringing ourselves under self-accusation.

23. Jesus said that this rule is the message of "the law and the prophets." The directive is the substance of whatever is written in the law that God revealed to humankind in ancient times, and in all the principles "that God announced long ago through his holy prophets." Everything in the law and prophets can be condensed in this short maxim: "In everything do to others as you would have them do to you." Rightly understood, this command comprises the entire religion that our Lord came to establish upon the earth.

24. This rule can be understood in either a positive or negative sense. If understood in a negative way, the meaning is, "Whatever you do not want others to do to you, do not do to them." Here is a simple rule that is constantly at hand and always easy to apply. In all circumstances connected with your neighbors, consider their circumstances to be your own. Conjecture that the circumstances were changed and that you were in your neighbor's place. Take caution that you assume no attitude or opinion, do nothing, and take no step that you would condemn in others if they were in your place. If we apply this rule in a direct and positive sense, its clear meaning is, "Whatever you could reasonably expect of others if you were in their circumstances, to the best of your ability act this way toward every other human being."

25. Let us apply this rule in one or two clear examples. It is certain to everyone that we would not want others readily to judge us or unjustly to think evil about us. Much less would we want anyone to malign us or spread abroad our real faults and infirmities. Apply this standard to yourself. Do nothing to others that you would not want them to do to you, and you will never judge your neighbors. Never think evil of neighbors quickly or without cause. And certainly you will not slander others. You will never mention even the real failings of an absent person, unless you are convinced that doing so is absolutely necessary for the good of other people.

26. As another example, we want everyone to love us, respect us, and treat us fairly, mercifully, and truthfully. It is reasonable for us to expect them to do all the good for us they can without harming themselves. According to this rule, in outward things their surpluses should be directed to our comfort, and their comforts to our need, and their needs to our desperate emergencies. Let us live by the same rule. Let us do to all people as we want them to do to us. Let us love and honor everyone. Let justice, mercy, and truth govern your minds and actions. Let your surpluses give way to your neighbors' comfort. (Who would then have any surpluses remaining?) Let your comforts give way to your neighbors' needs, and your needs to their desperate emergencies.

27. This way of living constitutes spotless and genuine morality. Do these things and you will live. As for those who will follow this rule,—peace be upon them, and mercy; for they are "the Israel of God." But recognize that unless we first love God we cannot live by the rule that calls us to love our neighbors as ourselves (nor has anyone ever been able to do so). And we cannot love God unless we believe in Christ and have redemption through his blood. The Spirit of God must bear witness with our spirits that we are children of God.

Therefore, faith is still the foundation of all true religion and of present and future salvation. Always, we must say to every sinner, "Believe on the Lord Jesus, and you will be saved." You will be saved now, so that you can be saved forever—saved on earth so that you can be saved in heaven. Believe in Jesus Christ, and your faith will work through love. You will love the Lord your God because he has loved you, and you will love your neighbor as you love yourself. Then, it will be your honor and joy to exercise this love and grow in it. You will not merely abstain from what is contrary to love, such as every unkind thought, word, and deed. You will also bestow all the kindness upon everyone that you want them to show to you.

Notes

1. Jackson, *Wesley's Works*, 8:321.
2. *Explanatory Notes upon the New Testament*, Matt. 7:1.
3. *Explanatory Notes upon the New Testament*, Matt. 7:11.
4. Roman Emperor, 222–235.
5. Wisdom of Solomon 5:9-14.

UPON OUR LORD'S SERMON ON THE MOUNT

Discourse 11

This discourse continues the teaching of Jesus about those things that obstruct the spiritual progress of his disciples. Having dealt with inward sin, the Sermon on the Mount next turns to the outward pressures of bad examples and poor advice. Jesus declared that there are two contrasting ways—the wide gate opening to an easy road and the narrow gate that leads to a hard road. He said that most people follow the easy way that leads to destruction and that only a few enter the narrow gate and take the hard road that leads to eternal life.

This sermon also examines the teaching of Jesus about the way of death and the way of life. Wesley preached this message often, addressing it to congregations consisting of wealthy and privileged people and to congregations consisting of poor and neglected people. On one occasion he recorded in his journal, "I preached at Doncaster, in one of the most elegant Houses in England, and to one of the most elegant congregations. They seemed greatly astonished; and well they might; for I scarce ever spoke so strongly on, 'Strait is the gate, and narrow is the way, that leadeth unto life.'"[1] On another occasion he wrote, "The evening congregation at Greencock was exceeding large. I opened and enforced these awful words, 'Strait is the gate, and narrow is the way, that lead-eth unto life.' I know not that ever I spoke more strongly. And some fruit of it quickly appeared; for the House, twice as large as that at Glasgow, was thoroughly filled at five in the morning."[2]

Here, Wesley instructs and encourages Christ's followers to overcome all the obstacles that would cause them to turn back into the world system. He divides this discourse into three "heads." (1) The Lord's clear explanation of the essential charac-teristics of the wide gate and easy road that lead to destruction. (2) The Lord's solemn teaching about the essential characteristics of the narrow gate and the hard road. (3) The Lord's inspiring appeal to enter through the narrow gate and travel the hard road that leads to eternal life.

This sermon also contains a severe warning to the City of London—an admonition that applies to any secularized culture. The moral contamination left in the wake of the reign of King Charles II was shockingly evident throughout England, especially among the upper classes. Wesley exclaims, "Although it is with shame and sorrow that we have to admit it, we cannot deny that even in this Christian nation many are walking in the way of destruction. The majority of every age, gender, vocation, occupa-tion, rank, and social station are taking the broad way that leads to death."

In 1724, just before Wesley began his public ministry, the Bishop of Lichfield preached before the Society for the Reformation of Manners. That sermon confirms Wesley's assess-ment of the low state of public morals. The bishop declared, "The Lord's day is now the devil's market day....Strong liquors are become the epidemic distemper of [London]....Sin, in general, is grown so hardened and rampant, as that immoralities are defended, yea, justified on principle. Obscene, wanton, and pro-fane books find so good a market as to encourage the trade of publishing them. Every kind of sin has found a writer to teach and vindicate it, and a bookseller and hawker to divulge and spread it."[3]

From Wesley's point of view, as bad as was the scandal of the sinful behavior of secular people, an even greater offense to God was the spiritual and theological apostasy within the established church. In 1713 a bishop reported, "The much greater part of those who come to be ordained are ignorant to a degree not to be apprehended by those who are not obliged to know it....They can give no account, or at least a very imperfect one, of the contents even of the gospel, or of the catechism itself." Canon John H. Overton said, "A low standard existed all round, and the clergy as a body rose a little, though only a very little, higher than the general level."[4] Historian John Stoughton wrote, "The public have long remarked with indignation that some of the most distinguished coxcombs [vain people], drunkards, debauchees, and gamesters...are young men of the sacerdotal order [clergymen]."[5]

Wesley deplored the state of affairs that existed in the nation and church, and here he speaks directly to these evils. He does not root his message in the cultural trends or religious vogues of his day. Indeed, he insists that dominant social currents are always contrary to the gospel of Christ. The sermon's message rests on the words of Jesus, which people cannot understand apart from the enlightening work of the Holy Spirit. Only by the light of God's word and the assistance of his Spirit can Christians rise above the deceitful words of blind leaders in the world and false teachers in the church. This sermon contains a powerful message for both a corrupt culture and an unfaithful clergy.

In a burst of passionate pleading, Wesley closes this discourse by saying, "Be roused with sorrow and shame for having traveled so long with the unthinking crowd, utterly neglecting if not despising the holiness without which no one will see the Lord....If necessary, be ready to cut off your right hand and to tear out your right eye and throw them away. Be ready to endure the loss of possessions, friends, and health, everything on earth in order to enter into the kingdom of heaven."

Sermon 31

UPON OUR LORD'S SERMON
ON THE MOUNT

Discourse 11

"Enter through the narrow gate; for the gate is wide and the road is easy that leads to destruction, and there are many who take it. For the gate is narrow and the road is hard that leads to life, and there are few who find it."

(Matthew 7:13-14)

1 Earlier in the Sermon on the Mount, our Lord warned us about the dangers that easily besiege us when we first enter into real religion. These obstacles naturally arise from *within* us, because they stem from the sinfulness of our own hearts. In this text, Jesus proceeds to acquaint us with the hindrances that come from *without*, particularly from bad examples and poor advice. These obstacles have caused thousands who once ran well to draw back into damnation. Indeed, many of those who fell from grace were not novices in religion; they had made some progress in righteousness. Therefore, with all possible seriousness our Lord urges caution upon us so that we become aware of these hindrances to

our faith. Out of his concern that we do not let his warning slip from our minds, he repeats himself in a variety of ways. Therefore, to protect us from bad examples, he said, "Enter through the narrow gate; for the gate is wide and the road is easy that leads to destruction, and there are many who take it. For the gate is narrow and the road is hard that leads to life, and there are few who find it." To protect us from bad advice, he said, "Beware of false prophets." Here, we will consider only the matter of bad advice.

2. Our blessed Lord said, "Enter through the narrow gate; for the gate is wide and the road is easy that leads to destruction, and there are many who take it. For the gate is narrow and the road is hard that leads to life, and there are few who find it."

3. In the first place, in these words Jesus showed us the central characteristics of the road to hell. He said, "The gate is wide and the road is easy that leads to destruction, and there are many who take it." Second, Jesus explained the central characteristics of the way to heaven: "The gate is narrow and the road is hard that leads to life, and there are few that find it." Third, Jesus added a serious appeal grounded on what he had described—"Enter through the narrow gate."

I. The wide gate and the easy road to hell

1. First, we can recognize the central characteristics of the road to hell: "The gate is wide and the road is easy that leads to destruction, and there are many who take it."

2. The gate to hell is sin and the road to hell is wickedness. How wide a gate to hell is the gate of sin! How broad the way to hell is the way of wickedness! God's law is extremely comprehensive. It extends to all our actions and to every word that arises within our hearts and falls from our lips. Sin is equally far-reaching, because any transgression of the law is sin. Indeed, sin is a thousand times more extensive than the law. There is only one way to keep God's law. However, we will fail to keep it properly unless our manner of keeping it and all the other circumstances are correct. There are a thousand ways to break every commandment, so sin is indeed a wide gate.

3. Let us consider this matter in more detail. Our basic sins reach out widely because they are the source of all the rest of our sins. Our basic sin is "the mind that is set on the flesh and hostile to God." It includes a proud heart, stubbornness, and the love of the world. Who can limit the bounds of these sins? Do they not permeate all our thoughts and blend into all our attitudes? Are they not, as it were, the leaven that permeates all our affections? On a close and faithful examination of ourselves, can we not perceive these roots of bitterness continually springing up, infecting all our words, and defiling all our actions? In every age and nation, how innumerable are the fruits produced by our basic sins! They are enough to cover the entire earth with "haunts of violence."

4. Who can possibly enumerate sin's loathsome fruits! Aside from the sins that our imagination might describe, who could add up all our sins against God and neighbor that are a daily experience of sadness to us all? We do not need to range throughout the earth to find them. Survey any kingdom, country, city, or town. How vast is the harvest of sin! It need not be an area still enveloped with Mohammedan or pagan darkness. Sin abounds in areas that name the name of Christ and profess to understand the light of his glorious gospel.

Go no farther than England, the kingdom to which we belong, or London, the city where we now are. We call ourselves Christians of the purest kind. We are Protestants and heirs of the Reformation. But what a pity! Who among us will apply our doctrines to our hearts and lives? Do we not need further reformation? How innumerable are our sins—sins of the deepest sort! From day to day, do not the most outrageous abominations of every kind abound in our midst? Do not sins of every description cover the land, as the waters cover the sea? Who can count them? It would be easier to count the drops of rain or the sands on the seashore. Certainly, it is true that the gate is wide and the road is easy that leads to death.

5. Concerning the road to destruction, Jesus said, "There are many who take it." Almost as many pass through the easy gate of destruction as those who die and "go down to the chambers of

death." Although it is with shame and sorrow that we have to admit it, we cannot deny that even in this Christian nation many are walking in the way of destruction. The majority of every age, gender, vocation, occupation, rank, and social station are taking the broad way that leads to death. Most of the inhabitants of this city even now live in sin. They engage in some blatant, habitual, and known transgression of the law they profess to observe. They sin outwardly in some variety of flagrant and visible irreverence, unrighteousness, or public violations of their duties to God and others. No one can deny that these people are all taking the way that leads to destruction.

Add to these people the number who "have a name of being alive," but have not yet come alive to God. Outwardly, to others they appear to be principled people. However, inwardly they are filled with all uncleanness. They are full of pride, conceit, anger, vindictiveness, appetite for fame, and greed. These people are lovers of themselves, lovers of the world, and "lovers of pleasure rather than lovers of God." They indeed may be highly esteemed by others, but they are an abomination to the Lord. And how greatly will these "saints of the world" increase the number of the children of hell! Then, add to these people those who have only "an outward form of godliness." They are "ignorant of the righteousness that comes from God, and, seeking to establish their own, they have not submitted to God's righteousness." Taking all these considerations together, how terribly true is our Lord's assertion: "The gate is wide and the road is easy that leads to destruction, and there are many who take it."

6. This dire declaration of Jesus concerns not only the common masses consisting of the poor, menial, foolish part of humankind. No indeed. Prominent people in the world who own much land and have many farm animals do not qualify to be exempt from the warning of Jesus. On the contrary, the world, the flesh, and the devil beckon many of those who are "wise by human standards, powerful, and of noble birth" onto the easy road. And they are not disobedient to that calling. Yes, the higher people are elevated in wealth and power, the deeper they sink into iniquity. The more blessings they receive from God, the more sins they commit. They

do not use their fame, wealth, learning, or wisdom as means for working out their salvation. Instead, they use these advantages to excel in corruption—and in so doing they ensure their own destruction.

II. The lure of the wide gate and easy road

1. The reason so many people continue so securely on the easy road is because it requires no effort to do so. People take the easy road, even if it is an essential feature of the way that leads to destruction. Our Lord said, "There are many who take it." They take the easy way for the very reason that they should flee from it: "The gate is narrow and the road is hard that leads to life, and there are few who find it."

2. This declaration of Jesus calls attention to an essential feature of the way to heaven. The gate that opens into everlasting life is so narrow that nothing unclean or unholy can pass through it. Sinners cannot enter that gate until they are saved from all their transgressions—not only from outward sins, but also from "the futile ways inherited from their ancestors." It is not enough that one "ceases to do evil, and learns to do good." We must not only be saved from all sinful actions and evil and useless talk. We must also be *inwardly* changed and "be renewed in the spirit of our minds." Otherwise, we cannot pass through the gate of life and enter into glory.

3. The narrow gate that leads to life is the way of entire sanctification. Narrow indeed is the way of poverty of spirit, holy mourning, meekness, and hungering and thirsting after righteousness. Narrow is the way of mercy, genuine love, heart purity, doing good to others, and willingly suffering all manner of evil for righteousness' sake.

4. Jesus said, "There are few who find life." It is a pity how few attain even natural morality (practiced by the heathen)! How small is the number of those who do to others as they would have them do in return. Before God, not many people are innocent of unjust and unkind acts! What small numbers of people have not "sinned with the tongue" and speak nothing unkind or untrue!

How small is the ratio of humankind who are innocent of outward transgressions! And proportionally how much smaller are the numbers of those whose hearts are right before God—clean and holy in his sight!

Where can we find those who God knows to be so truly humble that they repent in dust and ashes in the presence of God their Savior? Where are those who are deeply and constantly serious, sensing their needs, and "living in reverent fear during their time on earth?" Where can we find those who are truly meek and gentle and who are not "overcome by evil, but overcome evil with good"?

How few utterly thirst for God and continually yearn to be renewed in God's likeness. How sparsely spread over the earth are those whose souls are full of love for everyone, who love God with all their strength, who have given him their hearts, and "desire nothing other than him on earth or in heaven." How few are those lovers of God and humankind that spend their entire strength in doing good to everyone. They are the ones who are ready to endure all things, even death, to save a single soul from eternal ruin!

5. Because there are so few on the road that leads to life and there are so many on the road to destruction, there is immense danger that the flood of their example might carry us along with them. Even a single example, if it is always before us, is prone to make a strong impression upon us. A bad influence is especially powerful when it has human nature on its side and when it accords with our own desires. Therefore, strong are the forces of many examples constantly before us. They work together, along with the power of our own inclinations, to carry us down the stream of natural desires! How difficult it is to stop the tide and to keep ourselves "unstained by the world!"

6. The difficulty is intensified even more when the evil influences and bad examples that crowd the downward road do not come from coarse and unrefined people (not entirely at least). Instead, these influences come from polite, aristocratic, genteel, and wise people who understand the world. They are people of knowledge and wide learning; they are both intelligent and

articulate. All or nearly all of these people oppose our entering the narrow gate.

How can we stand against them? Do they not utter enticing words? Have they not learned all the skills of gentle persuasion? They are at home with debate and intellectual controversy, and they are skilled in logic. Because the broad way is easy, it is a simple thing for them to demonstrate that it is right. They insist that the one who follows the majority cannot be wrong; they say that those who will not follow them are misguided people. They argue that your way must be wrong because it is narrow and because there are few who take it. These people will present evidence that evil is good, and that good is evil. They claim that the way of holiness is the road to destruction and the way of the world is the only road to heaven.

7. How difficult it is for unlearned and uneducated people to sustain their cause against such opponents! People of influence, however, are not the only ones with whom we must contend. On the road to destruction there are many strong, impressive, powerful, and wise people who have a shorter way of refuting you than by use of reason and argument. Usually, they do not apply their methods to the intellect. Rather, they strike at the *fears* of all who differ from them. This method seldom fails to succeed, even if intellectual debate is not successful. Their approach is effective with persons of every level of ability. Everyone can easily succumb to fear, whether or not they are skilled at logic. All who lack a firm trust in God and a secure confidence in his power and love cannot avoid the fear of offending those who hold the power of the world in their hands. It would not be surprising to learn that the examples of powerful people are virtual laws to all who do not know God!

8. Likewise, many rich people follow the easy road themselves. Persons of wealth influence the hopes and foolish desires of many, just as strongly and effectively as powerful and highborn people influence their fears. You can scarcely remain on the road to God's kingdom if you are not dead to everything in the world. You must covet God alone and be crucified to the world and the world crucified to you.

9. How dismal, uncomfortable, and forbidding seems the landscape on the opposite road! A narrow gate! A hard road! Few peo-

ple enter that gate and travel that road! Among this minority of people who take the hard road there are not many erudite people of learning and eloquence. They cannot debate strongly or clearly, and they are not able to frame a compelling argument. They do not know how to prove what they profess to believe or even explain what they say they experience. Surely such witnesses will never win approval for the cause they profess. Instead, they discredit it.

10. Furthermore, they are not highborn, distinguished people. If they were titled and eminent people, you might have patience with them. But from the world's perspective, they are not notable people of respect, authority, or worth. They are unimportant, menial, lowborn, and if they wanted to harm you they lack the power to do so. Therefore, there is nothing at all to be feared or hoped from them. Most of them can say, "'I have no silver or gold;' at the most I have a very modest amount." In fact, some of them have insufficient food to eat or clothing to wear. Because of the humble circumstances of their lives and because they constitute a minority, they are widely ridiculed and disregarded. Their very names are considered evil; they are persecuted in different ways and treated as "the rubbish of the world, the dregs of all things." In the light of these realities, your fears, hopes, desires (except those which you have immediately from God), and natural instincts steadily influence you to return to the easy road.

III. Encouragements to enter the narrow gate and travel the hard road

1. In view of all these considerations, our Lord earnestly entreats us, "Enter through the narrow gate." The same entreaty appears in Luke's Gospel: "Strive to enter through the narrow door." Here, the phrase *strive to enter* means "strive as one in agony." Our Lord said, "Agonize . . . for many, I tell you, will try to enter and will not be able." In effect, Jesus was saying, "If you lazily attempt the hard road, you will not be able to enter into salvation."

2. In the words that immediately follow, Jesus suggested what might seem to be another reason that some will not be able to

enter in. He added this statement: "When once the owner of the house has got up and shut the door, and you begin to stand outside and to knock at the door, saying, 'Lord, open to us,' then in reply he will say to you, 'I do not know where you come from.... Go away from me, all you evildoers!'"

3. A passing glance at these words of Jesus might suggest that the reason that some were not able to enter in was not their *manner* of striving, but their *failure* to strive at all. However, the result is the same. They were commanded to depart because they had all been "evildoers" who had walked the easy road. In other words, they had failed to agonize to enter in at the narrow gate. Probably they did seek to enter before the door was shut, but that degree of effort was not enough. Perhaps they did strive after the door was shut, but by then it was too late.

4. Today, therefore, "strive to enter through the narrow door." To do so, settle it in your heart and let it be constantly foremost in your thoughts that if you are on the easy road, you are in the way that leads to destruction. As sure as God is true, if legions of people are going with you, both they and you are going to hell. If you are walking as the majority of people walk, you are walking toward the bottomless pit. Are many wise, rich, powerful, or elite people traveling with you on the same road? By this clue, without going any farther, you know that the road does not lead to life. Before you deal with specifics, here is a short, simple, trustworthy rule: *In whatever business you are engaged, you must be singularly focused or you will be damned.*

The road to hell has nothing singular about it, but the way to heaven is thoroughly focused. If you take only one step toward God, you are not like other people. However, do not concern yourself about being alone. It is far better to stand alone than to fall into the pit of hell. "Run with perseverance the race that is set before you," even if you have only a few comrades in the race. It will not always be this way. In a short time you will come "to innumerable angels in festal gathering, and to the assembly of the first-born who are enrolled in heaven, and to a judge who is God of all, and to the spirits of just men made perfect."

5. Therefore, for now, "strive to enter by the narrow door," being permeated with the deepest recognition of the indescribable danger your soul is in for as long as you are on the easy way. You are in great peril as long as you lack poverty of spirit and all the inward religion, which the majority, the rich, and the wise, regard as insanity. Agonize to enter in. Be awakened with sorrow and shame for having traveled so long with the unthinking crowd, utterly neglecting if not despising "the holiness without which no one will see the Lord." Strive as in an anguish of holy alarm, for fear that you would fail to reach "the promise of entering his rest that remains for the people of God." Strive with fervent desire and "with sighs too deep for words." Agonize with unceasing prayer, always and everywhere lifting up your heart to God, and give him no rest until you "awake in his likeness and are satisfied."

6. I conclude. "Strive to enter through the narrow door." Strive in agony of soul, with confidence, anguish, humiliation, hope, fear, and persistent prayer. Also, strive by "going the right way," by walking with all your energy in the ways of God. It is the way of purity, piety, and mercy. "Abstain from every form of evil"; "work for the good of all"; "deny yourself and take up your cross daily." If necessary, be ready to cut off your right hand and to tear out your right eye and throw them away. Be ready to endure the loss of possessions, friends, and health, everything on earth in order to enter the kingdom of heaven.

Notes

1. Ward and Heitzenrater, *Wesley's Journal and Diaries*, July 15, 1776, 23:24.
2. Ibid, May 16, 1774, 22:407-08.
3. Quoted in Luke Tyerman, *The Life and Times of the Rev. John Wesley, M.A.*, 3 vols. (London: Hodder and Stoughton, 1870), 1:62.
4. Overton, John H. and Relton, Frederic. *The English Church From the Accession of George I to the End of the Eighteenth Century* (London: Macmillan and Co., 1906), p. 269.
5. Quoted in W. J. Townsend, "The Time and Conditions," *A New History of Methodism*, ed. W. J. Townsend, H. B. Workman, and George Eayrs, 2 vols. (London: Hodder and Stoughton, 1909), 1:118.

UPON OUR LORD'S SERMON ON THE MOUNT

Discourse 12

The previous sermon was based on Christ's instruction to enter through the narrow gate and travel the hard road. The present sermon is based on the Lord's warning to beware of wolves along the way who wear sheep's clothing. Wesley recorded in his journal an instance of preaching on this sermon's text: "I left Bristol on Friday, 28; came to Reading on Saturday, and to Windsor on Sunday morning. Thence I walked over to Egham, where Mr. — preached one of the most miserable sermons I ever heard: Stuffed so full of dull, senseless, improbable lies, of those he complimented with the title of 'False Prophets.' I preached at one, and endeavoured to rescue the poor text (Matt. vii. 15) out of [such] bad hands."[1]

This sermon defines false prophets as those who fail to teach the right way to heaven. Elsewhere, Wesley commented on the text, which warns against misguided teachers within the church: "Beware of false prophets who in their preaching describe a broad way to heaven. . . . All those are false prophets who teach any other way than that our Lord hath here marked out."[2] False prophets are those whose teaching does not lead to life and holiness, but to death and destruction.

270

Next, Wesley discusses the deceitful wiles of false prophets. By definition, counterfeit teachers are those who present themselves as something other than what they really are. Although they are wolves, they disguise themselves in sheep's clothing. They often have gentle and mild manners, and they show no marks of malice. They appear to do good, always hiding themselves under the cloak of religion. They may seem charming, loving, and caring. Nonetheless, they lead people into destruction because they teach a way other than that which Christ revealed.

This sermon addresses the question as to whether Christians should receive Holy Communion from members of the clergy who deny the essentials of the gospel, behave in ways contrary to the teaching of the Bible, or approve nonscriptural conduct in others. Wesley reiterates the same point that St. Augustine made centuries earlier: the validity of the church's sacraments does not depend on the worthiness of those who administer them. Rather, the power of the sacraments depends on the faithfulness of Christ who established them and promised to minister grace through the means that he ordained.

Article #26 of the Church of England's Thirty-nine Articles is titled, *Of the Unworthiness of the Ministers, which hinders not the effect of the Sacraments.* Wesley agreed with this theological position, and he preached, "God can and does give us his blessing even through those teachers who are themselves under God's curse." Wesley warns, however, that Christians should examine the teachings of misguided clergy members. Christians should reject false teachers, regardless of their ecclesiastical rank. This sermon advises, "Completely reject whatever differs from the scriptures and is not confirmed by them."

Finally, this sermon tells the reader how to detect false prophets and how to avoid their destructive influences. We can know people by their fruit and by the fruit they produce in others. Just as false prophets fail to produce good fruit, so do their followers. Only true prophets of God lead others to Christ and build them up in holiness. Wesley bluntly states that false prophets will be damned. By contrast, God's faithful witnesses will know the blessing of God here and hereafter.

The sermon concludes with a strong warning to false prophets: "How long will you say, 'God has spoken,' although God has *not* spoken through you? How long will you 'make crooked the straight paths of the Lord'?" Wesley summons all preachers to remain faithful to the word of God: "The word of God will be in your mouth as a hammer that breaks the rocks in pieces. Your fruit—the spiritual children that God gives you—will then demonstrate that you are the Lord's prophet. And you will lead many to righteousness, and shine like the stars forever and ever."

UPON OUR LORD'S SERMON ON THE MOUNT

Discourse 12

"Beware of false prophets, who come to you in sheep's clothing but inwardly are ravenous wolves. You will know them by their fruits. Are grapes gathered from thorns, or figs from thistles? In the same way, every good tree bears good fruit, but the bad tree bears bad fruit. A good tree cannot bear bad fruit, nor can a bad tree bear good fruit. Every tree that does not bear good fruit is cut down and thrown into the fire. Thus you will know them by their fruits." (Matthew 7:15-20)

1 It is hardly possible to express or conceive how many multitudes of souls have gone on to destruction because they refused to walk on the hard road, even though it is the way that leads to everlasting salvation. Daily, we can still observe the same thing. Such is the foolishness and insanity of humankind. Thousands of people continue to rush along the way to hell merely because it is an easy road. They walk this pathway because others walk it. Many people are perishing, and those who follow

273

their example will only increase their numbers. In this fact we see the amazing influence that an example exerts over weak and miserable people! The power of influence constantly populates the regions of hell and drowns numberless souls in everlasting destruction.

2. In order to warn humankind of this danger and to protect as many as possible against this spreading infection, God has instructed his watchmen. They are to speak out clearly and warn the people of the jeopardy they are in. In successive generations, God has sent his servants the prophets for this purpose. They point out the narrow way and plead with everyone to avoid being conformed to this world. However, what if the watchmen themselves fall into the snare about which they are supposed to warn others? What if "the prophets do not prophesy what is right?" What if they "lead the people astray by their lies and their recklessness?" What will happen if they teach as the way to eternal life a way that is in truth the way to eternal death? What will happen if they admonish others to walk as they themselves walk—in the easy way instead of the hard way?

3. Are false teachers little known and rare? No. God knows that they are not the exception. The examples of false teachers are almost innumerable. We can find them in every age and nation. How appalling it is when the ambassadors of God become agents of the devil! How tragic when those who are commissioned to teach people the way to heaven do in fact teach them the way to hell! These false teachers are like the locusts of Egypt that "devoured the last remnant left after the hail." False teachers devour even the traces of the people who had escaped and were not destroyed by the bad examples of others. Therefore, it is for good reason that our wise and gracious master so solemnly cautions us against them: "Beware of false prophets, who come to you in sheep's clothing but inwardly are ravenous wolves."

4. This warning is of supreme importance. In order for this counsel more effectively to settle into our hearts, let us examine (1) who these false prophets are, (2) in what way they present themselves, and (3) how we can discern false prophets, despite their attractive demeanor.

I. False prophets identified

1. First, we will investigate who these false prophets are. It is necessary to examine this matter diligently because they have carefully schemed to "twist scripture to their own destruction" (and not their destruction alone). Therefore, in order to end all dispute I will not create a furor (as some do) or use any careless or verbose proclamations to mislead ordinary people. Rather, I will speak strong, clear truths, which no one who has retained intelligence or humility can deny. I will present those truths that are most closely associated with the full meaning of the scripture that precedes the words of Jesus that we are now considering. All too often, many people have interpreted these closing words of the Sermon on the Mount without taking into account the verses that came before them.

2. Here (as in many other passages of Scripture, particularly in the New Testament), the word "prophets" does not mean those who foretell things to come. Rather, prophets are those who speak in the name of God; they are messengers who claim to be sent by God to teach others the way to heaven. *False prophets* are those who teach a wrong way to heaven. In sum, what they teach is not true because it does not lead to heaven.

3. Every easy road is a false one. Therefore, here is a clear and certain rule: *False prophets are those who teach people to walk on an easy road that many travel.* Once again, the true road to heaven is a hard one. Therefore, here is another clear and certain rule: *False prophets are those that do not teach others to walk on the hard road and become single-minded in their quest for God's kingdom.*

4. To be more specific, the only true way to heaven is the way given in the Sermon on the Mount. False prophets, therefore, fail to teach others to walk in this way.

The way to heaven, presented in the preceding sermon, is the way of humility, sorrowing, meekness, and holy desire. The way to heaven consists of loving God and neighbor, doing good, and overcoming evil for Christ's sake. Anyone is a false prophet who teaches that the road to heaven is any other way.

5. It does not matter what people call an alternate way. They might call it "faith," "good works," "faith and works," "repentance," or "repentance, faith, and new obedience." All these words are good ones. But if by using these words or any other words people teach others a way different from the way that Jesus taught, they are properly false prophets.

6. If these teachers condemn the right way, how much more do they fall under the condemnation of being false prophets! Above all, false prophets teach the exact opposite way—the way of pride, frivolity, lust, worldly desires, loving pleasure more than God, unkindness to our neighbors, disregard for good works, enduring no wrong, and having no persecution for righteousness' sake!

7. Someone may ask, "Who ever has taught such a thing? Who teaches that we should do these evil things as the way to get to heaven?" I answer that ten thousand learned and important people in all denominations teach this very thing. They encourage proud, frivolous, lustful lovers of the world to think that they are on the road to heaven. They assure pleasure-loving, unfair, cruel, comfortable, reckless, benign, useless creatures that endure no persecution for righteousness' sake that they are going to heaven. Such teachers are false prophets in the fullest sense of the word.

These false prophets are traitors to God and all people. They are the first-born of Satan, the eldest children of *Apollyon* the destroyer. They are far worse than ordinary murderers because they assassinate human souls. They are continually populating the kingdoms of darkness. When they follow the poor souls they have destroyed, "hell beneath will be stirred up to meet them."

II. The wiles of false prophets

1. Second, do the false prophets appear to us as they really are? By no means. If people were to see their true nature, they could not destroy as they do. If you saw them as they actually are, you would become alarmed and flee for your life. Consequently, they present themselves as quite the opposite of their true selves. "False prophets who come to you in sheep's clothing are inwardly ravenous wolves."

2. Appearing, as they do, "in sheep's clothing" means first that they have the bearing of apparent harmlessness. They come in the most gentle and mild manner, without any mark or sign of malice. Who would think that these calm creatures would harm anyone? Perhaps they might not be as zealous and active in good works as one would wish they were. Nevertheless, you see no reason to suspect that they have any wish to do any harm. However, this is not the case.

3. Second, they come with the appearance of usefulness. Indeed, the church particularly called and appointed them to do good. They are especially designated to watch over your soul and to train you up to eternal life. Their only apparent work is to "go about doing good and healing all who are oppressed by the devil." You have always been in the habit of looking at them in this light, as messengers of God sent to bring you a blessing.

4. Third, they come under the guise of religion. They assure you that everything they do is for the sake of their conscience! They are making God a liar, and yet they assure you that they are acting out of zeal. Out of "true concern for religion," they work to destroy it root and branch. They insist that everything they say is out of a love for truth and a fear that it might suffer harm. They pretend that they have high esteem for the church and desire only to defend her from all her enemies.

5. Above all, these wolves in sheep's clothing deceive with an appearance of love. They seem to work as hard as they do only for your good. They would not trouble themselves about you if they did not "have such a compassion for you." They will make profuse declarations of their goodwill. They feign concern about the danger you are in, and they pretend an earnest desire to protect you from error and devilish doctrines. They profess sorrow at seeing those who mean so well becoming excessively zealous, bothered by peculiar and incoherent notions, or deluded into religious fanaticism. Therefore, they counsel you to settle into a simple, untroubled life. They warn against "being too righteous," for fear of "destroying yourself."

III. How to discern false prophets

1. Third, despite the fair appearance of false prophets, how can we discern what they actually are? Our blessed Lord saw how necessary it is for everyone to determine who are false prophets, however disguised they may be. Likewise, Jesus saw how incapable most people are of understanding a truth through the long train of consequences flowing from it. He therefore gave us a short and simple rule, easily understood by people of the most modest endowments. This rule applies to every situation: *You will know them by their fruits.*

2. You can easily apply this rule on every occasion. It is easy to detect whether all who speak in the name of God are true or false prophets. First, what are the fruits of their doctrines in their own lives? What effect has it had in them? Are they holy and unblemished in everything? What effect has their doctrine had within their hearts? Does it appear from the general course of their conduct that their spirits are holy, heavenly, and godly? Do they have "the same mind that was in Christ Jesus"? Are they meek, humble, diligent lovers of God and people? Are they "zealous of good deeds"?

3. Second, you can easily observe the fruits of their doctrine in those who hear them. (That is, in *many* of their followers, if not in all. The apostles themselves did not convert everyone who heard them.) Do their followers have "the very mind that was in Christ"? And do they walk just as he walked? And was it by listening to these teachers that they began to do so? Were they inwardly and outwardly wicked until they heard them? If so, it is a conspicuous proof that these leaders are true prophets and teachers sent from God. However, if people have no fruit and do not effectively teach themselves and others to love and serve God, it is unmistakable proof that these teachers are false prophets and that God has not sent them.

4. "This teaching is difficult; who can accept it?" Our Lord knew that this truth was hard to grasp, so he accommodated himself to our need for proof by giving several clear and convincing arguments. He asked, "Are grapes gathered from thorns, or figs from thistles?" By this analogy he meant, "Do you expect that these evil men could bring forth good fruit? You had just as soon

expect thorns to produce grapes or figs to grow on thistles!" Jesus also declared, "A good tree cannot bear bad fruit, nor can a bad tree bear good fruit." Jesus meant that every true prophet or teacher he has sent bears the good fruit of holiness. The false prophet or teacher that he has not sent bears only the fruit of sin and wickedness. "A good tree cannot bear bad fruit, nor can a bad tree bear good fruit." True prophets and teachers sent from God bear good fruit not only sometimes, but always. They bear good fruit not accidentally, but by necessity.

In the same way, a false prophet whom God has not sent always and inevitably fails to bear good fruit. Jesus went on to say that every tree that does not bear good fruit is cut down and thrown into the fire.

This end will come unfailingly to those prophets who do not bear good fruit. They do not bring sinners to repentance or save souls from sin. Therefore, let this eternal rule stand forever: *You will know them by their fruits.*

Good teachers and prophets lead the proud, lustful, cruel lovers of the world to become humble and kind lovers of God and others. God himself confirms their word. On the other hand, those are false prophets whose unrighteous hearers remain unrighteous still. At the least, lest they remain void of the righteousness which "exceeds that of the scribes and Pharisees." They are false prophets and God has not sent them. Consequently, their word falls to the ground. Without a miracle of grace, they and their hearers together will fall into the bottomless pit.

5. Therefore, Jesus warned, "Beware of false prophets, who come to you in sheep's clothing but inwardly are ravenous wolves." They only destroy and devour the flock. They tear the sheep into pieces, if no one helps them. They cannot and will not lead you on the road to heaven. How could they, when they do not know the way themselves? Be on guard that they do not lead you astray and cause you to "lose what you have worked for."

6. Perhaps you will ask, "If there is such danger in hearing them, should I ever listen to them at all?" That question is an important one and it deserves the deepest consideration. The question should not be answered except after the most even-tempered

thought and cautious reflection. For many years, I have been almost afraid to speak to this question because I have not been able to decide one way or the other or to make a judgment about it. There are many reasons that quickly come to mind which incline me to say, "Do not ever listen to false teachers and prophets." Yet, what our Lord said about the false prophets in his day seems to suggest the opposite. Jesus said to the crowds and to his disciples, "The scribes and the Pharisees sit on Moses' seat" (those ancient leaders are analogous to the assigned teachers in the church today). Jesus continued: "Therefore, do whatever they teach you and follow it; but do not do as they do, for they do not practice what they teach."

Throughout the entire course of the ministry of Jesus he demonstrated that these scribes and Pharisees were false prophets. Concerning them, he said, "They do not practice what they teach." The disciples of Jesus could easily discern these teachers because everyone saw their fruits. Accordingly, Jesus repeatedly warned us to be on guard against false prophets. Still, Jesus did not forbid his followers to hear even the scribes and Pharisees. He said, "Do whatever they teach you and follow it." For unless the disciples heard them, they could not know their teaching and follow it. In these words, then, our Lord himself gives a clear direction. In some circumstances, his apostles and all who follow our Lord are to hear those who are recognized as false prophets.

7. It may be said that Jesus only instructed his followers to hear the false teachers when they read the scripture to the congregation. I answer that when these teachers read the scriptures they usually explained them as well. Jesus did not intimate that we should hear only their reading of scripture and not their comments as well. The phrase, "whatever they teach you, follow it" excludes only a partial hearing of these teachers.

8. In addition to teaching, those who are undeniably false prophets also frequently have charge of administering the sacraments. (How grievous! Surely, it ought not to be this way.) Therefore, to forbid people from hearing these teachers would essentially keep believers from God's sacrament. We must remember this truth that we know: The validity of the sacrament does

not depend on the goodness of the one who administers it. Rather, the worth of the sacraments depends on the faithfulness of God who ordained them and promised to meet us in his appointed ways. Therefore, on this account I hesitate to say that we should never listen to false prophets. God can and does give us his blessing even through those teachers who are themselves under God's curse. Experientially, we have found the communion bread they break to be "a sharing in the body of Christ" and the cup that God blessed, even by their unholy lips, was to us "a sharing in the blood of Christ."

9. In sum, my advice is that in every case wait before God in humble and fervent prayer, and then act according to the best light you have. Do what you are persuaded on the whole will best contribute to your spiritual advantage. Take great caution that you do not judge hastily, and too freely believe that others are false prophets. When you have complete proof that they are, see that you nourish no anger or scorn in your heart. Then, in the presence and fear of God, make your own judgments. I can only say that if by experience you find that hearing them harms your soul, then do not listen to them. Quietly avoid them and listen to those who benefit you. On the other hand, if you find that listening to them does not harm your soul, then you can continue to hear them.

However, "pay attention to how you listen." Be cautious of them and of their doctrine. Hear with fear and reverence, so that you are not deceived and given up to a powerful delusion, as they are. Because they continually combine truth and lies, how easy it is for you to accept both together! Listen with fervent and ceaseless prayer to Jesus who alone teaches us wisdom. See to it that you compare whatever you hear with the ancient biblical teaching and instruction. Receive nothing that has not been tested; it must first be in agreement with the doctrine of the church. Believe nothing that teachers say unless it is clearly confirmed by plain passages from the Bible. Completely reject whatever differs from the scriptures and is not confirmed by them. Particularly, reject with the utmost aversion any teaching about the way of salvation that differs from, or falls short of, the way our Lord has prescribed in the preceding words of the Sermon on the Mount.

10. I cannot conclude this sermon without directing a few simple words to those false teachers about whom we have been speaking. O, you false prophets, you dry bones: for once, hear the word of the Lord. How long will you falsify in the name of God? How long will you say, "God has spoken," although God has *not* spoken through you? How long will you "make crooked the straight paths of the Lord"? How long will you "put darkness for light and light for darkness"? How long will you teach the way of death and call it the way of life? How long will you deliver to Satan the souls that you profess to bring to God?

11. "Woe to you, blind guides." "You lock people out of the kingdom of heaven. For you do not go in yourselves, and when others are going in, you stop them." Those who want to strive to enter in at the narrow gate you call back onto the easy road. Those that have barely taken one step into the ways of God you diabolically warn against "going too far." You caution those who are just beginning to hunger and thirst after righteousness not to be "overly righteous." You cause seekers to stumble at the very threshold of God's kingdom. You make them fall and not rise again. Why do you do this thing? What do you gain from their eternal destruction? It is of no advantage to you at all. God declares, "Those wicked persons shall die for their iniquity; but their blood I will require at your hand."

12. Where are your eyes and comprehension? Have you deceived others to such an extent that you are also deceiving yourselves? Who has required you to teach a way that you never knew? Are you "given over to such a powerful delusion" that you not only teach a lie but actually believe it? Can you possibly believe that God has sent you as his messengers? If the Lord had sent you, his work would prosper in your hands. As the Lord lives, if you were messengers of God he would "fulfill the word of his messengers." However, the work of the Lord does not prosper in your hand; you bring no sinners to repentance. The Lord does not confirm your word, because you save no one from death.

13. How can you possibly escape the force of our Lord's abundant, powerful and explicit words? How can you escape "knowing yourselves by your fruits"? Evil fruits come from evil trees!

How can it be otherwise? "Are grapes gathered from thorns, or figs from thistles?" Receive this word within yourselves, you to whom it belongs. O you barren trees, why are you wasting the soil? "Every good tree bears good fruit." Can you not see that there is no exception? Grasp the fact that you are not good trees because you do not bear good fruit. "The bad tree bears bad fruit." Always, you have borne bad fruit. Your claims to speak for God have only confirmed your hearers in demonic attitudes and deeds. O receive warning from him in whose name you speak, before he passes sentence on you: "Every tree that does not bear good fruit is cut down and thrown into the fire."

14. My dear colleagues, do not harden your hearts. Too long you have closed your eyes to the light. Open your eyes before it is too late and God throws you into outer darkness. Do not give regard to any transient consideration. Eternity is at stake. You have run before you were sent. O, do not continue your way. Do not persist as you are; you damn yourselves and those who hear you! You have no fruit for your labors. Why? Because the Lord is not with you. Can you succeed in your own strength? No, you cannot.

Therefore, humble yourselves before God. Plead with him out of the dust, praying that he will first grant life to your soul and give you the faith that works through love. Ask him for a faith that is humble, meek, pure, merciful, and zealous of good works. Pray for a faith that rejoices in the midst of adversity, indignity, misfortune, and persecution for righteousness' sake. Then "the spirit of glory, which is the Spirit of God, will rest on you." Only then will it become evident that God has sent you. Indeed, then you will "do the work of an evangelist, and carry out your ministry fully." The word of God will be in your mouth. So shall the word of God in your mouth be "a hammer that breaks the rocks in pieces." Your fruit—the spiritual children that God gives you—will then demonstrate that you are the Lord's prophets. And you will "lead many to righteousness, and shine like the stars forever and ever."

Notes

1. Curnock, *Wesley's Journal*, January 30, 1743, 3:65.
2. *Explanatory Notes upon the New Testament*, Matt. 7:15.

UPON OUR LORD'S SERMON
ON THE MOUNT

Discourse 13

John Wesley often preached from the text of this sermon, Matthew 7:21-27. The following journal account appears: "After preaching at eight, I went to St. Saviourgate Church. Towards the close of the Prayers, the Rector sent the sexton to tell me the pulpit was at my service. I preached on the conclusion of the Gospel for the day, 'Not every one that saith unto me, Lord, Lord, shall enter into the kingdom of heaven; but he that doeth the will of my Father which is in heaven.' I did not see one person laugh or smile, though we had an elegant congregation."[1]

On another occasion, the rector of a church invited Wesley to preach because he appeared in the congregation in his clerical dress, although the rector did not know who Wesley was. Earlier, the rector had warned his congregation against hearing "that vagabond Wesley." Following the sermon, the rector asked the clerk if he knew the name of the stranger. The clerk replied, "It is that vagabond Wesley, against whom you warned us." The rector replied, "Aye, indeed, we are trapped this time; but never mind, we have had a good sermon."[2] Ten years later, the same priest invited Wesley to preach a second time in his church. On this occasion, Wesley preached on the Beatitudes from the Sermon on the Mount. Wesley found that his preaching on texts from Christ's Sermon on the Mount was usually attended by special blessing. Concerning the teaching of Jesus, Wesley wrote, "He taught...the multitudes, as one having authority—With a dignity and majesty peculiar to himself as the great Lawgiver, and with the demonstration and power of the Spirit: and not as the scribes—who only expounded the law of another; and that in a lifeless, ineffectual manner."[3]

This sermon is the last of Wesley's series of thirteen sermons on Christ's Sermon on the Mount. It explains the foolishness of building upon the sand and the wisdom of building upon a rock. Wesley shows that we cannot reach heaven merely by using proper words, believing in the creeds of the church, professing faith, praying, or following the liturgy. Neither do we reach heaven by offering praise to God, preaching the glories of God's kingdom, or winning people to Christ. Further, we do not earn salvation by avoiding outward sin or by doing good works. Heaven awaits only those who trust in Christ and obey him faithfully. Once, after preaching this sermon, Wesley recalled, "In the evening I preached at Bradford, on the Wise Man that builds his house upon a rock; that is, who builds his hope of heaven on no other foundation than doing these sayings contained in the Sermon on the Mount; although, in another sense, we build not upon his sayings, but his sufferings."[4] This sermon explains that those who build on a rock have become aware of their sin and have trusted God's grace and pardoning love as the sole basis for salvation. Trials will come. The rain will fall. Floods will rise. The winds will blow and beat upon these trusting ones. Jesus Christ assures us that they will not fall because they have built upon a firm foundation.

The last section of the sermon summarizes the entire Sermon on the Mount, and this section of the discourse is a splendid survey of vital Christian discipleship. Wesley declares, "In a word, let your religion be the religion of the heart. Let it reside deep within your innermost soul. In your own eyes, be small, humble, low and wretched, beyond what words can express....Let the entire stream of your thoughts, words, and actions flow from the deepest conviction that you stand on the edge of the great gulf (along with everyone else) just ready to drop into it, either into everlasting glory or everlasting flames. Let your soul be filled with gentleness, tenderness, patience, and forbearance toward everyone. At the same time, let everything within you thirst for the living God, while yearning to awake in his likeness. Be content with this aim. Be a person who loves God and all humankind. In this spirit, do and endure everything. Demonstrate your faith by your works, and in this way you will do the will of your Father in heaven."

Sermon 33

UPON OUR LORD'S SERMON ON THE MOUNT

Discourse 13

"Not everyone who says to me, 'Lord, Lord,' will enter the kingdom of heaven, but only the one who does the will of my Father in heaven. On that day many will say to me, 'Lord, Lord, did we not prophesy in your name, and cast out demons in your name, and do many deeds of power in your name?' Then I will declare to them, 'I never knew you; go away from me, you evildoers.' Everyone then who hears these words of mine and acts on them will be like a wise man who built his house on rock. The rain fell, the floods came, and the winds blew and beat on that house, but it did not fall, because it had been founded on rock. And everyone who hears these words of mine and does not act on them will be like a foolish man who built his house on sand. The rain fell, and the floods came, and the winds blew and beat against that house, and it fell—and great was its fall!"

(Matthew 7:21-27)

1 In his Sermon on the Mount our divine teacher first declared the whole counsel of God about the way of salvation. Next, he talked about the chief hindrances facing those who want to walk in his way. Now, so that his words will stand firm for all generations, in this text he closes the sermon with important words that set his seal upon his declarations and stamp his entire authority on what he delivered.

2. The Lord declared the way of salvation so that no one would ever need to think that there is any other way than the one he taught.

> "Not everyone who says to me, 'Lord, Lord,' will enter the kingdom of heaven, but only the one who does the will of my Father in heaven. On that day many will say to me, 'Lord, Lord, did we not prophesy in your name, and cast out demons in your name, and do many deeds of power in your name?' Then I will declare to them, "I never knew you; go away from me, you evildoers.'"

And everyone who hears my words and does not act on them will be like a foolish man who built his house on sand. The rain fell, and the floods came, and the winds blew and beat against that house, and it fell—and great was its fall!

3. In this sermon I intend (1) to consider the standing of the one who builds on the sand, (2) to show the wisdom of the one who builds on a rock, and (3) to give a practical application.

I. The standing of those who build on the sand

1. First, I will consider the standing of the one who builds on the sand. Our Lord said, "Not everyone who says to me, 'Lord, Lord,' will enter the kingdom of heaven." Indisputably, this pronouncement will abide forever. Therefore, it is supremely important for us completely to comprehend the force of what Jesus said. What are we to understand by the expression, "Not everyone who says to me, 'Lord, Lord'"? Undoubtedly our Lord is referring to anyone who thinks of going to heaven by any other way than that which he has given.

To begin with, this scripture applies to all our words and discourse about religion. It includes whatever creeds we recite, professions of faith we make, prayers we repeat, or litanies of thanksgiving we read or say to God. We may participate in the daily offices and proclaim God's steadfast love for everyone. Day after day we may speak about all God's mighty acts and recount his salvation. We may explain the meaning of the Bible, "interpreting spiritual things to those who are spiritual." We may clarify "the mysteries of God's kingdom that have been hidden throughout the ages and generations." Rather than speaking as mortals, we may speak in the tongues of angels about the deep things of God. We may announce to sinners, "Here is the Lamb of God who takes away the sin of the world." Yes, we may preach with such a demonstration of the Spirit and power as to save many souls from death, and cover a multitude of sins.

Yet it is very possible that all this speech is nothing more than merely saying to Jesus, "Lord, Lord!" After I have successfully preached to others, I can myself still be disqualified. With God's help, I might rescue many souls from hell and yet drop into hell when I have finished. I might bring many others to the kingdom of heaven and yet myself never enter heaven. Reader, if God has ever blessed my preaching to your soul, pray that he will be merciful to me, a sinner!

2. Second, saying "Lord, Lord" to Jesus may include the fact that you do not harm others. We may abstain from every flagrant sin and every kind of outward evil. We may refrain from all the ways of acting or speaking that scripture forbids. We may be able to say to everyone among whom we associate, "Which of you convicts me of sin?" Outwardly, we may have a clear conscience toward God and all people, as well as a life that is free from all impurity, irreverence, and unrighteousness. St. Paul wrote, "As to righteousness under the law, we might be blameless." However, we still may not be justified. Avoiding evil deeds might count for no more than just saying, "Lord, Lord!" If we go no further than avoiding wrongdoing, we will never "enter the kingdom of heaven."

3. Third, one's merely saying "Lord, Lord" may include what many people call doing good works. One may partake of the

Lord's Supper, hear many excellent sermons, and miss no opportunity to participate in all the other ordinances of God. I might do good to my neighbor, give my bread to the hungry, and clothe the unclothed. I might be so zealous of good works as even to "give away all my possessions." Yes, I might do all these things with a hope of pleasing God and a true conviction that I do please him with my works. Such is undeniably the case with those our Lord describes as saying to him, "Lord, Lord." Nevertheless, I still may have no part in the glory about to be revealed."

4. If anyone wonders at what I have been saying, let that one admit that he or she fails to understand the entire religion of Jesus Christ. In particular, that one fails to grasp the perfect picture of true religion that Jesus sets forth in his Sermon on the Mount. Speaking upright words and performing good deeds fall far short of the true righteousness and holiness that Jesus described in his sermon! How very far are these things from the inward kingdom of heaven that God opens to the believing soul! The kingdom of God is first sown in the heart like a small mustard seed. But when it has grown it sends out large branches on which grow a harvest of righteousness of every good disposition, word, and work.

5. Although Jesus clearly and frequently repeated the message that no one will enter heaven who does not have the kingdom of God within, he knew well that many people would not receive his words. Therefore, he again confirmed his message:

> On that day many will say to me, "Lord, Lord, did we not prophesy in your name, and cast out demons in your name, and do many deeds of power in your name?" Then I will declare to them, "I never knew you; go away from me, you evildoers." (Matt. 7:22, 23)

Jesus said that *many* would miss the way, not just one or a few. In the day of judgment they will declare:

> We have said many prayers; we have spoken your praise; we have refrained from evil; we have given ourselves to doing good works. And even more importantly, we have prophesied in your name. In your name have we cast out demons; in your name we did many wonderful works. We have prophesied; we have announced your

will to humankind; we have shown sinners the way to peace and glory. And all these things we did in your name according to the truth of your gospel and on your authority—you who confirmed the Word with the Holy Spirit whom you sent down from heaven. In your name and through the power of your Word and Spirit, we cast demons out of the souls which the demons had long claimed as their own and over whom they had quiet control. And in your name and by your power (not our own) we have done many wonderful works. Even the dead heard the voice of the Son of God speaking through us and they lived.

Jesus said, "Then I will declare to them, 'I never knew you; go away from me, you lawless ones.' I did not know you even when you were casting out devils in my name, because your heart was not right toward God. You were not meek and humble; you did not love God and others; you were not renewed in the image of God. You were not holy as I am holy. Depart from me. Despite your claims, you are 'workers of iniquity.' You are transgressors of my law of holy and perfect love."

6. In order to place his words beyond all possibility of contradiction, our Lord established them with an appropriate comparison: "Everyone who hears these words of mine and does not act on them will be like a foolish man who built his house on sand. The rain fell, and the floods came, and the winds blew and beat against that house." Invariably, sooner or later everyone will experience the floods of outward affliction or inward temptation and the storms of pride, anger, fear, or lust. Jesus continued, "And the house fell—and great was its fall!" It perished forever. This great fall will be the destiny of all those who rest in anything short of the religion that Jesus revealed. Their fall will be all the greater because they heard the words of Jesus but did not heed them.

II. The wisdom of the one who builds on a rock

1. Second, I will demonstrate the wisdom of those who heed the words of Jesus and build their houses on rock. One is indeed wise who does the will of the Father in heaven. Those are truly wise whose "righteousness exceeds that of the scribes and Pharisees."

They are poor in spirit, knowing themselves even as God knows them. They see and feel all their sin and guilt until it is washed away by Christ's atoning blood. They are conscious of their lost condition, the wrath of God toward them, and their complete inability to help themselves. By trusting in Christ, they are filled with peace and joy in the Holy Spirit. They are meek, gentle, and patient toward everyone; they never "repay evil for evil or abuse for abuse. On the contrary, they repay with a blessing," until they "overcome evil with good."

Their souls thirst for nothing on earth other than the living God. They have compassion for everyone and they are prepared to lay down their lives for their enemies. They love the Lord their God with all their hearts, with all their souls, with their entire minds, and with all their strength. Only those will go to heaven who do good to everyone in this spirit of love. For the sake of Jesus Christ they are despised and rejected by others, hated, criticized, and persecuted. Even so, they rejoice and are glad because they know the one in whom they have put their trust. They are confident that our light, momentary afflictions "are preparing us for an eternal weight of glory."

2. How truly wise are these people! They know themselves to be eternal spirits who have come from God, now in houses of clay, and called not to do their own will, but the will of him who sent them. They realize that the world is the location where they are to spend a few days or years, not as citizens, but as strangers and sojourners on their way to eternal mansions. Accordingly, they do not abuse the world but they use the world. They understand that "the present form of this world is passing away." They know God as Father, friend, and author of all good. He is "the God of the spirits of all flesh" and the only happiness of all intelligent beings. Clearer than the light of the midday sun, these followers of Jesus Christ see that the purpose of humankind is to glorify God. He made us for himself, to love and enjoy him forever.[5] And with equal clarity they see the means to that end, which is to delight in God in heaven. The means to that end is to know, love, and imitate God, and to believe in Jesus Christ whom he has sent.

3. Such persons are wise in God's reckoning because they build their houses on the rock. This rock is the eternal Rock of Ages, the Lord Jesus Christ, the everlasting rock that never changes. "Jesus Christ is the same yesterday and today and forever." The psalmist and the apostle who quotes him both bear witness to Jesus Christ:

> In the beginning, Lord, you founded the earth,
>   and the heavens are the work of your hands;
> they will perish, but you remain;
>   they will all wear out like clothing;
> like a cloak you will roll them up,
>   and like clothing they will be changed.
> But you are the same,
>   and your years will never end. (Ps. 102:25-27; Heb. 1:10-12).

Wise, therefore, are those who build on Christ and establish him as their only foundation. They trust only in his blood and righteousness and in what he has done and suffered for us all. Wise persons fix their faith on this cornerstone and rest the entire weight of their souls upon it. God teaches them to say, "Lord I have sinned and I deserve the lowest hell. However, I am 'justified by your grace as a gift, through the redemption that is in Christ Jesus.'" They say, "The life I now live in the flesh I live by faith in the Son of God, who loved me and gave himself for me. The life I now live is a divine, heavenly life, which is "is hidden with Christ in God.'" It is a life of pure love toward both God and others. It is a life of holiness and happiness, praising God and doing everything for his glory.

4. Yet, these obedient ones should never think that they will not see any more spiritual warfare or that they are beyond the reach of temptation. It remains for God to test the grace he has given. God will refine believers as gold is refined in the fire. They will be tempted no less than those who do not know God; perhaps they will be even more abundantly tested. Satan will never fail to tempt to the limits those he is not able to destroy. Therefore, the rain will descend furiously. It will fall when and how it seems good both to the prince of the power of the air and to God whose "kingdom rules over all." Deluges and floods will create waves, and they will rage frightfully.

However, the Lord "sits enthroned over the flood" and "he reigns as king forever." He will say to the floods, "Thus far shall you come, and no farther, and here shall your proud waves be stopped." Jesus said, "The rain fell, the floods came, and the winds blew and beat on that house." The elements will attack as though they would rip the house from its foundation. But they cannot prevail. "The house did not fall, because it had been founded on rock." Those who are wise build on Christ by faith and love, and they will never fall. They declare, "God is our refuge and strength, a very present help in trouble. Therefore we will not fear, though the earth should change, though the mountains shake in the heart of the sea, though its waters roar and foam, though the mountains tremble with its tumult." Those who trust Jesus and obey God "live in the shelter of the Most High and abide in the shadow of the Almighty."

III. A practical application

1. How important then is it for all human beings realistically to apply these teachings to themselves! To determine whether we are building on rock or on sand, we need diligently to examine the foundation on which we build! How profoundly important it is for us to ask ourselves, "What is the foundation of my hope?" On what basis am I building my expectation of entering into the kingdom of heaven? Am I building on sand? Am I resting on my orthodoxy or right opinions (which, after a manner of speaking, I have called *faith*). Am I trusting in my system of opinions, which I think are more rational or scriptural than those of others?

How pitiful! What insanity! Surely, to trust in these things is to build on sand—or rather on the foam of the sea! Suppose I am convinced that these things are not a sufficient foundation. Am I not in danger of putting my hope on something else that is equally unable to support it? Perhaps I am resting my hope on belonging to an excellent church that is reformed according to the true scriptural model, blessed with the purest doctrine, the most ancient liturgy, and the most apostolic form of government. Without doubt, because these things may serve as helps to holiness, they are all reasons for praising God. But they are not holiness itself. To the extent that they are disconnected from holiness they will not benefit me. No. Even more, they will leave me without excuse and exposed to all the "greater condemnation." Therefore, if I build my hope on this foundation I am still building upon sand.

2. You cannot and dare not rest on any of these things. What next will you turn to as a basis for your hope of salvation? Will you look to your being innocent of doing harm? Will you rest on your not harming or mistreating anyone? Suppose this claim is true. Suppose you are fair in all your dealings, utterly honest, and you pay others what you owe them. Suppose you neither cheat nor steal and that you act honestly toward everyone. Suppose you have a good conscience toward God and that you do not live in any known sin. All these marks are good ones. However, you still lack a sufficient foundation for hope. You may go this far and yet never arrive in heaven. When all this innocence flows out of a right belief, it is still the least part of the religion of Christ. However, in you it does not flow from a proper faith, and therefore your good works and human achievements are not a part of vital religion. Therefore, in grounding your hope of salvation on these things you are still building on sand.

3. Do you go still farther? Do you add to doing no harm your participation in all the ordinances of God? At every opportunity do you partake of the Lord's Supper? Do you exercise public and private prayer, fast frequently, and hear, study, and meditate on the Scriptures? These things likewise you ought to have done from the time you first set your face toward heaven. Yet by themselves, as a means of getting to heaven, these things also amount to nothing. Without the weightier matters of the law, which are justice, mercy, and faith, they are useless. You have forgotten these more important matters. You do not experience faith, mercy, love for God, holiness of heart, and heaven opened within the soul. Consequently, you are building your hope on sand.

4. Over and above all your religious accomplishments, are you "zealous for good deeds"? As you have opportunity, do you "work for the good of all"? Do you feed the hungry, clothe the

naked, and "care for orphans and widows in their distress"? Do you care for the sick and relieve those in prison? Do you welcome strangers? Friend, come up still higher. Do you prophesy in the name of Christ? Do you preach the truth as it is in Jesus? And does the anointing of the Holy Spirit accompany your word and make it "the power of God for salvation"? Does God enable you to bring sinners "from darkness to light and from the power of Satan to God"?

If not, then go and learn for yourself what you have so often taught others: "For by grace you have been saved through faith." "He saved us, not because of any works of righteousness that we had done, but according to his mercy." Learn to hang exposed upon the cross of Christ, counting everything you have done as but filth and refuse. Devote yourself to him in the spirit of the dying thief, as did the prostitute with her seven demons. Otherwise, you are still building on sand, and after saving others you will lose your own soul.

5. Lord, if I now believe, increase my faith! Give me faith at least the size of a mustard seed. "If you say you have faith but do not have works, can faith save you?" Never! Any faith that does not have works (both inward and outward holiness) that fail to stamp the whole image of God on the heart is not saving faith. Our faith must purify us as he is pure. Faith must produce the whole of the religion described in the foregoing chapters or else it is not the faith of the gospel. Anything less than this religion is not the Christian faith that leads to heaven. Above all other snares of the devil, be cautious of resting on unholy faith that does not save you! If you lay stress on this kind of faith you are lost forever. You are building your house on sand. "The rain falls, and the floods come, and the winds blow and beat against that house, and it falls—and great will be its fall!"

6. In view of what Jesus has said, build your house upon rock. By the grace of God know yourself. Know and feel that you were born guilty and that you were a sinner from the time your mother conceived you. Know that you have been heaping sin upon sin ever since you could distinguish good from evil. Acknowledge that you are sentenced to eternal death. Renounce all hope of ever

being able to save yourself. Place all your hope on being washed in Christ's blood and cleansed by his Spirit. Christ himself "bore our sins in his body on the cross." If you understand that he has taken away your sins, all the more humble yourself before him in a continuous sense of your total dependence on him for every good thought, word, and work. Understand your complete inadequacy to do any good thing unless God "waters you every moment."

7. Weep over your sins and agonize after God until he turns your heaviness into joy. Weep with those who weep and for those who do not weep for themselves. Agonize over the sins and sufferings of humankind. See that just before your eyes is the immense ocean of eternity that has no bottom or shore. Eternity has already swallowed millions and millions of people and it is yawning to devour those who are still alive. On the one hand, while you still have the opportunity, see the house of God that is eternal in the heavens. On the other hand, see hell and destruction that have no covering. Consider these things and grasp the importance of every moment. Time appears briefly, and then it is gone forever!

8. To your seriousness, add the humility of wisdom. Keep your emotions in balance—especially anger, sorrow, and fear. Calmly consent to whatever is God's will. "Learn to be content with whatever you have." Be gentle toward good people; be kind toward everyone, especially toward evil and unthankful people. Be on guard against outward expressions of anger, such as calling someone *raca*, which means "you fool."

Also, be on guard against every emotion that is contrary to love, even if the emotion goes no further than the heart. Be angry at sin because it is an insult to the grandeur of heaven. However, love the sinner. Become like our Lord who "looked around at the Pharisees with anger and was grieved at their hardness of heart." He was angry at the sin, but he grieved over the sinners. Therefore, "be angry but do not sin."

9. Do not work for the food that perishes, but for the food that endures for eternal life. Trample underfoot the world and the things of the world, including all its riches, honors, and pleasures.

Of what value is the world to you? Follow Christ, the true image of God, "and let the dead bury their own dead." If a blessed thirst for God has already been aroused in your soul, be on guard against quenching it by what is commonly understood as "religion." Do not pursue a poor, apathetic sham of religion that consists of form and outward pretense. It only leaves the heart clinging to the dust and just as earthly and unspiritual as ever. Let nothing satisfy you other than the power of godliness—a religion that is spirit and life. True religion is dwelling in God and God in you. It is being a citizen of eternity, having entered "the inner shrine behind the curtain" by Christ's sprinkled blood, and "sitting with him in the heavenly places."

10. Because you can "do all things through Christ who strengthens you," "be merciful, just as your Father is merciful." "Love your neighbor as yourself." Love friends and enemies as your own soul. And let your love be uncomplaining and patient toward everyone. Let love inspire you with the most pleasant sweetness and the most fervent and kind affections. Let your love rejoice in the truth that is in accordance with godliness, wherever it is found. Enjoy whatever brings glory to God and promotes peace and goodwill among everyone. Let your love "bear all things;" speak nothing but good of the dead and the absent. Love "believes all things" that may in any way tend to vindicate another's character. Love "hopes all things" in a neighbor's favor, and it "endures all things," enabling you to triumph over all opposition. Genuine love "never fails," either in time or eternity.

11. Be "pure in heart," cleansed by faith from every unholy affection. "Cleanse yourself from every defilement of body and of spirit, making holiness perfect in the fear of God." By deep poverty of spirit, through the power of God's grace be cleansed from pride and anger. By your meekness and mercy be cleansed from every unkind or violent passion and from all desires other than to please and enjoy God. Hunger and thirst for righteousness. "Love the Lord your God with all your heart, and with all your soul, and with all your mind, and with all your strength."

12. In a word, let your religion be the religion of the heart. Let it reside deep within your innermost soul. In your own eyes be

small, humble, low and wretched, beyond what words can express. Be amazed and humbled to the dust by the love of God in Christ Jesus. Be serious. Let the entire stream of your thoughts, words, and actions flow from the deepest conviction that you stand on the edge of the great gulf. Along with everyone else, you are almost ready to drop into it, either into everlasting glory or into everlasting flames. Let your soul be filled with gentleness, tenderness, patience, and forbearance toward everyone. At the same time, let everything within you thirst for the living God, while yearning to awaken in his likeness. Be content with this aim. Be a person who loves God and all humankind. In this spirit, do and endure everything. Demonstrate your faith by your works, and in this way you will do the will of your Father in heaven. As you now walk with God on earth, you will also reign with him in glory.

Notes

1. Ward and Heitzenrater, *Wesley's Journal and Diaries*, July 20, 1766, 22:51.
2. Sugden, Edward H., *The Standard Sermons of John Wesley*, 2 vols. (London: Epworth Press, 1961), II, 23.
3. *Explanatory Notes upon the New Testament*, Matt. 7:29.
4. Curnock, *Wesley's Journal*, April 26, 1776, 6:103.
5. Westminster Shorter Catechism, Question #1; Augustine, *Confessions*, I, 1.

Index

Abba, 158
Abraham, 41, 216
Addison, Joseph, 70
adultery, 82-84, 213, 221, 230
affections, 20, 59, 82,148, 152, 190, 191, 193, 197, 200-201, 203, 207, 215, 227, 229, 244, 262, 298
alcohol, alcoholism, 14-15, 20
alms, almsgiving, 140, 143, 146, 148-49, 153-55, 187, 194, 199
altar, 62
angel, angels, 64, 68, 90, 107, 155, 159, 218, 229, 268
anger, 44, 56, 59, 60, 61, 62, 71, 76, 121, 166, 184, 263, 291, 297, 298
Antinomianism, 17-18, 34, 101-3
anxiety, 221, 231, 235
arrogance, 44
atonement, 179, 191
Augustine, 15, 271
awaken, 9, 47, 136, 147, 207, 299

backsliding, 94
Barnabus, 71, 128, 185, 191
bearing witness. See Witness
beatitudes, 55-56, 61, 103, 284, Sermons #21, #22, and #23
blindness, 195, 251
Bready, J. Wesley, 15
Bristol, 34, 78, 270
broad way, Sermon #31

Cameron, Richard M. (cited), 15
Cannon, William R. (cited), 13-14
charity, 68, 75
 works of, 148, 153, 155, Sermons #27 and #28

Christian community, 128, 191
Christian conference, 23
Christian ethics. See ethics
Collins, Kenneth, 16
communion, 143, 146
compassion, 37, 70, 86, 159, 167, 170, 253, 277
condemnation, 40, 46, 49, 62, 166, 248, 276
controversy, 266
creation, creator, 12-15, 25, 28, 29, 51, 65, 84, 113, 158, 162, 193, 213
cross bearing, 22
Cudworth, William, 34

damnation, 45-46, 181, 245, 260, Sermon #13
darkness, outer, 134-35, 283
debt, 14, 165-66, 206-7
deceit, 63, 76, 122, 193, 271
decree, 37, 125, 175, 184
devil. See Satan
discipline, 12, 19, 22, 34, 59, 172-74, 177, 182, 191, 199
disciplined living, 12, 19-24
disease, 64, 158, 165, 210
divine authority, Sermon #33
drunkenness, 29, 66, 134, 221, 230

Edward VI, 94
empty words, 149, 156
endure, endurance, 60, 63, 75, 99, 108, 132, 147, 162, 164, 168, 265, 297, 299
error, 59, 60, 68, 72, 92, 101-2, 119, 203, 277
ethics, 9-18, 22-24, 26-30, 33